The Places and Spaces of News Audiences

Historically, or so we would like to believe, the story of everyday life for many people included regular, definitive moments of news consumption. Journalism, in fact, was distributed around these routines: papers were delivered before breakfast, the evening news on TV buttressed the transition from dinner to prime time programming, and radio updates were centred around commuting patterns. These habits were organized not just around specific times but occurred in specific places, following a predictable pattern.

However, the past few decades have witnessed tremendous changes in the ways we can consume journalism and engage with information – from tablets, to smartphones, online, and so forth – and the different places and moments of news consumption have multiplied as a result, to the point where news is increasingly mobile and instantaneous. It is personalized, localized, and available on-demand. Day-by-day, month-by-month, year-by-year, technology moves forward, impacting more than just the ways in which we get news. These fundamental shifts change what news 'is'. This book expands our understanding of contemporary news audiences and explores how the different places and spaces of news consumption change both our experiences of journalism and the roles it plays in our everyday lives. This book was originally published as a special issue of *Journalism Studies*.

Chris Peters is Associate Professor of Media and Communication at Aalborg University's Copenhagen campus, Denmark. His research explores the ways people get and experience information in everyday life and the sociocultural impact of transformations in the digital era. His publications include *Rethinking Journalism*, *Rethinking Journalism Again*, and *Retelling Journalism*.

Journalism Studies: Theory and Practice

Edited by
Bob Franklin
Cardiff School of Journalism, Media and Cultural Studies, Cardiff University, UK

The journal *Journalism Studies* was established at the turn of the new millennium by Bob Franklin. It was launched in the context of a burgeoning interest in the scholarly study of journalism and an expansive global community of journalism scholars and researchers. The ambition was to provide a forum for the critical discussion and study of journalism as a subject of intellectual inquiry but also an arena of professional practice. Previously, the study of journalism in the United Kingdom and much of Europe was a fairly marginal branch of the larger disciplines of media, communication, and cultural studies; only a handful of Universities offered degree programmes in the subject. *Journalism Studies* has flourished and succeeded in providing the intended public space for discussion of research on key issues within the field, to the point where in 2007 a sister journal, *Journalism Practice*, was launched to enable an enhanced focus on practice-based issues, as well as foregrounding studies of journalism education, training, and professional concerns. Both journals are among the leading ranked journals within the field and publish six issues annually, in electronic and print formats. More recently, 2013 witnessed the launch of a further companion journal, *Digital Journalism*, to provide a site for scholarly discussion, analysis, and responses to the wide ranging implications of digital technologies for the practice and study of journalism. From the outset, the publication of themed issues has been a commitment for all journals. Their purpose is first, to focus on highly significant or neglected areas of the field; second, to facilitate discussion and analysis of important and topical policy issues; and third, to offer readers an especially high quality and closely focused set of essays, analyses and discussions.

The *Journalism Studies: Theory and Practice* book series draws on a wide range of these themed issues from all journals and thereby extends the critical and public forum provided by them. The Editor of the journals works closely with guest editors to ensure that the books achieve relevance for readers and the highest standards of research rigour and academic excellence. The series makes a significant contribution to the field of journalism studies by inviting distinguished scholars, academics, and journalism practitioners to discuss and debate the central concerns within the field. It also reaches a wider readership of scholars, students and practitioners across the social sciences, humanities and communication arts, encouraging them to engage critically with, but also to interrogate, the specialist scholarly studies of journalism which this series provides.

Mapping the Magazine: Comparative Studies in Magazine Journalism
Edited by Tim Holmes

The Future of Newspapers
Edited by Bob Franklin

Language and Journalism
Edited by John Richardson

The Future of Journalism
Edited by Bob Franklin

Exploration in Global Media Ethics
Edited by Muhammad Ayish and Shakuntala Rao

Foreign Correspondence
Edited by John Maxwell Hamilton and Regina G. Lawrence

How Journalism Uses History
Edited by Martin Conboy

Lifestyle Journalism
Edited by Folker Hanusch

Environmental Journalism
Edited by Henrik Bødker and Irene Neverla

Online Reporting of Elections
Edited by Einar Thorsen

The Future of Journalism: Developments and Debates
Edited by Bob Franklin

Cross-continental Views on Journalistic Skills
Edited by Leen d'Haenens, Michaël Opgenhaffen and Maarten Corten

Cosmopolitanism and the New News Media
Edited by Lilie Chouliaraki and Bolette Blaagaard

The Press and Popular Culture in Interwar Europe
Edited by Sarah Newman and Matt Houlbrook

Community Journalism Midst Media Revolution
Edited by Sue Robinson

Digital Technologies and the Evolving African Newsroom: Towards an African Digital Journalism Epistemology
Edited by Hayes Mawindi Mabweazara

Making Sense of Mediatized Politics: Theoretical and Empirical Perspectives
Edited by Jesper Strömbäck and Frank Esser

The Future of Journalism in an Age of Digital Media and Economic Uncertainty
Edited by Bob Franklin

The Places and Spaces of News Audiences
Edited by Chris Peters

Theories of Journalism in a Digital Age
Edited by Steen Steensen and Laura Ahva

Journalism in an Era of Big Data: Cases, Concepts and Critiques
Edited by Seth C. Lewis

The Places and Spaces of News Audiences

Edited by
Chris Peters

LONDON AND NEW YORK

First published 2017
by Routledge

2 Park Square, Milton Park, Abingdon, Oxfordshire OX14 4RN
711 Third Avenue, New York, NY 10017

Routledge is an imprint of the Taylor & Francis Group, an informa business

First issued in paperback 2018

Copyright © 2017 Taylor & Francis

All rights reserved. No part of this book may be reprinted or reproduced or utilised in any form or by any electronic, mechanical, or other means, now known or hereafter invented, including photocopying and recording, or in any information storage or retrieval system, without permission in writing from the publishers.

Notice:
Product or corporate names may be trademarks or registered trademarks, and are used only for identification and explanation without intent to infringe.

British Library Cataloguing in Publication Data
A catalogue record for this book is available from the British Library

ISBN : 978-1-138-69191-9 (hbk)
ISBN: 978-0-367-02537-3 (pbk)

Typeset in MyriadPro
by diacriTech, Chennai

Publisher's Note
The publisher accepts responsibility for any inconsistencies that may have arisen during the conversion of this book from journal articles to book chapters, namely the possible inclusion of journal terminology.

Disclaimer
Every effort has been made to contact copyright holders for their permission to reprint material in this book. The publishers would be grateful to hear from any copyright holder who is not here acknowledged and will undertake to rectify any errors or omissions in future editions of this book.

Contents

Citation Information ix
Notes on Contributors xi

Introduction: The places and spaces of news audiences 1
Chris Peters

1. News Now: Interface, ambience, flow, and the disruptive spatio-temporalities of mobile news media 12
Mimi Sheller

2. Toward New Journalism(s): Affective news, hybridity, and liminal spaces 27
Zizi Papacharissi

3. Locative News: Mobile media, place informatics, and digital news 41
Gerard Goggin, Fiona Martin, and Tim Dwyer

4. News Media Old and New: Fluctuating audiences, news repertoires and locations of consumption 60
Kim Christian Schrøder

5. News Media Consumption in the Transmedia Age: Amalgamations, orientations and geo-social structuration 79
André Jansson and Johan Lindell

6. News in the Community? Investigating emerging inter-local spaces of news production/consumption 97
Luke Dickens, Nick Couldry, and Aristea Fotopoulou

7. Citizens of Nowhere Land: Youth and news consumption in Europe 115
Shakuntala Banaji and Bart Cammaerts

Index 133

Citation Information

The chapters in this book were originally published in *Journalism Studies*, volume 16, issue 1 (February 2015). When citing this material, please use the original page numbering for each article, as follows:

Introduction
Introduction: The places and spaces of news audiences
Chris Peters
Journalism Studies, volume 16, issue 1 (February 2015) pp. 1–11

Chapter 1
News Now: Interface, ambience, flow, and the disruptive spatio-temporalities of mobile news media
Mimi Sheller
Journalism Studies, volume 16, issue 1 (February 2015) pp. 12–26

Chapter 2
Toward New Journalism(s): Affective news, hybridity, and liminal spaces
Zizi Papacharissi
Journalism Studies, volume 16, issue 1 (February 2015) pp. 27–40

Chapter 3
Locative News: Mobile media, place informatics, and digital news
Gerard Goggin, Fiona Martin, and Tim Dwyer
Journalism Studies, volume 16, issue 1 (February 2015) pp. 41–59

Chapter 4
News Media Old and New: Fluctuating audiences, news repertoires and locations of consumption
Kim Christian Schrøder
Journalism Studies, volume 16, issue 1 (February 2015) pp. 60–78

Chapter 5
News Media Consumption in the Transmedia Age: Amalgamations, orientations and geo-social structuration
André Jansson and Johan Lindell
Journalism Studies, volume 16, issue 1 (February 2015) pp. 79–96

CITATION INFORMATION

Chapter 6
News in the Community? Investigating emerging inter-local spaces of news production/consumption
Luke Dickens, Nick Couldry, and Aristea Fotopoulou
Journalism Studies, volume 16, issue 1 (February 2015) pp. 97–114

Chapter 7
Citizens of Nowhere Land: Youth and news consumption in Europe
Shakuntala Banaji and Bart Cammaerts
Journalism Studies, volume 16, issue 1 (February 2015) pp. 115–132

For any permission-related enquiries please visit:
http://www.tandfonline.com/page/help/permissions

Notes on Contributors

Shakuntala Banaji is Associate Professor in the Department of Media and Communication and Director of the Master's Programme in Media, Communication, and Development at the London School of Economics, UK. Her research focuses on the lives of children and young people in different geographical and class contexts, with a critical take on the ways in which rhetorical conceptions of citizenship, development, engagement, and digital media construct and position child and youth subjectivities. She is the editor of the *Global Media and Communication* book series.

Bart Cammaerts is Associate Professor and Director of the PhD programme in the Department of Media and Communications at the London School of Economics, UK. His current research looks at activist cultures and how a media and communication saturated environment impacts on activist identities; the nature of protest; community radio regulation; and the consequences of different patterns of consumption of, and value attributed to, music for alternative labels and artists.

Nick Couldry is Professor of Media, Communications and Social Theory at the London School of Economics, UK. He approaches media and communications from the perspective of the symbolic power that has been historically concentrated in media institutions, and how these institutions contribute to various types of order. He is the editor of *Ethics of Media* (with Madianou and Pinchevski, 2013), as well as the author of *Media, Society, World: Social Theory and Digital Media Practice* (2012) and *Why Voice Matters: Culture and Politics After Neoliberalism* (2010).

Luke Dickens is Departmental Lecturer in Human Geography at the University of Oxford, UK. His research interests include the politics of urban experience and spatial practice. In particular, his research seeks to develop critical understandings of the relationships between the performance of difference and identity, and the material conditions and contingencies driving unequal processes of urban change.

Tim Dwyer is Associate Professor and Chair of the Department of Media and Communications at the University of Sydney, Australia. His research focuses on the critical evaluation of media and communications industries, regulation, media ethics, and law and policy in an era of convergent media. His most recent books are *Convergent Media and Privacy* (2016) and *Legal and Ethical Issues in the Media* (2012).

Aristea Fotopoulou is Research Fellow in the Department of Media and Film at the University of Sussex, Brighton, UK. She works at the intersections of media and cultural studies with science and technology. She has written about information politics, knowledge production, digital engagement, digital networks, and feminism.

NOTES ON CONTRIBUTORS

Gerard Goggin is Professor of Media and Communications and ARC Future Fellow at the University of Sydney, Australia. He is the author of *Disability and the Media* (with K. Ellis, 2015) and the editor of *Mobile Technologies* (with R. Ling and L. Hjorth, 2016). His research focuses on social, cultural, and political aspects of digital technologies, especially with regard to the Internet, mobile phones, and the media.

André Jansson is Professor of Media and Communication Studies at Karlstad University, Sweden, where he also directs the PhD programme. His research is oriented towards questions of media use, identity, and power from an interdisciplinary perspective. His work links various theoretical strands including social phenomenology, human geography, and the sociology of culture.

Johan Lindell is a post-doctoral researcher in the Department of Geography, Media and Communication at Karlstad University, Sweden, where he recently completed his PhD on Cosmopolitanism in a Mediatized World. His research is driven by a media sociological vision that insists on understanding media and communication in social contexts, and the power dynamics at work in those contexts.

Fiona Martin is Senior Lecturer in Convergent and Online Media in the Department of Media and Communications at the University of Sydney, Australia. She is the editor of *The Value of Public Service Media: RIPE@2013 Reader* (with G. Lowe, 2014). She researches the uses, politics, and regulation of online media, and the implications of these technologies for change in the media industry.

Zizi Papacharissi is Professor and Head of the Department of Communication at the University of Illinois at Chicago, USA. Her book, *A Private Sphere: Democracy in a Digital Age* (2010), discusses how we practice politics in a digital age. Her latest book, *Affective Publics: Sentiment, Technology and Politics* (2014), won the Best Book award for the Human Communication and Technology Division of the National Communication Association in 2015.

Chris Peters is Associate Professor of Media and Communication at Aalborg University's Copenhagen campus, Denmark. His research explores the ways people get and experience information in everyday life and the sociocultural impact of transformations in the digital era. His publications include *Rethinking Journalism* (with Marcel Broersma, 2013), *Rethinking Journalism Again* (with Marcel Broersma, 2016), and *Retelling Journalism* (with Marcel Broersma, 2014).

Kim Christian Schrøder is Professor in the Department of Communication, Business and Information at Roskilde University, Denmark. His most recent books are *Transformations: Late Modernity's Shifting Audience Positions* (with Nico Carpentier and Lawrie Hallett, 2014), and *Museum Communication and Social Media: The Connected Museum* (with Kirsten Drotner, 2013).

Mimi Sheller is Professor of Sociology and the Director of the Center for Mobilities Research and Policy, at Drexel University, Philadelphia, USA. She is a co-founder of the journal *Mobilities*, the author of *Citizenship from Below* (2012) and *Aluminium Dreams: The Making of Light Modernity* (2014), and the editor of *Mobile Technologies of the City* (2006) and *The Routledge Handbook of Mobilities* (2013).

INTRODUCTION
The places and spaces of news audiences

Chris Peters

Having the means to access "news" at any moment without much hassle likely changes the experience of journalism for many people. Beyond this, one might even say that the way we interact with information on a daily basis transforms through this phenomenon. Considering such changes in what is often referred to as "everyday life" provides a useful starting point for research into media use. It guides us towards a number of considerations, from how we structure our day through certain habits and patterns of media consumption; to the development of technology and the formation of new rituals; to shifting dynamics of communicative flows across societies and their impact; and to the processes whereby the emergent becomes the familiar. Obviously such analyses are not bound to the disciplinary confines of media studies and the term "everyday life" enjoys a rich, if vague and complicated, twentieth-century history.[1] Indeed, a quick Google Scholar search of "everyday life" takes us on a whirlwind interdisciplinary tour of academia, from sociology to cultural studies, psychology to political science, anthropology to economics. There is good reason for this, in that thinking through consistency and change—patterns and disruptions—across the passage of time forms the analytic foundation for much scientific research. But while "everyday life" adorns the cover of many a noted book (e.g. Goffman 1959; de Certeau 1984), a comparable term is almost nowhere to be found. "*Everywhere* life" not only draws the Google equivalent of a blank stare, even writing it down or saying it aloud feels a little awkward. This is almost certainly no discursive anomaly but is rather indicative of the subjugation of spatial thinking to temporal analysis within academia (Soja 1989). While space has been "treated as the dead, the fixed, the undialectical. Time, on the other hand, was richness, fecundity, life, dialectic" (Foucault 1980, 70). Journalism studies is not immune from this tendency. Yet if we want to understand much of what *makes media use meaningful for people*, it is important *to accentuate not only its everydayness, but its everywhereness as well.*

This special issue on the places and spaces of news audiences presents an initial attempt to do this; to see how the everyday digital geographies of contemporary media, communication, and information flows intersect with the everywhere "lived" geographies of individuals, and how this impacts audience perceptions of news, of storytelling, of journalism. The past few decades have seen a tremendous increase in the number of different devices and platforms through which we can get journalism—from tablets to smartphones, Twitter, online news, and so forth—and the different possible places and moments of news consumption have multiplied in concert. Although it is not certain just how robust traditional practices such as reading newspapers or watching the evening news will be in the future, to whatever extent they may have been stable in the past, what does seem clear is that old audience habits are certainly becoming de-ritualized and it is unclear what will replace them (Broersma and Peters 2012). As consumptive possibilities gradually spread to any conceivable instant and every potential location we desire, it seems fairly self-evident that conceptualizing the news media diet of audiences as something clearly distinguishable from other mediated forms of communication is problematic. Similarly, as the temporal and spatial architectures of media use are increasingly unshackled from the distributional constraints of unidirectional, programmatic mass media, audiences are slowing catching up to the possibilities. This changing ecology of digital media may appear quite disruptive, its scale and impact being perceived most strongly early on in its introduction (until such emerging practices and ways of living with media become habitual and taken-for-granted). Coming to grips with the impact this has on journalism requires a scholarship attuned to these different spatio-temporal affordances.

This is not to say that efforts to theorize the dynamics of place and space have been entirely absent from the study of journalism, of course. Many of the classic ethnographies which helped establish the field were attuned to how the newsroom functioned as a place that captured and combined information from a variety of geographic locales before redistributing these back out (e.g. Tuchman 1978). Research into the content of news has also looked more closely into how the world is portrayed on the pages of newspapers and what this signals in terms of how different regions and places are represented and understood (e.g. Wanta, Golan, and Lee 2004). And much current research into news and journalism which centres on the breakdown of distance seems to implicitly recognize the importance of "where" when it comes to content, production, distribution, and reception in an increasingly networked, connected, and participatory digital age.

Yet for all the talk of the emerging and dynamic spaces of news, many of the examples that seem to investigate its significance for journalism employ conceptions that are quite two-dimensional, ignoring established theories of space or imbuing the concepts with dictionary-like meaning. A closer look reveals that the way space and place are treated in many analyses that brand themselves around their consideration is often based upon a Euclidian approach that makes these ideas synonymous with a "plottable" location, albeit one increasingly marked out by virtual coordinates (i.e. "going on to Facebook"). This sort of "GPS" perspective of space can easily miss the inherent sociality that produces it (cf. Lefebvre 1991) and often treats spatiality, sociality, and temporality as separate factors for analytic purposes. This risks mistakenly conceptualizing space as something that "pre-exists" human interaction—as a steady location in which "action" occurs or passes through.

This approach becomes especially problematic when it comes to figuring out what the foundational stakeholder of journalism, namely the audience, "does" with its media use, as new technologies allow users to blur familiar boundaries and co-create new communicative spaces. While media has always possessed this affordance to some degree, in the current changing media landscape even those especially sensitive to accusations of technological determinism must certainly acknowledge that something fairly fundamental has changed, and that former habits will have a tendency to transform. The ubiquity and personal proximity of recent digitalization increasingly means experiencing multiple places simultaneously and continuously and it is unclear how this impacts our perception and experience of information and the world in general. Here challenging questions arise, such as: How do familiar places like work and the home change from the lived materiality of new technologies? What about more abstract but supposedly social aggregates like communities or neighbourhoods? Do these change alongside non-relational, "non-places" like airports, commuter transport, motorways, supermarkets, and shopping centres

(Augé 1995)? If we think of places as layered, textured environments created by social interaction, human intervention, and technological extension in the broadest sense, how does news use fit into this broader equation? Do different potential places of consumption and habits within them change what news is and can news use change our meaning of different spaces? As social scientists and humanities scholars, the intriguing questions likely are not really about the absolute spaces and coordinates where such practices occur, but rather about *the integration of media use within everywhere life*.

Terms and concepts familiar to journalism studies scholars, like "public sphere" or "network society", initially sound like they are closely attuned to such complexities of space and certainly have the possibility to offer such insights. But oftentimes scholarship which relies on these notions de-emphasizes such spatial aspects for other considerations. To briefly elaborate, public sphere is a potentially useful abstraction to shape understanding of how people learn about things and form opinions, which is without doubt of great relevance to journalism scholarship. But when we apply it to news consumption, the spatial significance is often lost or relegated, the focus is placed on the substance of content and orientation to discussion within it, and this becomes detached—or conflated— with experience. In a digital age, increasingly we look to participation via online or social media attached to journalism, say in comment fields, live blogs, and via Twitter, and deem this a virtual public sphere; but surely where, when, and why people are participating is as foundational to their experience and proclivity for engagement as the content they read or produce. The idea of network seems more sensitive to these issues, and is also a potentially useful metaphor to explain the flow of information and the shifting forms and infrastructures of communication. However, the predominance of trying to map how the network operates and discern its structure tends to drown out any useful consideration of the lived materiality of news use, and how this is spatially situated.

In scholarship, it is a necessary evil that we ignore some factors to stabilize our object of study and this selectivity is unavoidable rather than an intellectual shortcoming. The previous observations should accordingly be viewed not as polemic or admonishment but rather as invitation. Just as we in journalism studies frequently pause and take stock of key developments in terms of production, content, values, economics, and technology, we should devote comparable attention to taking a nuanced, processual approach to the spatialized aspects of news and experiment with different ways to operationalize them methodologically. The lack of attention employed to tease these out, when considered in conjunction with a general acknowledgement that an "audience" or "user" turn is necessary in journalism studies (see Madianou 2009; Bird 2011; Costera Meijer 2013), means that we are in danger of ignoring much of what grounds the financial viability and democratic remit of journalism.

The argument put forth in constituting this special issue of *Journalism Studies* is that a concomitant emphasis on both is an analytic necessary if we aim to understand the broader context of news and journalism within society. All economic, social, and cultural phenomena are the result of highly complex spatio-temporal articulations and interrelations. Journalism—not only in terms of its production and content but its often overlooked consumption—is no different. This point is at the heart of the seven contributions which form this special issue of *Journalism Studies*, and in this respect the common claim they make may seem quite uncontroversial on the surface: if we want to appreciate the changing ways audiences are engaging with news and information, (social) space is inseparable from the equation. Nevertheless, for all the apparent obviousness of this claim, what the contributions in this issue demonstrate is just how complex a task embracing this idea can be; concomitantly, they illustrate the added richness of analysis which occurs when such "spatial thinking" is incorporated.

News Use in *Everywhere Life*

The so-called "spatial turn" in scholarship, which has had an increasing interdisciplinary influence over the past couple of decades (Warf and Arias 2008), incorporates a greater effort to approach analysis by treating space and time as equally crucial analytic considerations. Embracing such thinking means discarding the dominant understanding of space as something simply locational, and instead demands thinking of the sociality of space and meanings of place. This sort of "human geography" is an established but not hegemonic paradigm, indeed, even within geography—a discipline in which it seems reasonable to expect that space would be approached in a fairly nuanced and complex manner—the social aspect is still often overlooked for a more "absolute" mathematical conception of space which views phenomena as existing "pre-place" (Hubbard and Kitchin 2011). This seems a case of substituting positivistic simplicity for the "messiness" that shapes different places. As Urry (2004, 13) notes,

> [P]lace can be viewed as the particular nexus between, on the one hand, propinquity characterized by intensely thick co-present interaction, and on the other hand, fast flowing webs and networks stretched corporeally, virtually and imaginatively across distances.

Applying this thinking to contemporary news consumption means not only thinking about the different ways that far-off places have become closer, but the materiality, meaning, and practices of situated moments of "news" use. Cresswell's (2009, 1) helpful description of the tripartite components of "place" is useful in this regard:

> Place is a meaningful site that combines location, locale, and sense of place. Location refers to an absolute point in space with a specific set of coordinates and measurable distances from other locations. Location refers to the "where" of place. Locale refers to the material setting for social relations—the way a place looks. Locale includes the buildings, streets, parks, and other visible and tangible aspects of a place. Sense of place refers to the more nebulous meanings associated with a place: the feelings and emotions a place evokes.

If we think about the significance and meaningfulness of media consumption for most people, not only in the current digitalized, online era but historically, much of this derives not only from its "time-shifting" qualities but from its parallel "emplaced" nature (Peters 2012). Mediated communication can be conceptualized in terms of its fit within the continuous and sensorial experience of moving through life (Pink and Hjorth 2012), and this awareness alerts us to the dynamics behind the personal integration of established and emerging platforms for news and changes which may occur. Old distinctions, such as personal versus mass communication, are being reconfigured in the digital age as the form and function of new technologies change the (a)symmetry of communication practices, interactional structures, and the lived materiality of their use (Lüders 2008). By considering the everywhere alongside the everyday, we place ourselves in a much better position to understand the purpose and meanings people actually make from their interactions with news and information.

Historically, or so we would like to believe, the story of everyday life for many people included definitive moments of news consumption, in regular, set places. The industrial practices of journalism, in fact, were (and sometimes still are) distributed around these spatio-temporal routines: newspapers were delivered to the home before breakfast or to embarkation points for public transit before the morning and evening commutes. Television news buttressed the transitions from work to home (early evening news) and home to bed (nightly news) and the set was frequently the radial point in the central "living room" in most houses. Radio news updates, in terms of both duration and frequency, centred around commuting patterns and the automobile. To understand these habits and the sociology of news media distribution/consumption demands seeing the synergy between these patterns and their enactment. What stands out about the "Golden Age" of mass communication is that there was a certain stability and predictability to media consumption, and the notion of ritual—habitual, formalized actions which reinforce the "symbolic power" of media institutions—provided a good fit to explain the significance of these practices.

Today, these scenarios seem increasingly anachronistic, at least with Western societies. The places, spaces, times, and further social aspects of news consumption are all changing, but we know very little about the impact this has on journalism's various audiences/consumers/users/citizens or on how people process, access, and discuss information. This shortcoming is quite troublesome in an age when, according to many authors, the spaces of everyday life are all becoming mediated (Livingstone 2009; Couldry 2012). News is increasingly mobile, instantaneous, and available "on demand". It is participatory and personalized; locational and localized. Accordingly, this special issue aims to provoke discussion on these themes through a series of theoretically-engaged contributions that are all grounded in empirical research projects. Mimi Sheller employs insights on the materiality, mobility, and infrastructure of digital social media to show how the mobile production, dissemination, and consumption of news produces new spatio-temporalities. Zizi Papacharissi looks at how the hybrid forms of news co-production produce affective news streams which function as social spaces that support marginalized and liminal viewpoints, what she calls "electronic elsewheres". Gerard Goggin, Fiona Martin, and Tim Dwyer highlight how the locational capabilities of mobile media devices to determine, sense, incorporate, and conjure with the relative locations of reporting and audiences have emerged as key to news-gathering and dissemination ventures. Kim Christian Schrøder provides insights into the cross-media challenges facing news audiences, as they seek access to, navigate in, and make sense of the multitude of news sources across print, broadcasting, online, and mobile media platforms. André Jansson and Johan Lindell look at how individuals navigate and orient themselves through representational spaces and flows, and how their media practices amalgamate with other activities in everyday life. Luke Dickens, Nick Couldry, and Aristea Fotopoulou demonstrate how community reporting practices lead to the emergence of new, inter-local spaces of news production and consumption and discuss how such practices, while emerging from the place of local community, also extend across wider communities of interest. Shakuntala Banaji and Bart Cammaerts look at the experiences of news by a diverse group of young European citizens, decentring the technologies of watching or reading news to reposition the relationships between political news-seeking, trust in journalism, meaning-making, and socio-economic status within a framework of local experiences of politics and civic life.

These insightful contributions highlight two distinguishable but overlapping lines of research—the mobility and flow of everywhere life; and the politics and scale of everywhere life—which are shown to be promising avenues for further exploration. The remainder of this introduction uses the papers comprising this special issue as a foundation to flesh out these themes further in relation to the "places and spaces of news audiences". While these lines are by no means exhaustive nor exclusive, together they form a useful interdisciplinary starting point to introduce the key ideas in this issue, combining perspectives from human geography, audience and reception studies, mobilities research, the sociology of media, new and digital media studies, and political communication. The seven papers bring these traditions into conversation with journalism studies, interweaving key considerations on issues surrounding engagement, citizenship, identity, and belonging.

The Mobility and Flow of *Everywhere Life*

In a world where convenient updates are not just the norm but an expectation, how informational flows transect and shape the day has significant impact on the spatio-temporal expectations of journalism and its real-time integration. As I have argued elsewhere, it changes what news "is" (Peters 2012). Sheller goes one step further and argues that the constantly updated flow of "news now" and mobile news "'prosumption' practices such as agglomeration, curation, crowd-sourcing, updating, tagging, and sharing" go far beyond just remaking news. Indeed, she argues this is a more fundamental change, as "the rise of on-demand, on-location, participatory capabilities has also changed the content, form, style, and temporality of news as event." She rightfully points out that the "mobility" of mobile phones is not by itself remarkable for journalism, as newspapers have traditionally acted as a mobile interface that interacts both with the reader and with the surrounding social space in which it is consumed. What is telling about the data-sharing possibilities of contemporary digital technologies like smartphones is that they change the spatio-temporality of news events themselves; reporting becomes co-temporaneous and "may even precede the full unfolding of 'the news'". These changes in news circulation, she argues, transform "the very ground beneath our feet: ambient flows of news re-situate how we understand where we are, who we are connected with, what our 'present' moment actually is. The now-ness of news, in other words, offers a new sense of the present."

Papacharissi picks up on similar themes about "ambient news streams" (see also Hermida 2010), and how the interactive possibilities of personal media allow people to infuse personal meaning into storytelling and, though its mobile nature, traverse public and private spaces. This altered "experience of involvement", both for consuming and producing news, leads to different forms of engagement and differing degrees and modes of attachment (Peters 2011). More specifically, Papacharissi examines "how the affordances of technologies change both the scale and experience of space while at the same time reproducing a degree of familiarity that permits audiences to somehow claim (their own) place". By this she refers not just to control over how one connects to others, or how one experiences public and private spaces and the movement between these, but how audiences find their place within news stories. She explains that,

> geo-social, hybrid, and mediated environments can be understood as *elsewheres* that presence alternative viewpoints, voices, and stories. For citizens, the liminal form of space

is crucial, as it permits them to access content in transition and find their own place in the story, alongside journalists, who already possess an institutionally assigned place in the story.

This recognition of the complexity of liminality also alerts us to the increasing importance of location and movement—as opposed to just frequency of use—when it comes to practices of consumption. Goggin, Martin, and Dwyer argue that this is a cardinal aspect of engagement, as "audiences now expect to be able to search and aggregate news based on locational indicators and also to position themselves *vis-à-vis* events and places, via location annotated posts to social media". They look beyond the mere technological capacities of mobile technology to explore "locative news" as "a new way of marshalling, mediating, and making sense of place; evidenced in the new kinds of information created through projects of emplacement". However, they note that audience experimentation with locative forms is often held back by clunky design and other factors. They provide a cautionary note that there is still a "yawning chasm between, on the one hand, the social imaginaries of locative news, and, on the other hand, the materialities, path-dependency, industrial settings, political and cultural economies of the places and spaces of mobile audiences and their unfolding futures".

This is similarly reflected in Schrøder's findings about mobile news consumption in Denmark, which show that while its reported use is on the rise, its function as an in-depth platform is far less significant. And even if these uses are changing, he raises a wise caveat for researchers, namely that the serious future methodological "challenge for the study of the places and spaces of (news) media use derives from the difficulty of—ethnographically—tracing the footsteps of individuals as they traverse the terrain of everyday life". Modernizing the uses and gratifications perspective via the concept of "worthwhileness", Schrøder points to the necessity of longitudinal, multi-method studies that investigate news use within our broader media repertoires and alongside "a multitude of other processes that are more indigenous and often more vital to everyday life". In this respect, we should keep in mind that mobile phones are only one aspect of a more broadly accelerated mobilization of life that encompasses goods, services, ideas, information, transport, travel, and communications (Elliott and Urry 2010).

The Politics and Scale of *Everywhere Life*

The notion of being able to experience the far-away clearly and instantaneously is something we now take for granted. Indeed, one could query whether the "far-away" is still "far" or now both "near-and-far" due to the ability to transcend geographic scale with increasing ease, precision, and quality. This and the flip side of this scalar equation, namely the coverage of "the local", is the focus of much journalism studies scholarship when it comes to how different places are presented *within* the news. However, if we switch focus to depart from the perspective of the audience, the idea of place takes on added significance beyond the textual. For the reduction of space is felt and experienced differently and is not uniform.

This is quite evident in the contribution by Jansson and Lindell, whose study of the dynamics of news navigation in Sweden demonstrates a clear differentiation "in terms of how individuals navigate and *orient* themselves through representational spaces and flows, and how their media practices *amalgamate* with other activities in everyday life". While they find that cosmopolitan and local orientations to the world are largely reproduced in a new media age, they note this is differentiated in terms how media options are amalgamated within the places of everyday life. Opportunities for consuming and circulating news while on the move are unevenly distributed in social and geographic space and their study raises a thought-provoking observation, namely that "the ways in which they [media practices] are carried out *in space*, contribute to the social classification of media users and their lifestyles". This relates to the socially contingent "power geometry" (cf. Massey 1991) of media use; people are placed differently in relation to geographic scale, in terms of movement, communication, and the control they exert over both. As Jansson and Lindell note, "the very same technological affordances that enable media users to expand their views towards *cosmos* and the distant other (if they have any such ambitions) are the affordances that may tie people closer to the *hearth*".

In this respect, then, the political is inextricably associated with the scale of everywhere life and questions of power. Dickens, Couldry, and Fotopoulou address this theme quite explicitly by looking at how practices of content generation and gaining skills in media production change the experience of locality, in a very positive sense, for community reporters. Looking to the new spaces of news circulation, they investigate how the "news production/consumption" practices of these reporters is not a case of "a centralised valorisation of 'user-generated content' or … a decentred hyperlocalism" but is "a more complex relationship whereby local stories are produced and linked within an inter-local exchange; yet it is often audiences' feelings of *not* being recognised in national news agendas that drives them to generate *and consume* news stories more locally". In considering their findings, perhaps we can draw a parallel with Smith's (2008) observations that spatial patterns, like exports and migration, are not simply cases of linear movement but are aspects of relative space that are quite political. The flow of information via journalism (and its uneven development in certain areas) is in this respect no different. Dickens, Couldry, and Fotopoulou find the localized practices of being a community reporter seem "to *change* how locality is understood, and in the process build a different material geography of news production/consumption". If "legacy" media institutions are gradually losing their symbolic power as a "meeting place" for information, we might view these community reporting practices as trying to recreate this on a local level by "restructuring" the mediaspace, employing "inter-local" connection practices and exchanges, grounded in a critical consumption of news practices.

These sorts of "information-rich" socio-economic neighbourhoods and "information-poor" ghettos are explored even more explicitly in the final article in this issue, where Banaji and Cammaerts question the relationship between socio-economic status and the local experiences of politics and civic life for European youth *vis-à-vis* news use. Drawing upon a wide set of data, they find a substantial interest in politics and civic engagement among all youth especially "in the world around them, specifically in relation to their local communities, leisure spaces (or lack thereof), school, employment and housing prospects". However, they note significant divergences in terms of access to political power, including media representations. Banaji and Cammaerts find that "youth who are most pathologised by news and who perceive themselves as being negatively represented both personally and via association with a particularly stigmatised locality or cultural space, are also most likely to have negative views about the news". Their results challenge the "crude" assumption that "all citizens are equal, live how they wish to live and are equally powerful actors in the public sphere should they only choose to be". Tuan (1977) observes that feelings of personal freedom are closely tied to the power to move and having sufficient room to act. These phenomenological ideas on the self-perception of spaciousness appear to parallel the descriptions of informational representation and lived (geographic) realities described by the different youth demographics in Banaji and Cammaerts' piece. Simply put, it seems that geographic descriptions do not only represent different places, through its representation news socially produces the spaces of everywhere life.

Place, Space, and Information in *Everywhere Life*

The articles in this issue raise our attentiveness to the importance of space and place when it comes to audiences/users of journalism, and identify a number of key shifts that bear further investigation. This is not to claim that we are undergoing, necessarily, an entire transformation of the media field. However, this issue underscores the importance of the "spatial turn" when addressing significant questions regarding the public–private dichotomy and its reconfiguration; the flow of news and information, especially as it pertains to social issues and civic awareness on different scales; and the uses of (news) media for structuring, patterning, or ritual purposes. These questions relate to prominent issues of connection, engagement, enjoyment, affordances, and storytelling that are already being explored by a number of scholars *vis-à-vis* news use. Overhanging all of this are the rapid changes we have witnessed with technology, which does not determine social identities, knowledges, and experiences but certainly has a profound influence "that shapes and controls the scale and form of human association and action" (McLuhan 1964, 9).

This special issue was convened around the coupling of "audiences" and "space", but its results point to the complexity of this relationship. The idea of "space" is not at the absolute forefront of every article in this special issue, instead appearing as a poignant consideration that arises from time to time. Similarly, most contributions point to the difficulty, both conceptually and methodologically, of separating audiences from producers. Many also highlight the danger of simply substituting an amalgamation of the two concepts, which can ignore the motivations and experiences of media use and fairly substantial power relations that shape the particularities of access to, and control over, media. These challenges are not insubstantial, and their presence within this special issue reinforces a broader academic point I wanted to make when I went about assembling the different contributions that comprise it. If we are to overcome a tendency in journalism studies to have production and content dominate the consideration of audiences, if analysis is to avoid privileging temporal concerns over spatial, if the possibilities of technological development should not obscure the actual lived materiality of its use, this means, almost by definition, that scholarship will be messy.

We must embrace the necessary subtlety and multifaceted aspects of change this demands, I would argue, rather than forcing the point. The assorted flavour and conceptual terrain of the articles in this issue point to having space as a consideration, but avoid making it a substitute concern rather an augmenting one. It is something to be contemplated alongside and intertwined with (really, inseparable from) more familiar tropes such as media use; audience consumption, participation, and co-production; and the temporal flow of information. Indeed, advocating for the importance of space does not mean casting aside everything we know. Rather, it points to increasing this as a key concern, especially if we want to understand the flow, material integration, and (social) significance of news and information consumption. Increasingly, the idea of being able to communicate whenever, wherever, and while in motion is unremarkable, and the fact that one can combine and mix forms of auditory, oral, written, and visual communication while "on the go" is expected. In such a seemingly "fluid" mediascape, thinking "spatio-temporally" helps us distinguish the unique from the routine, the extraordinary from the ordinary, the significant from the mundane. This is imperative if we wish to capture the diverse meanings, connections, structures, and experiences that audiences create out of the mediated content they consume, engage with, and augment. Day-by-day, month-by-month, year-by-year technology moves forward and its development and integration, and the impact of this development and integration, mean considering the fundamental shifts this imparts on how people conceive of informational integration within their everyday and everywhere lives.

ACKNOWLEDGEMENTS

My thanks to Stuart Allan for alerting me to Highmore's (2002, 1) discussion of the term "the everyday", and also to Marcel Broersma and Kirsten Kolstrup for their comments on this piece.

NOTE

1. As one might expect, the scholarly usage of "everyday life" is quite disparate and it is not often clear what distinguishes the analytic use of the term from what we might call "the everyday" itself. Highmore (2002, 1) notes the term is used with "unspecific gravity" to denote everything from literal day-to-day practices, to "everdayness" as a value (positively or negatively qualified), to that which goes unnoticed. He notes that elements of boredom, mystery, and rationalism form a central constellation that configures the idea of everyday life in Western modernity.

REFERENCES

Augé, Marc. 1995. *Non-places: Introduction to an Anthropology of Supermodernity*. London: Verso.
Bird, Elizabeth. 2011. "Seeking the Audience for News: Response, News Talk, and Everyday Practices." In *The Handbook of Media Audiences*, edited by Virginia Nightengale, 489–508. Hoboken, NJ: Wiley.
Broersma, Marcel, and Chris Peters. 2012. "Introduction." In *Rethinking Journalism: Trust and Participation in a Transformed News Landscape*, edited by Chris Peters and Marcel Broersma, 1–12. London: Routledge.
Costera Meijer, Irene. 2013. "Valuable Journalism: The Search for Quality from the Vantage Point of the User." *Journalism* 14 (6): 754–770. doi:10.1177/1464884912455899.
Couldry, Nick. 2012. *Media, Society, World: Social Theory and Digital Media Practice*. Cambridge, MA: Polity.
Cresswell, Tim. 2009. "Place". Elsevier. Accessed September 1, 2013. http://www.elsevierdirect.com/brochures/hugy/SampleContent/Place.pdf
de Certeau, Michel. 1984. *The Practice of Everyday Life*. Berkley: University of California Press.
Elliott, Anthony, and John Urry. 2010. *Mobile Lives*. London: Routledge.
Foucault, Michel. 1980. *Power/Knowledge*. London: Harvester Wheatsheaf.
Goffman, Erving. 1959. *The Presentation of Self in Everyday Life*. New York: Anchor.

Hermida, Alfred. 2010. "Twittering the News." *Journalism Practice* 4 (3): 297–308. doi:10.1080/17512781003640703.

Highmore, Ben. 2002. *Everyday Life and Cultural Theory: An Introduction.* London: Routledge.

Hubbard, Phil, and Rob Kitchin, eds. 2011. *Key Thinkers on Space and Place.* London: Sage.

Lefebvre, Henri. 1991. *The Production of Space.* Oxford: Blackwell.

Livingstone, Sonia. 2009. "On the Mediation of Everything: ICA Presidential Address 2008." *Journal of Communication* 59 (1): 1–18. doi:10.1111/j.1460-2466.2008.01401.x.

Lüders, Marika. 2008. "Conceptualizing Personal Media." *New Media & Society* 10 (5): 683–702. doi:10.1177/1461444808094352.

Madianou, Mirca. 2009. "Audience Reception and News in Everyday Life." In *The Handbook of Journalism Studies*, edited by Karin-Wahl Jorgensen and Thomas Hanitzsch, 325–337. London: Routledge.

Massey, Doreen. 1991. "A Global Sense of Place." *Marxism Today* 35 (6): 24–29.

McLuhan, Marshall. 1964. *Understanding Media: The Extensions of Man.* Cambridge, MA: MIT Press.

Peters, Chris. 2011. "Emotion Aside or Emotional Side?: Crafting An 'Experience of Involvement' in the News." *Journalism: Theory, Practice and Criticism* 12 (3): 297–316. doi:10.1177/1464884910388224.

Peters, Chris. 2012. "Journalism to Go: The Changing Spaces of News Consumption." *Journalism Studies* 13 (5–6): 695–705. doi:10.1080/1461670X.2012.662405.

Pink, Sarah, and Larissa Hjorth. 2012. "Emplaced Cartographies: Reconceptualising Camera Phone Practices in an Age of Locative Media." *Media International Australia, Incorporating Culture & Policy* 145: 145–155.

Smith, Neil. 2008. *Uneven Development: Nature, Capital, and the Production of Space.* Athens, GA: University of Georgia Press.

Soja, Edward. 1989. *Postmodern Geographies: The Reassertion of Space in Critical Social Theory.* London: Verso.

Tuan, Yi-Fu. 1977. *Space and Place: The Perspective of Experience.* Minneapolis: University of Minnesota Press.

Tuchman, Gaye. 1978. *Making News: A Study in the Construction of Reality.* New York: Free Press.

Urry, John. 2004. "The Sociology of Space and Place." In *The Blackwell Companion to Sociology*, edited by Judith Blau, 3–15. Hoboken, NJ: Wiley-Blackwell

Wanta, Wayne, Guy Golan, and Cheolhan Lee. 2004. "Agenda Setting and International News: Media influence on public perceptions of foreign nations." *Journalism & Mass Communication Quarterly* 81 (2): 364–377. doi:10.1177/107769900408100209.

Warf, Barney, and Santa Arias, eds. 2008. *The Spatial Turn: Interdisciplinary Perspectives.* London: Routledge.

NEWS NOW
Interface, ambience, flow, and the disruptive spatio-temporalities of mobile news media

Mimi Sheller

This article explores how mobile consumption practices afforded by new mobile media have transformed the spatialities and temporalities of news media through processes such as proliferation, participation, personalization, cross-platform flow, geolocation, and mapping. Expanding journalism studies to encompass digital social media and the interdisciplinary field of mobilities research, the approach taken here gives greater attention to the making and unmaking of materialities and infrastructure in order to show how the mobile production, dissemination, and consumption of news produces new spatial temporalities and scales. With the emergence of various mobile interfaces and personalized networks connected via mobile social media, news is not only constantly accessed "on demand" from miniature mobiles, but also tagged, curated, aggregated, and easily re-distributed, fostering "ambient journalism" (Hermida) and on-location "citizen witnessing" (Allan). Through a historical analysis of changes in the New York Times *since the 1990s and a consideration of emerging modes of on-demand, on-location, participatory news production, it is argued that the redistribution of the places, spaces, and timing of news production and consumption has transformed not only the content, form, and style of news, but also the very temporality of news as an event. Through an analysis of the impact of these changes on the reporting of recent natural disasters, the article seeks to envision an enlivened terrain of mobile news that is live, active, immersive, pervasive, and constantly updating, yet also attentive to the implications of infrastructural disruption, data-mining, and surveillance.*

Introduction

In the recent turn toward "materialist approaches" to media and mobility there has been an effort to investigate the significance of communication not simply as image, message, or content to be relayed from one point to another, but rather as an embodied spatial practice that produces space/time and is itself constitutive of social orders (Packer and Wiley 2012). Such an approach builds on the early work of James Carey on the materiality of communication, especially in its relation to transportation networks such as the train and the telegraph (Packer and Robertson 2007), while also incorporating more recent mobilities theory which also pays attention to the material infrastructures and "moorings" of mobility and communication systems, and their spatio-temporal effects (Sheller and Urry 2006; Hannam, Sheller, and Urry 2006). News media are especially dependent on various infrastructural moorings, including communications and transportation networks of various kinds, that enable news to flow. This article draws on the interdisciplinary field of mobilities research to think about the mobile production, dissemination, and consumption of news, and in particular how new interrelations between the spaces and times for news production and consumption produce new *spatial temporalities* for the "flow" of news (a term discussed in more detail below).

Chris Peters argues that there has been a lack of spatial awareness in journalism scholarship and especially in regard to mobile consumption practices afforded by new mobile media, which have transformed the spatial experience of news (Peters 2012). With the emergence of various mobile interfaces and personalized networks connected via mobile social media, news can not only be constantly accessed from "miniature mobiles" (personal devices that are always to hand), but can also be tagged, curated, aggregated, and easily re-distributed. This has affected the places, spaces, and timing of news production and consumption (in particular the use of travel time and waiting time), as well as contributing to the changing temporalities of news production, dissemination, and circulation. Furthermore, as Peters suggests, it has changed what news *is*.

This article will explore these issues first by considering the idea of print media as a "mobile interface", focusing on a brief case-history of the *New York Times* based on my own participant-observation there as an employee from 1990 to 1997. The second part develops this analysis of the changing spatio-temporalities of news today, focusing in particular on the disruptive impacts of social media which led to what Alfred Hermida defines as "ambient journalism", producing further changes in traditional print media outlets like the *New York Times*. The third section draws on the concept of "flow" as developed in the work of Kathleen Oswald and Jeremy Packer in their updating of Raymond Williams's prescient analysis of twentieth-century televisual culture, to further consider "instantaneous" and "on-demand" news in which mobile social media sources are incorporated into broadcasting. Finally, a brief case-study is provided of disaster and emergency news, based on my research experience in Haiti after the January 2010 earthquake, as well as subsequent work on lessons learned from Japan's disaster response after the March 2011 earthquake and tsunami.[1]

My overall aim is to show how the specific temporalities produced by mobile social media, and in particular the emergence of continuous real-time streaming of interactive and participatory news, produces a kind of constantly updated flow of "news now"—one that is simultaneously produced, consumed, and re-distributed by the audience through a variety of mobile spatial practices. Mobile news "prosumption" practices such as agglomeration, curation, crowd-sourcing, updating, tagging, and sharing have not simply enabled the repackaging and mobile distribution of news to tailored audiences. More fundamentally, I argue, the rise of on-demand, on-location, participatory capabilities has also changed the content, form, style, and temporality of news as event.

Print News as Mobile Interface

Traditional print news has always been associated with the production of "imagined communities", as Benedict Anderson ([1983] 2006) first reminded us, due to the daily production of a distributed readership who shared a ritual of simultaneous collective awareness as they opened the daily newspaper. Such rituals take place in specific places, but they are not simply sedentary. Newspapers are a mobile medium. The diurnal ritual of reading the paper in the morning and the evening connects readers to a wider public, one that is not present spatially but is an imagined community. Yet this imaginary public is also spatially located, for the newspaper reader observes "exact replicas of his own paper being consumed by his subway, barbershop, or residential neighbours", continually reassuring him "that the imagined world is visibly rooted in everyday life" (Anderson [1983] 2006, 36). This grounding of an imagined community in everyday places and their mobilities suggests a collective spatio-temporality enacted through the act of reading the news. Historically, this medium spread nationally and transnationally through colonial empires with increasingly fast delivery systems in the nineteenth century—from stagecoach to railway, from sailing ship to steam packet ship, and so on. Mobility and communication systems were intertwined, and producing and distributing the newspaper was a key component of this mobility system.

In the twentieth century, this temporal proximity of what is in the news (the event) and what is on the news (the report) was furthered in the case of print news by the use of new communication technologies such as satellite phones and electronic news services in newspaper production. The telegraph, the ticker-tape, and the radio brought an increasing approximation of "instantaneous news", which was reported on closer-and-closer to the time of the event itself, culminating with live television coverage of unfolding events. At the *New York Times* in the pre-social media era,[2] for example, while local reporters hit the streets and brought stories back to the newsroom each day, national and international news reporting came in from reporters and "stringers" around the world via email, teletext, telephone, sat-phone, and Associated Press or Reuters electronic news wires. Stories would flow into the newsroom up until about 3 pm, when the front-page meeting would take place to decide the lead stories of the day. These news stories of the day would be stitched together and edited from around 2 to 9 pm, with updates being added until the last minute. The paper was then "put to bed" and sent to the printing presses, with further significant updates or major new events coming in after 10 pm being added to the late editions up until about midnight. By 11 pm the editors would have already circulated a so-called "post-mortem" on the paper, highlighting errors. By the time paper deliveries landed on newsstands or people's doorsteps in the morning, it was still felt that this news was "fresh" and up-to-date. Yet for those working in the newsroom, the next day's paper was already effectively yesterday's news.

Newspapers are crucial to understanding the development of what we now call "mobile interfaces" (such as smartphones). Although mobile social media are often understood to be relatively new technologies, usually defined as "software, applications, or services accessed through mobile devices that allow users to connect with other people and to share information, news, and content" (Humphreys 2013, 21), we should not forget the cultural histories of newspaper being read during "in-between" times of transit (and of radio news being targeted for car-drivers especially during the morning and evening commute), and in those collective spaces noted by Anderson such as barbershops or cafes. The newspaper broadsheet (and especially tabloid) was itself a mobile object designed to be carried through the streets and read on trains, platforms, or subway cars, not simply in isolation, but *in a connected social space*.

Adriana de Souza e Silva and Jordan Frith remind us that in the nineteenth century readers also used newspapers (and paperback books) to manage their interactions in public spaces such as railway carriages, waiting areas, or park benches. "For 150 years after the first paperback novel was printed", they argue, "books and newspapers remained the most effective mobile technologies for filtering experience of public space" (De Souza e Silva and Frith 2012, 40). Immersion in reading a newspaper may allow "readers to carve a more private experience out of the shared public space of a crowded street", but it should not be thought of as a "privatization" of public space, because the "reader still must position herself physically in relation to other people in the space and must recognize to some degree the dynamics of the shared space", including noise, talk, and interruptions (59).

De Souza e Silva and Frith therefore describe mobile interfaces as something beyond specific technologies, and beyond communication mediators: they are "symbolic systems that filter information and actively reshape communication relationships, and also reshape the space in which social interaction takes place" (De Souza e Silva and Frith 2012, 4). Thus there is a double relation within the interface between the more interior-oriented relation between the reader and the information they are accessing, which can occur in various locations and during travel, and the more exterior-oriented relation between reader-equipped-with-mobile-object and a surrounding social space in which they interact both with the object and with the physical and social space. Interfaces are in part a physical device with a particular materiality, including software that produces an interactional space with specific affordances, but they also imply a deeper social shaping of how we interact with space, place, and others.

Today the tempo of the old *New York Times* newsroom seems far from instantaneous, while Anderson's sense of an authoritative national view and imagined community has largely receded. The rise of the internet certainly disrupted this model of print news, as did transformations in twentieth-century modes of broadcast television news. While I cannot fully explore the role of television here, I want to turn to the implications of mobile locative social media for effecting distinctive new processes for the organization of news production, distribution, and consumption. These changes not only transformed the spaces in which news is produced and the places in which it is consumed, but also the temporalities of each and the relation between them. In the transition from newsprint to mobile communication devices, what makes mobile social media so compelling, according to Lee Humphreys, is not just their mobility or their relation to space or even their social shaping of place—all of which are relevant to newsprint as well—but "because the means of media production, distribution, and consumption are on the same device" (Humphreys 2013, 23). Mobile social media intertwine both spatial processes and temporalities of news in new ways while using (and producing) new materialities.

Ambient Journalism

News production, distribution, and consumption has been transformed by new mobile interfaces, at first simply due to the digital delivery of content to internet platforms, but now especially by the proliferation of those that are socially connected and interactive. We are all familiar with the rise of internet news aggregation and commentary through Web platforms such as the Huffington Post, Slate, or The Daily Beast; and of course traditional media sources like the *New York Times* had to develop their own Web platforms for digital content. Initially, these were envisioned as desktop computer experiences. But even these news services have had to adapt quickly to mobile platforms and the rise of social media, which promote a kind of grazing across sites. Further adaptation is spurred on by the rise of hybrid socially networked, magazine-like news feeds such as BuzzFeed, or curated micro-blogging Twitter streams like BrainPicker, as well as applications for tablets and smartphones that use algorithms to deliver personalized news from across the Web on topics chosen by the reader, such as Zite. Micro-blogging allows brief blasts of information, especially accessed on mobile devices, which displaced the role of the newspaper as a key mobile interface in public space. These transformative mobile media thus changed not only where news is consumed, but also where and how it is produced and distributed.

In a study of these developments, Alfred Hermida (2010, 298) argues that "new para-journalism forms such as micro-blogging are 'awareness systems', providing journalists with more complex ways of understanding and reporting on the subtleties of public communication". He argues that

> these broad, asynchronous, lightweight and always-on communication systems are creating new kinds of interactions around the news, and are enabling citizens to maintain a mental model of news and events around them, giving rise to what this paper describes as ambient journalism. (Hermida 2010, 298)

In particular, they have been disruptive of traditional print news organizations, requiring new policies and practices concerning their use:

> Of particular concern has been how journalists should adopt social media within existing ethical norms and values (Posetti 2009), leading news organizations such as the *New York Times* (Koblin 2009), *Wall Street Journal* (Strupp 2009), and Bloomberg (Carlson 2009) to institute Twitter policies to bring its use in line with established practices. (Hermida 2010, 299)

Arguably, though, the traditional newsroom is not capable of adapting to the new situation simply by incorporating it (and the recent sales of the *Boston Globe* and the *Washington Post* suggest more radical digital strategy changes are needed for the industry to survive).

Representative of the digital revolution's impact on traditional media is the evolution of the *New York Times* over the last 20 years. When I first arrived there as a "copy girl" in 1990 they were still using the old Harris computer terminals, with a green glowing screen and line-by-line commands for type-setting articles; there was also still a ticker-tape feed with business news updates; and even pneumatic tubes for delivering important messages on scraps of paper to departments within the building. Finished articles were sent to composers and printing presses in the basement of the 43rd St. building at Times Square, operated by unionized workers, and loaded onto trucks for delivery. In the mid-1990s, the *New York Times* transitioned to actual desktop personal computers for editing and moving around copy, while incorporating Bloomberg news terminals, and Associated Press and Reuters news wires for constantly updated news feeds coming into the building. These transitions were followed by the introduction of digital typesetting, and finally the move of their entire printing operation to New Jersey and eventually the entire company moving out of the historic Times Square building.

As the means of production was transformed (including painful reductions in journalist and editorial staff), so too did the "interface" for receiving the newspaper also shift from newsprint on paper to website, and finally to tablet and mobile delivery of Web content. This was accompanied by the rise of enhanced visual media (both photographic slide shows and video Timescasts), more interactive features, and the development of near real-time blogs such as the Lede, with constantly updated stories. Live-blogging has also transformed the role of newspaper journalism at competitors like *The Guardian*, possibly becoming what some identify as a "pivotal platform" for digital journalism (Thurman and

Walters 2013). While @NYTimes had 2 million followers on Twitter in March 2011 (Lasorsa, Lewis, and Holton 2012, 22), by August 2013 this had grown to more than 9 million. The *New York Times* also allowed for personalization, in which subscribers could choose topics to receive special email updates on, subscribe to tailored lists of articles they might be interested in, and access easy tools for sharing stories on social media platforms. The newspaper that once addressed and imaginatively tied together a national public sphere through a universal daily product with "all the news that's fit to print" is now fragmented into a multiplicity of individualized experiences, places for consumption, and varied interfaces not only for engaging its content, but more significantly for engaging with wider social spaces and mobile publics while "consuming" (and actively re-distributing) news; i.e., people are micro-blogging and reading news anytime, anywhere, grazing snippets at work, at play, and in transit, with information coming to them from a diverse range of public and personalized sources.

One of the most important aspects of this transformation of interface is not merely the shifting location in which news is accessed now, but the changing ways in which, as an interface to public space, it changes the "systems that enable people to filter, control, and manage their relationships with the spaces and people around them" (De Souza e Silva and Frith 2012, 5). Sources like Twitter have especially begun to influence news that pertains to emergency situations such as terrorist attacks, political uprisings or suppression, and natural disasters. BBC reporting on the Mumbai bombings in 2008, coverage of the Iranian elections in 2009 (Hermida 2010, 300), and all of the various events involved in the "Arab Spring", for example, heavily incorporated Twitter feeds into mainstream journalistic practices, even while professional journalists reflected on the problematic nature of the unverified information. Hermida describes such ambient journalism as "an awareness system that offers diverse means to collect, communicate, share and display news and information, serving diverse purposes" (301). Such always-on asynchronous communication systems offer a new kind of immersion in the time-space of news as event, which becomes especially acute in emergency situations, which I will focus on in the final section because they are indicative of some of the most extreme transformations taking place.

Ambient journalism (see also Burns 2010) then rebounds back on the production of news itself. As popular *New York Times* columnist Maureen Dowd writes of her conversation with James Gleick on a piece he wrote for *New York* magazine following the Boston Marathon bombings (media reflecting on media reflecting on media):

> The TV audience used to be isolated and passive," he said. "Now everybody is tweeting and texting to everybody else, and sometimes the viewers know more than the hapless microphone-wielding faces on TV. During the drama of the Boston manhunt and car chase, it never occurred to me to turn on the TV. The screen I needed was on my iPhone, where I followed the tweets of newspaper reporters running through the streets of Boston and Cambridge residents listening to gunfire in real-time. The Internet is messy, pointillist, noisy, often wrong. But if you had a visceral need for instantaneity, TV couldn't compete. (Dowd 2013)

The tethering of television production to a single production crew on location, or a distant newsreader in a studio, make it uncompetitive in the race to get ambient news instantaneously from every direction. Print news media, even slower off the mark in filing, editing, and publishing stories, resorts to reporting on what is happening on micro-blogging sites, which become part of the news itself; or the story becomes live-blogging about television coverage that already incorporates live social media. Traditional reporting in such a context begins to seem distanced, somewhat out of touch, and less up-to-date than what the audience already knows.

Within the field of journalism studies these transformations have mainly been approached in terms of their impact on the norms and practices of journalists, who have had to adapt to the new digital context in a variety of ways (Burns 2010; Hermida 2010; Lasorsa, Lewis, and Holton 2012). Although these are all interesting questions, here I am less interested in professional practices, journalistic ethics, or questions of fact verification, transparency and gatekeeping, and more concerned with the broader impacts of these disruptive transformations on the underlying spatial and temporal formations of news and what we understand it to be. When is something news? What is our relation to events? The connectivity of audiences (and broadcast news producers) to live socially sourced information raises questions of the relation between news, locational mobility, and spatio-temporality, which we can pursue in terms of the concept of flow.

News Flow Now

In their recent analysis of the materiality of digital media, Kathleen Oswald and Jeremy Packer build on Raymond Williams' conceptualizations of "mobile privatization" and "flow" while developing them in new directions for the analysis of contemporary practices, technologies, and corporate organization of multi-platform, on-demand, digital media. They argue that:

> digital screens need to be understood outside the conventions of media specificity; that is we should no longer treat film, television, the computer, and telephone as separate entities ... we examine how the use of multiple screens orchestrate the individual's material flow through space according to a fluid set of temporal programs ... In our conception, flow is the process by which subjects and attendant data move seamlessly through the world in unison. (Oswald and Packer 2012, 277)

The implications of this approach for the analysis of news production and consumption is, first, that it is far more fluid than in the past, shifting across screens and devices as consumers move through time and space, so that "increasingly this means following the shifting flow of the user in time and space across devices" (Oswald and Packer 2012, 283). In other words, it is significant not only that viewers/readers/listeners are "more distributed than ever before, but that they are time shifting, format shifting, and screen-shifting" (279). The "media" actually overflow their medium—news crosses media platforms, slipping easily from one format to another, and the formats themselves are increasingly losing their technological distinctiveness when newspapers and TV are on your computer and your phone, the internet is on your TV or in your car, and all information can be carried around on phones, tablets, even glasses.

Second, news consumption should be conceived of as *on-demand*, which Oswald and Packer (2012, 279) identify "as the model of communication that best describes a new set of tele-practices, and ultimately, a new model of flow". In contrast to Williams's analysis of the 1970s television media, in which the viewer was "mentally or cognitively moved through media content, while their bodies remain fixed in place" (277), it is now crucial to attend to how the bodies of viewers move through space as they call up content on various devices on demand. And the consumption of news content, in particular, may flow between digital text and digital video delivered "on-demand" to various moving screens, as well as audio content delivered by conventional radio, digital radio, and on-demand services such as "podcasting" delivered to personal media players in various locations. Whereas Williams' concept of flow occurred within the individual television program, across a scheduled series of programs and advertisements, and in relation to the temporal flow of the viewer's workday and leisure time, Oswald and Packer suggest how flow must now be extended out into an even more scaled-up notion of movement across devices, spaces, and moments of news consumption, which reflects a new organization of capital, labor, and consumer-subjects.

There is a third component of flow, however, to which Oswald and Packer give less attention, which is the production, curating, and sharing of media content by the "audience", which has been accompanied by the rise of "aggregation" by specialists with a particular sensibility or ethos. With the explosion of social media tools for sharing content (in this case news especially), media analysts such as Ben Adler writing in the *Columbia Journalism Review* describe four overlapping and mutually reinforcing trends:

- *Proliferation* of news sources, formats, and new technologies for media consumption.
- *Participation* by consumers in the dissemination and creation of news, through social media sharing, commenting, blogging, and the posting online of photos, audio, and video.
- *Personalization* of one's streams of news via email, mobile apps, and social media.
- *Source promiscuity*—rather than having strong relationships with a handful of media brands, young people graze among a vast array of news outlets Adler (2013).

News is now being "pushed" out to audiences via social media sites including Facebook, Twitter, and Tumblr, where it is mixed with commentary and recommendations from personal social networks, and where the audience/consumer can easily add comments, share items, and re-distribute it to their social networks. These aspects of flow amongst "empowered and participatory news consumers" and "citizen witnesses" (Allan 2013) indicate a far wider destablization of older tele-practice models of temporality and spatiality, and the need for the study of news to hybridize with the fields of locative media and social media studies, as well as mobilities research. This idea of flow relates to recent perspectives in mobilities research that also consider how place itself is "in play", with the flows of mobility re-shaping spaces and places, not just moving through them (Hannam, Sheller, and Urry 2006). This idea of flow, therefore, is less like water running smoothly down a channel, and more like an entire terrain forming in the manner of lava spreading unevenly, bubbling up and overflowing, and melting some structures even as it hardens into other structural forms. In other words, we can combine Hermida's idea of ambient journalism with Packer and Oswald's reinterpretation of media flow, to envision an enlivened terrain of mobile news that is live, active, immersive, pervasive, and constantly updating: what I call "news now".

These forms of flow are not just re-shaping news distribution, but also content itself. As Adler points out, young audiences are increasingly consuming news on smartphones or tablets, which promotes short-form, summary presentation with easily clickable links to longer stories. The moving body, the capabilities of the thumb, and the distribution of attention to the physical and the digital world are all re-shaping not just the delivery systems to be on-demand, but also the stylistic form of news to be easily consumable on-location. As "symbolic systems that filter information and actively reshape communication relationships, and also reshape the space in which social interaction takes place", to return to De Souza e Silva and Frith's definition, new mobile interfaces are reshaping not only how we filter and access news, but also how we engage in communication and shape social space, and hence how news itself is packaged, presented, and connected to location, proximity, and place.

Fourth, these practices have further implications for the temporality of news as well as for content. As news audiences participate in the production of news streams, commenting and sharing, they not only become "amateur journalists" (content producers) and aggregators (content distributors), but in certain key instances have become *part of the news itself*—"citizen witnesses" whose acts of citizenship are as important as their acts of witnessing (Allan 2013). That is to say, during events being covered "in the news", the instantaneous circulation of *on-location* information, pictures, and video can contribute to the unfolding event, shifting the audience to being "on the news", as noted above by Gleick. Audience commentary is not simply occurring after the fact, but is also being picked up by news producers from those "tweeting on the ground" as part of the production of stories in progress. This has occurred in relation to unfolding political events (e.g., the Arab Spring uprisings, or the Occupy Movement); emergency response during disasters (e.g., during and immediately after the Haiti earthquake of 2010 or the Japanese earthquake and tsunami of 2011); or in the tracking of criminal or terrorist suspects (e.g., the killing of Osama bin Laden in 2011, or coverage of the Boston Marathon bombings in 2013, in which live social media were incorporated into mainstream media broadcasts— and FBI and police intelligence—of the apprehension of suspects as it unfolded).

In other words, there is a breaking of the "proscenium",[3] so to speak, not only between the producers of news content and the audience of the news, who are now mixed together in processes of co-producing and sharing content, but also between the event itself and the news of the event, which are now mixed together in the dynamic temporality of the news cycle. Even traditional newsrooms have started using social media alongside their own hired reporters, feeding that information into new reporting, online broadcasts as well as onto their own mobile platforms. The audience is now part of the news production cycle. Reporting on the event no longer follows the event, but is co-temporaneous and in some ways may even precede the full unfolding of "the news". This, of course, presents problems of source verification, rumor, and viral transmission of false information in ways that were in the past far more controlled by news organizations. As Gleick suggested, "Crowd-sourcing quickly turned into witchhunting ... and bits of intelligence surfaced amid 'new forms of banality'" (Dowd 2013). It has also created new opportunities for dramatic intelligence leaks, as we have seen in the cases of Bradley Manning's relationship with Wikileaks, and National Security Agency (NSA) leaker Edward Snowden's relationship with the *Guardian* reporter Glen Greenwald.

The merging of event and news has been especially marked in the occurrence of natural disasters (and other emergency situations), in which there is an urgency to locating and contacting victims, identifying aid distributions, and conveying accurate overviews to broader media outlets. While these kinds of urgent events differ from everyday news coverage, they offer an interesting example of the furthest-reaching efforts to completely blur the production, consumption, and distribution of news into a single flow of ambient live updates of an ongoing situation. In the final section, therefore, I will briefly discuss news flow during disaster response, especially in relation to the spread of new infrastructures for mobile communication in the Global South, and issues of the breakdown of infrastructure and disruption of communication networks just when they are most needed.

Disaster Now

The incorporation of social media into user-generated and user-shared news coverage has especially important implications for disaster news, which combines highly localized events and immediate impacts with very wide, often global, audiences. This has generated not only a new space for news audiences, but a new kind of crowd-sourced (but partially verified) means of news collection, with a new temporality of flow for both production and consumption. Crowd-sourced news based on localized reports are now being curated into open-source GIS mapping platforms (particularly as used during disaster response), such as Ushahidi. Ushahidi's Crisis Map of Haiti is described as:

> the most comprehensive and up-to-date crisis map available to the humanitarian community. The information here is mapped in near real time and gathered from reports coming from inside Haiti via: SMS, Web, Email, Radio, Phone, Twitter, Facebook, Television, List-serves, Live streams, Situation Reports. Volunteers at Ushahidi's Situation Room at the Fletcher School, in Washington DC, Geneva, London and Portland are mapping the majority of the reports submitted to Ushahidi in near real-time. The volunteers then identify GPS coordinates for the reports and geo-tag the reports on the Ushahidi map, using OpenStreetMap, which is then made available under a Creative Commons License (Attribution-NonCommercial-Share Alike).[4]

This kind of mapping project is suggestive of the ways in which micro-level news is now being made accessible and searchable by location, so that interested parties can share information, and zero in on specific sites or types of information. Users can add their own filters or over-lays to such open-source news maps, concentrating for example on where buildings have collapsed or where water is in short supply. This kind of "zeroing in" is suggestive of some of the ways in which ambient news flows more generally allow the user to zoom in at different scales, dipping into locations marked with different proximity to the events. One can switch scales and perspectives between different eye-witnesses, aggregators, local sources, or national commentators.

Secondly, there are political questions surrounding infrastructure and how it is produced, including the infrastructure for producing, distributing, and accessing news during disasters.[5] As Heather Horst notes, building on Susan Leigh Star's foundational work drawing attention to infrastructure (Star 1999), communications companies operate in the Global South with a certain degree of latitude that gives them leverage over state capacities to regulate them; at the same time states may try to exercise control "from above" while citizens try to appropriate, hack, or game the system "from below" (Horst 2013). The telecom company Digicel, for example, "transformed the telecommunications industry in Jamaica (Horst and Miller 2006) and subsequently moved into other 'island markets' in the Caribbean and the Pacific" (Horst 2013, 149). Companies like Digicel disrupt the business model of "national carriers" and a state monopoly over national space, with implications for news flow, imagined communities, and the creation of public space. Horst and her collaborators have studied the complex relations of mobile communication on the Haitian–Dominican border, as users tried to navigate the use of competing infrastructures (Baptiste, Horst, and Taylor 2011). This work reminds us of the material grounding and spatial frictions of infrastructure, and the constellations of people, devices, networks, laws, and regulations that together enable any communication (and specifically for our purposes "news") to be unevenly produced, distributed, and consumed. Flows, in other words, and the ways in which they shape space, states, and subjects, are highly uneven, and even turbulent. While these issues are often "backgrounded" in highly developed countries, we should remember that all communication infrastructures, including mobile interfaces, are "a dynamic process that is simultaneously made and unmade" (Horst 2013, 151), by companies, by audiences, and by regulators. The questions raised about NSA surveillance of national and global telecommunications flows, for example, suggest interesting avenues of inquiry about the spatio-temporalities produced by ambient media.

Following the Japanese earthquake, tsunami, and nuclear meltdown of March 2011, there was a further problem highlighted in regard to the breakdown of infrastructure, leading to difficulties in actually getting news reports out of the affected regions because of the loss of cell towers and power lines. News agencies and first responders resorted to Google, Facebook, Ustream, and Twitter to find local information, but they also needed to go to the field to update real information on the ground. Toyota donated a 1000 watt electric vehicle to send out "Information Rangers" who could not only get to affected places, but could also generate power for communicating. They gathered and collected information into a bigger context map, using smartphones to load short location-tagged video clips. Thus they were able to produce both "macro-level" news for newspapers and television, as well as "micro-level" news for people trying to find family members or responders trying to find out where food deliveries were needed. Ushahidi crisis mappers also started a Japanese version, called Shinsa Info.[6] Insofar as news broadcasting depends on flows of mobile social media in the future, questions of resilience and continuity of flows in the face of disruption will become increasingly significant for all types of news.

The experience in Japan indicated that emergency evacuation centers were not very well prepared to use social media. First, many users of social media were concentrated in urban areas, so there was less news coming from rural areas. More people needed training in social media use, and especially how to collect and curate local news into a useful platform. And second, there were also physical and material aspects of flow that need to be addressed. Evacuation centers need back-up power sources and wireless base stations. Back-up battery cells could help in re-charging hand-sets, but also back-up bandwith is needed and communications service competitors need to share each other's infrastructure to expand a network temporarily. Although we have the expectation that news will come "instantaneously" from on-the-ground eye-witnesses, we actually do not have a resilient enough infrastructure to provide such capabilities once a major incident has occurred. The experience of many other emergency situations in the past suggests that cell-phone bandwith is frequently overwhelmed in the immediate vicinity of an emergency, as happened in Lower Manhattan during 9/11; cell-towers may be knocked out, or public access may be closed down entirely for security reasons, as happened following the Boston Marathon bombings.

Subsequent follow-up reporting on disasters may also rely significantly on social media and crowd-sourcing, and increasingly the recent turn toward data-mining. Data from Digicel on cell-phone usage in Haiti, for example, helped support indications of the number of people who moved out of Port-au-Prince and into provincial areas in the weeks immediately after the event, but also showed their eventual return to the city (Lu, Bengtsson, and Holme 2012). Carrying our cell phones with us, and connecting to different cell towers, we become tracers of population movements. Visualizations of such traffic data (of people, or cars, or air traffic, or shipping lanes) have provided a new dimension of reporting who and what is moving where, offering new kinds of global and regional knowledge. Mobile social networks, moreover, may be highly localized yet also span international borders, playing an important role in spreading news across diasporas which are connected emotionally and imaginatively to a homeland, but live elsewhere. Rather than remaining regional or national, such diasporic imagined communities create their own news networks distributed across social media, forming important new transnational spaces for news production, aggregation, dissemination, and consumption.

Finally, location itself can become an important kind of news source. Open crowd-sourced maps created on Google Earth have offered an increasingly utilized means for geo-tagging information that can be shared with others and frequently updated, thus becoming a new news medium. Locative mobile social networks such as Foursquare are used to find local user-annotations on specific places and points of interest, creating a genre of highly place-specific news. Foursquare and Twitter platforms also allow for highly event-specific and location-based exchange of rapid flows of information and commentary amongst users during a particular happening, while short message platforms like WhatsApp can enable news to flow without archiving any meta-data on producers or locations. These developments in proximity services all have spatial and temporal implications for the way current mobile interfaces are potentially re-shaping social spaces and forms of communication associated with the production and consumption of news. Location, proximity, instantaneity, and sharing have all become hallmarks of news flows today.

Conclusion

This article has suggested some of the ways in which journalism and communications scholarship has begun to address the shifting spaces and places of news production and consumption, as well as the mobilities and temporalities of distribution and cross-platform flow. Building on the concept of mobile interfaces as part of news making, I first showed some of the continuities from traditional print media to contemporary mobile media. In both cases, I argued, it is important to attend to how space and place are shaped by these filtering systems, both as physical devices for seeking information in portable contexts and as screens and portals for managing social interaction in public space. In delineating the impacts of digital media on traditional news organizations such as the *New York Times*, I sought to also show the disruptions taking place in journalistic practice and print news publishing. How audiences get news (and spread news) shapes social space and place-based imagined communities, but also refracts back on news production itself, changing the processes of news media as corporate structures, as national media, and as gatekeepers of what is news.

Then, through the concepts of ambient journalism and flow, I explored how the spatio-temporalities of news production and consumption are changing, including the impact on news making of processes of proliferation, participation, personalization, and promiscuity of sources. Micro-blogging and ambient awareness offer key modalities of the new news environment. Insofar as news is now on-demand, on-location, and accessed via mobile devices, it reflects new forms of organization of capital, labor, and consumer-subjects, which I have not fully explored here, but which are relevant to thinking about how news flows are uneven, place-specific, and productive of social relations and spatio-temporalities. As the circulation of news changes, I have argued, it transforms the very ground beneath our feet: ambient flows of news re-situate how we understand where we are, who we are connected with, what our "present" moment actually is. The now-ness of news, in other words, offers a new sense of the present.

Finally, I have argued that these changing interfaces and temporalities of news flow are especially relevant in consideration of disaster and emergency news, including situations in the Global South and non-Western contexts. By paying more attention to these extreme situations, we may also gain a better sense of infrastructural issues that are left in the background in more everyday contexts, but are actually crucial aspects of political and ethical debate. Locational tagging of information especially offers great powers to zero in and zoom out of a vast range of situations, yet at the same time it implicates information flows in potentially controversial situations of surveillance, unwarranted tracking and data-mining by powerful agencies, which all create imbalances of power between those with those capabilities and those without. Secondly, the potential disruption of communications infrastructures, whether by government interference or natural disaster, signals our complete dependence on the everyday working of infrastructural systems. The more we depend on proliferation and participation to be our "eyes and ears", the more we need to be concerned with the resilience of our means of communication.

While this is only a very preliminary overview of these issues, I hope to have suggested the ways in which a "material turn" in journalism studies that includes an emphasis on perspectives from the fields of mobilities research and digital media can contribute to a better understanding of how news now is being produced, distributed, and consumed. We are in the midst of a still emergent paradigm shift, an unsettling of older media regimes and the rise of new ones, with important lessons to be learned from the making and unmaking of infrastructures, spatio-temporalities, and the potential impacts of disruptions. In addition to attending to the technologies, infrastructures, and materialities of news mobilities, I would further conclude that studies of the new flows of ambient journalism will make their greatest contribution if they keep linking the transformation of spatio-temporal structures of news-making back to the guiding history of press freedom, democratic publics, and citizenship. The re-making of news does not mean it is automatically stronger or weaker, better or worse, than in the past, but only that we must find new ways to continue to guard against its suppression and maintain its vital role in the changing global media regime.

NOTES

1. My involvement in Haiti arises from a National Science Foundation grant NSF-RAPID: "Supporting Haitian Infrastructure Reconstruction Decisions with Local Knowledge", PI Franco Montalto, Co-PI's Michael Piasecki, Patrick Gurian, and Mimi Sheller, No. 1032184, April 2012 to March 2013; and as an expert advisor from Janaury to May 2012 to the World Bank's Global Facility for Disaster Risk Reduction, meeting at the World Bank, Tokyo, Japan, and at the Earthquake Engineering Research Institute in Oakland, CA, to help produce a report on "Lessons from the Japanese Earthquake and Tsunami for Developing Countries".

2. This account is based on my experience of working in at the *New York Times* as a news clerk and news assistant in the mid-1990s.
3. The proscenium is the wall that separates the stage from the auditorium and provides the arch that frames it.
4. Accessed December 29, 2011, at http://haiti.ushahidi.com/page/index/1.
5. For a critique of uneven access to such online tools in post-earthquake Haiti, based on my own research there in 2010, see Sheller (2012).
6. Information on Japan comes from my participation in the World Bank Seminar "Disaster Risk Management and Social Media", January 17, 2012, Tokyo, including presentations by Mr. Junya Ishikawa, Board Member, Tasukeai Japan, and CEO Dreamdesign Co. Ltd., Mr. Toru Takanarita, Professor, Sendai University, and Mr. Hiroyasu Ichikawa, SocialCompany Inc.

REFERENCES

Adler, Ben. 2013. "Streams of Consciousness." *Columbia Journalism Review*, May 1. http://www.cjr.org/cover_story/steams_of_consciousness.php?page=all.

Allan, Stuart. 2013. *Citizen Witnessing: Revisioning Journalism in Times of Crisis*. Cambridge: Polity.

Anderson, Benedict. ([1983] 2006). *Imagined Communities: Reflections on the Origins and Spread of Nationalism*. New ed. London: Verso.

Baptiste, Espelencia, Heather Horst, and Erin Taylor. 2011. "Earthquake Aftermath in Haiti: The Rise of Mobile Money Adoption and Adaptation." *Lydian Journal* (7) (May).

Burns, Alex. 2010. "Oblique Strategies for Ambient Journalism." *Media-Culture Journal* 13 (2). http://journal.mediaculture.org.au/index.php/mcjournal/article/view/Article/230.

De Souza e Silva, Adriana, and Jordan Frith. 2012. *Mobile Interfaces in Public Space: Locational Privacy, Control, and Urban Sociability*. London: Routledge.

Dowd, Maureen. 2013. "Lost in Space." *The New York Times*, April 23. http://www.nytimes.com/2013/04/24/opinion/dowd-lost-in-space.html?_r=0.

Hannam, Kevin, Mimi Sheller, and John Urry. 2006. "Mobilities, Immobilities, and Moorings." *Mobilities* 1 (1): 1–22. doi:10.1080/17450100500489189.

Hermida, Alfred. 2010. "Twittering the News." *Journalism Practice* 4 (3): 297–308. doi:10.1080/17512781003640703.

Horst, Heather. 2013. "The Infrastructures of Mobile Media: Towards a Future Research Agenda." *Mobile Media and Communication* 1 (1): 147–152.

Horst, Heather, and Daniel Miller. 2006. *The Cell Phone: An Anthropology of Communication*. Oxford: Berg.

Humphreys, Lee. 2013. "Mobile Social Media: Future Challenges and Opportunities." *Mobile Media and Communication* 1 (1): 20–25.

Lasorsa, Dominic L., Seth C. Lewis, and Avery E. Holton. 2012. "Normalizing Twitter." *Journalism Studies* 13 (1): 19–36. doi:10.1080/1461670X.2011.571825.

Lu, Xin, Linus Bengtsson, and Petter Holme. 2012. "Predictability of Population Displacement After the 2010 Haiti Earthquake." *Proceedings of the National Academy of Sciences of the United States of America*, June 18. http://www.pnas.org/content/early/2012/06/11/1203882109.full.pdf+html.

Oswald, Kathleen, and Jeremy Packer. 2012. "Flow and Mobile Media: Broadcast Fixity to Digital Fluidity." In *Communication Matters: Materialist Apporaches to Media, Mobility and Networks*, edited by J. Packer and S. C. Wiley, 276–287. London: Routledge.

Packer, Jeremy, and Craig Robertson. 2007. *Thinking with James Carey: Essays on Communications, Transportation, History*. New York: Peter Lang.

Packer, Jeremy, and Stephen Crofts Wiley, eds. 2012. *Communication Matters: Materialist Apporaches to Media, Mobility and Networks*. London: Routledge.

Peters, Chris. 2012. "Journalism to Go." *Journalism Studies* 13 (5–6): 695–705. doi:10.1080/1461670X.2012.662405.

Sheller, Mimi. 2012. "Islanding Effects: Mobility Systems and Humanitarian Logistics in Post-Earthquake Haiti." *Cultural Geographies* 20 (2): 185–204. special issue on Islanding Geographies, eds. Eric Clark and Godfrey Baldaccino. doi:10.1177/1474474012438828.

Sheller, Mimi, and John Urry. 2006. "The New Mobilities Paradigm." *Environment and Planning A* 38: 207–226. doi:10.1068/a37268.

Star, Susan L. 1999. "The Ethnography of Infrastructure." *American Behavioral Scientist* 43 (3): 377–391. doi:10.1177/00027649921955326.

Thurman, Neil, and Anna Walters. 2013. "Live Blogging – Digital Journalism's Pivitol Platform?" *Digital Journalism* 1 (1): 82–101. doi:10.1080/21670811.2012.714935.

TOWARD NEW JOURNALISM(S)
Affective news, hybridity, and liminal spaces

Zizi Papacharissi

Research indicates that information sharing and conversational uses of online media by journalists, news organizations, and individual users render complex and networked social awareness systems that evolve beyond traditional ecologies of journalism. This essay examines the form of news "prodused" through networked platforms that converge broadcast and oral traditions of storytelling into contemporary news practices. Synthesizing existing research, I argue that the shape news takes on is affective, the form of production is hybrid, and that spaces produced discursively through news storytelling frequently function as electronic elsewheres, or as social spaces that support marginalized and liminal viewpoints. Affective news streams are defined as news collaboratively constructed out of subjective experience, opinion, and emotion all sustained by and sustaining ambient news environments. They provide liminal layers to storytelling, but also a way for storytelling audiences to feel their own place into a developing news story.

Introduction

In *Vers une architecture* (Towards an Architecture), Le Corbusier, a pioneer of modern architecture, famously proclaimed a new direction for architects, meant to fundamentally reshape how we design and interact with buildings. Envisioning style as the direct outcome of socio-cultural context, and as such, always in flux, he directed architects to focus on form instead. Thus the stylized contraptions of art deco and eclecticism were to be abandoned for exterior forms that directly derived from the interior, with style to be organically set by the epoch. The technological advancements of engineering were beginning to enable architectural forms well beyond the scope of what architecture had previously perceived. Engineers, Le Corbusier (1931, 31) provoked, "overwhelm with their calculations our expiring architecture." A new architecture must thus emerge, that utilizes technology to present solutions to how we organize walls and space, light and shade, in ways that are organic, living, and reflexive. Form thus becomes the result of this reflexivity, and not the result of an imposed style.

There is an important parallel to be drawn between how the advancements of engineering enabled architecture to become more organic, and how contemporary engineers of information sharing permit journalism to become grounded in organic necessity. Engineering advancements of the industrial revolution presented new ways of manipulating space, and Le Corbusier called for architects to rethink how they turn space into place. If journalism is to be understood as the contemporary practice of turning an event into a story, then on-going technological advancements afford new ways of letting information shape storytelling, and present new spaces that become the contemporary places of storytelling.

In this essay, I synthesize previous and on-going research to describe these new places of news storytelling, and the form that storytelling takes on as news audiences find their own place in it. I understand place as a particular location that bears significance for human agents, assembled and attained relationally, but also reflective of power structures and allowing potential for agency (Massey 1994; Couldry 2000). Attaining, and asserting, one's own place in a developing news story is effected through a variety of practices that blend news co-creation with the social practices of news sharing. Telling stories, about ourselves and others, has always formed the core of our socializing habitus. Telling, sharing, and commenting on news stories has its own place within this socializing infrastructure, and new(er) technologies expand our storytelling repertoire. Ultimately, telling a story represents an attempt to present one's own perspective on a particular course of events, and to thus frame how things happened. It represents an act of agency, although the extent to which this act grants the individual greater autonomy, and by consequence, power, depends on socio-cultural context and storytelling fluency. Socio-cultural context evolves an assemblage of components that set the stage for storytelling, inclusive of the affordances of technologies, which are always historically specific. Fluency derives from the ability of the individual to manipulate not just the affordances of technologies, but the greater socio-cultural context within which those are utilized. Storytelling becomes an exercise in power; one with uncertain outcomes but exciting potential.

Because all, and especially new(er), media become meaningful to the extent that they enable our own autonomy across time and space, I begin by describing what the new places of storytelling look like. For journalism studies, this permits us to understand how audiences employ news storytelling to develop their own takes on what makes a news story, and what counts as journalism. But audiences do not engage in practices of co-creation from the conventional spaces of news production and consumption. They tell stories from the spaces and places of their everyday lives, and tell them in ways that further infuse these spaces with meaning.

People navigate and organize these spaces so as to preserve storytelling autonomy, and tell stories as they traverse boundaries public and private, mobile and local. The affordances of technologies further remediate space and enhance, or discourage, particular narrative tendencies. In telling their own stories and engaging in meaning-making practices, storytelling audiences deconstruct and reconstruct storytelling conventions that blend the traditions of a primary and secondary orality. I trace how the form of these stories is grounded in affective gestures, invited by the platforms and re-appropriated by users to infuse stories with subjectivity, thus producing a historically specific variety of affective news streams. The liminality inherent in these practices permits citizens to make space for their own place in the story, and potentially lay claim to how these stories combine to form histories.

The New Places of News Storytelling

Research indicates that information sharing and conversational uses of online media by journalists, news organizations, and individual users render complex and networked social awareness systems that evolve beyond traditional ecologies of journalism. The practices populating these evolving ecologies blend the production and consumption of news storytelling and have been describe as *produsage*. "Prodused" feeds of storytelling emerge out of user-led collaborative content creation, driven by citizens and journalists using networked media in ways that challenge the traditional dichotomies of production and consumption (Bruns 2008). The term is meant to describe, in a theoretically relevant manner, a set of practices that typically develop organically, as people share, forward, and comment on the news. While the resulting patterns of news sharing challenge our existing hierarchies of news production, consumption, and distribution, it is questionable whether people themselves consciously and constantly perceive themselves as *produsers* within the context of their everyday normality. The term serves as a reminder that the tenuous distinction between producers and consumers of content has faded, and thus underlines the hybrid nature of production and consumption. What is of most interest, as *produsage* lends form to developing news stories, is the extent to which the resulting and remediated places and spaces of news audiences evolve organically out of the everyday rhythms of sociality.

Through these patterns of communication, hybridity is introduced into the news system, by further blurring boundaries between information, news, and entertainment and by creating "subtle, but important shifts in the balance of power in shaping news production" (Chadwick 2011, 6). Furthermore, the "broad, asynchronous, light-weight and always-on" aspect of networked platforms afford individuals "an awareness system [with] diverse means to collect, communicate, share and display news and information, serving diverse purposes ... on different levels of engagement (Hermida 2010, 301). Homophily frequently shapes information flows across and within platforms, meaning that like-minded actors tend to listen to like-minded others, frequently inducing what has been described as an echo-chamber effect.[1] At the same time, these articulated opinion silos frequently permit the expression of under-represented or marginalized points of view. Thus, homophily and intra-elite competition present dominant features within these developing systems, without at the same time excluding motivated and strategically oriented actors from influencing the resulting agenda of issues (Chadwick 2011). As a result, these platforms pluralize storytelling and may *presence* voices that are not readily visible through the conventional architectures of broadcasting and journalism (Couldry 2012). Thus the new networked spaces of storytelling afforded via online platforms may be understood as *prodused*, *hybrid*, and *ambient*.

The places constructed, as individual users infuse these practices with subjective meaning, can be better understood by applying the concept of mobile privatization. Williams (1974) introduced the concept of mobile privatization to describe the ways in which mass media allow mobility to be pursued from the privacy of one's home, thus enabling the witnessing from home and live, via television, events taking place at a different location. The concept was redeployed by Spigel (1994, 2001), who explained how television introduces elements of mobility in domestic spaces, thus enabling both a retreat to suburbia and a newer form of media-centered community. Du Gay et al. (1997) evoked the concept of mobile privatization to understand the ways in which a social technology, like the Walkman, permits individuals to manage public and private boundaries, while at the same time communicating in a variety of symbolic contexts. Hay (2003) re-deployed the concept as privatized mobility, to examine the domestic sphere as a sphere of self-governance, organized through multiple technologies.

Both concepts of mobile privatization and privatized mobility have been employed to describe how people use mobile technologies to traverse public and private spaces and attain autonomy in how they connect with others and express themselves (Papacharissi 2010). They are meaningful because they help describe how the affordances of technologies change both the scale and experience of space while at the same time reproducing a degree of familiarity that permits audiences to somehow claim (their own) place. The concept captures the tendencies and tensions of technologies that afford expression and connection across spheres public and/or private. It explains how audiences access and utilize storytelling practices, in ways that afford them locational, and potentially storytelling, autonomy. For audience storytellers, mobile connectivity recalibrates the social spaces of everyday life, utilized to both read and tell stories about the news (e.g., Peters 2012). News produsage practices, in an age of mobile media, locate humans at the center of journalistically informed storytelling, and are driven by customizing and repurposing of information (Westlund 2013). Technologies that afford mobility, private and privatized, permit both journalists and citizens to produse stories that attain geo-social relevance; they utilize mobility to both emphasize a users' location but also to afford a "sense of place," which "helps to conceptualise individuals' physical, psychological and/or social connections to particular geographic territory without necessarily locating them within these physical spaces" (Hess 2013, 49). Technologies of mobility thus provide both locative and storytelling autonomy, situating the narrator locally and permitting connection beyond locality. They enable storytellers to mark stories with their own boundaries and break those boundaries at the same time, by providing socially informed connectivity (Hess 2013). The places of ambient, hybrid, and prodused news storytelling are public and private, mobile and geo-social, actual and imagined. A reasonable question that thus emerges is, if place is everywhere and boundless, is it still place or does it lose specificity? I argue that it is, but that the specificity derives from the ability to infuse place with one's own subjectivity. People have always told stories as a way of both affirming their place in time and defining what this place is. New(er) technologies further enhance our storytelling abilities by presenting space as boundless and providing us with means to make it specific. In the next few paragraphs, I explain how this occurs within the context of news production, sharing, and consumption.

Liminality, News, and Subjectivity

On a first level, online networked platforms render ambient, always-on spaces where hybrid forms of news produsage take place. These spaces are frequently facilitated by processes of mobile privatization (Williams 1974, 1983), and more recently, privatized mobility (Hay 2003; Papacharissi 2010), through technologies that afford users (mobile) autonomy in choosing how and from where they connect to the rest of the world. On a secondary level, these spaces facilitate social conversations that produce user-generated arguments on what is news, or how a particular story might take the shape of news. For example, research and anecdotal evidence suggest that platforms like Twitter, Reddit, and a variety of blog and microblog services sustain collaborative storytelling, co-creation, and curation of news content (Schonfield 2010). These pluralized and collectively prodused news feeds, generated by citizens committing independent or coordinated acts of journalism, present an important alternative to the dominant news economy (Bruns and Highfield 2012). Social news climates like Reddit, Digg, and Twitter, in particular, generate collective news intelligence through a blend of social practices that include voting, filtering, and commenting on news (Meraz 2012). They generate news streams that blend cursory references to news with deeply personal and mostly affective reactions to how this news is covered. Resulting news streams are generated through socially infused conventions that enable engagement through broadcasting, but also through a variety of practices that derived out of how people pay attention, or "listen" to the news (Crawford 2009). These practices frequently involve gestures that we may understand as phatic. Nodding along online may be expressed as "digging" a preferred news item, pointing to an item of interest may involve retweeting an article or opinion of interest, so as to expose it to others, and "like" presents a form of affective attunement that is frequently expressed in interpersonal conversation with no more than a smile. Phatic practices that drive interpersonal conversations are weaved into and remediated through the affordances of the socially mediated news platforms. As a result, sociality drives phatic practices of broadcasting and listening to the news. News storytelling becomes increasingly dynamic and constantly evolving, driven by on-going conversations that turn events into evolving news stories.

Crises, breaking news situations, and in general, instances when news changes too quickly for mainstream media to develop a coherent and fully sourced narrative, bring ambient, always-on news platforms to the fore of news reporting. Different ways of covering crises and emergent events evolve out of different feelings associated with space, and different ways for making meaning out of space, thus turning into place. A variety of approaches to objectivity in news coverage emphasize distance, whereas practices like embedding are meant to infuse reporting with more of a sense of place. News streams generated by users reporting and conversing about what is happening blend various perspectives on space and place and, in doing so, frequently emerge as the primary alternative for information sharing and news dissemination (Papacharissi 2010; Howard 2011). Platforms like Twitter may be used to break news but to also monitor and edit rumors that are reported as fact (e.g., Jewitt 2009; Vis 2013). Furthermore, in situations where access to media is controlled, restricted, or otherwise not trusted, these platforms permit citizens to bypass traditional news gatekeepers and radically pluralize the news generation and dissemination process, through engaging in electronic word-of-mouth news sharing (e.g., Dahlberg 2009; Jansen et al. 2009). During times of conflict, the ability to broadcast, listen in on, and edit word-of-mouth news on these platforms affords a powerful way for individuals to articulate voice and presence concerns typically marginalized. Thus, individuals are able to change the dynamics of conflict coverage and shape how events are covered, and possibly, how history is written (Hamdy 2010). For example, research on the Egyptian uprisings of 2011 that led to the resignation of Hosni Mubarak has indicated that Twitter supported information flows that were networked, enabled connections with diasporic publics, and sustained engagement reflexively (Lotan et al. 2011; Papacharissi and de Fatima Oliveira 2012). Furthermore, social media in current and past uprisings in Egypt afforded visibility to marginalized voices and enabled alternative narratives of dissention (Hamdy and Gomaa 2012; Lim 2012). During ongoing Occupy and Los Indignados demonstrations, news streams generated by citizens participating and monitoring the movements sustained ambient conversations containing a mix of news updates, opinions, and other socially relevant information (Burns 2010; Hermida 2010)

It goes without saying that each event produces its own news stream, and this stream will vary depending on the medium used to propagate this stream. Collaboratively generated news streams through social media platforms produce unique digital footprints of the movements, conflicts, or events they pertain to. But they tend to be characterized by a unique mix of broadcasting conventions and interpersonal conversation tendencies. These tendencies blend print storytelling practices, described by Ong (1982) as a secondary orality, with the traditions of oral forms of storytelling, understood as a primary orality. The resulting streams blend news facts with the drama of interpersonal conversation, and combine news reports with emotionally filled and opinionated reactions to the news in a manner that makes it difficult to discern news from conversation about the news, and doing so misses the point. Tweets recurring on #egypt reflected the need for people to get their own story, in their own words, out (e.g., Papacharissi and de Fatima Oliveira 2012). The streams generated by people contributing to #egypt or #ows (Occupy Wall Street) were not meant to function as a substitute, nor as a complement to news provided by more conventional broadcast channels, even though they frequently did. They were *prodused* as collaboratively generated news stories, on a par with news stories reported on CNN, BBC, Al-Jazeera, and a variety of other news outlets. They do not replace or fill out, but rather, reconcile, the more deliberate and self-conscious storytelling invited by print and electronic media with the additive and participatory nature of oral storytelling practices, producing a form of orality we may understand as digital. The *liminality* inherent in these streams, which occupy the in-between space rendered as primary and secondary oralities meet, renders them ambiguous, which means that they contain both empowering and disempowering potential for those participating in them.

Liminality and Locating One's Own Place in Storytelling

Liminality refers to events, processes, or individuals that are pertaining to the threshold of or an initial stage of a process. The anthropologist Victor Turner drew from the work of Arnold Van Gennep (1909) on rites of passage, to present a theory of liminality, meant to describe stages of transition and in-between positions that liminal individuals occupy. Turner (1967, 97) understood liminality as a position of social and structural ambiguity, or as "the Nay to all positive structural assertions, but as in some sense the source of them all, and, more than that, as a realm of pure possibility whence novel configurations of ideas and relations may arise." A group of liminal actors is characterized by a lack of social markers and an in-between stage of social heterarchy that renders all actors equal, for the time being. Users participating in news gathering, listening, and disseminating processes are engaged in this process from a liminal point of access. Liminality is a middle point in a dialog about what is news, in a society. It is a transitional, but essential stage in finding one's own place in the story, and doing so from a position that allows autonomy and potential for agency. In order for this dialog to be rendered liminal, all previous hierarchy about what makes news must be abandoned, and therein lies the empowering potential of liminality. At the same time, the very function of liminality is to abandon structure so as to permit activity that will result in the birthing of a new structure, and therein lie both potential empowerment and disepowerment. Turner (1974, 225) understands "liminality as a phase in social life in which this confrontation between 'activity which has no structure' and its 'structured results' produces in men their highest pitch of self-consciousness."

Individuals participating in liminal forms of news storytelling engage in a variety of practices that both reproduce and forget past conventions of news production and consumption. I describe these stages of collaborative news co-creation as liminal because engagement relies on the temporary dismantling of news rituals so as to be able to collectively (re)produce new ones. It is easy to read these as processes of news production. But they are primarily about utilizing tools of news production and consumption to find ones' own place in the story (Robinson 2009). Liminality affords the opportunity for actors engaging and making meaning out of the story to approach the event on equal footing, and to feel their own place in the story. Engaged in various stages of *produsage*, storytelling audiences occupy a liminal space; a space of transition, as they contribute to turning an event into a story. But liminality is a temporary state, defined as the midpoint between beginning and end. It is set into motion as an initiated action attempts to undo social structures or conventions and ends as the initiated action is (re)integrated into social structure. The ambient, hybrid, and produced practices of liking, retweeting, liveblogging, endorsing, and opining frequently blended into social reactions to news events are also liminal. They present personal and temporary content injections that play their own part in turning a news event into a story. As such, they are inspired by the potential of what the produced story might look like, however temporary the lasting effect of these subjective content interpolations may be. In the next few paragraphs, I explain how their form is affective.

Affect, Mediality, and Discursive Spaces

Affective gestures are richly afforded by social media and present a first and primal step in meaning-making practices. Affect, or affection as used by Spinoza, is not to be confused with personal sentiment, although it may be inclusive of it. Affect refers "to the ability to affect and be affected. It is a prepersonal intensity corresponding to the passage from one experiential state of the body to another and implying an augmentation or diminution in that body's capacity to act" (Deleuze and Guattari [1980] 1987, xvi). Emotion is subsumed within affect, and perhaps the most intense part of affect. Yet affect itself extends beyond feeling, as a general way of sense making, that is inclusive of potentialities and:

> regimes of expressivity ... tied to resonant wordings and diffusions of feelings/passions—often including atmospheres of sociality, crowd behaviours, contagions of feeling, matters of belonging ... and a range of postcolonial, hybridized, and migrant voices that forcefully question the privilege and stability of individualized actants possessing self-derived agency and solely private emotions within a scene or environment. (Seigworth and Gregg 2010, 8)

Listening to, editing, rebroadcasting, reacting, or remixing electronic word-of-mouth news present affective gestures directed at shifting the shape of news content, so as to infuse it with the potential of subjectivity.

Affect is characterized by intensity, although the emotional root of that intensity will vary (Massumi 2002). As it is released through interaction, it marks forces and non-forces of encounter, belonging and non-belonging, in-between-ness and "accumulative beside-ness" (Seigworth and Gregg 2010). Because of its *not yet* element (Spinoza, in Seigworth and Gregg 2010), affect contains anticipation, promise, hope, and potential, or, what Seigworth and Gregg term "an inventory of shimmers" (9). In this sense, this liminality renders individuals powerful, and potentially powerless at the same time. The potentiality imparted through affective flows is communicative of affect's futurity. Affect is habitually rhythmic, via the connected assemblages of habituated interpretations and practices. Yet it is also performatively evocative of would-be reactions, which become a "bridge of not yet, to the next" (14). Affect is performed, enacted via many sites, fluid and always in motion, and defined by its own variation (Massumi 2002). Affective processes may breathe new meaning into the texture of a performance, frequently through linguistic play or reversal of norms (Sedgwick 2003). It is through the interaction with further bodies, thoughts, and ideas that affect promises additional interpretive layers, thus suggesting potential actions. Thus, affect is frequently evoked in esthetics, as it is more a matter of *manner* than of essence, of how, rather than what affects or is affected, thus lending itself to performativity (Seigworth and Gregg 2010). For online networked platforms, subtle remixing, rebroadcasting, and sharing of content may produce affective gestures of potentially powerful symbolic impact. A recent Human Rights campaign prompted thousands of Facebook pages to "turn red," replacing profile pictures with a red equals sign in support of marriage equality. This affective gesture, materialized through the sharing, remixing, and rebroadcasting of a simple image, produced a simple message, rich in intensity.

Affective News Streams

Affect refers to emotion that is subjectively experienced, and has been connected to processes of premediation, enabled by newer media, that frequently anticipate news or events prior to their occurrence (Grusin 2010). Premediation involves a variety of affective gestures or expressions, made in anticipation of an event. These anticipatory gestures afford emotive expression but also inform the shape an event will take, and of course are further shaped by ongoing events. Such anticipatory gestures are rendered by audiences, publics, governments, and the media, and characterize how we experience global public events. The concepts of mediality, affectivity, and premediation characterize the flow of information across networked mediated systems, and permit us to understand governmental and social agency in a more complex way, inclusive of the role of emotion in coloring public dispositions.

I employ affect theory to define *affective news streams* as news collaboratively constructed out of subjective experience, opinion, and emotion, all sustained by and sustaining ambient news environments. We may understand affective news as the product of hybrid news values and ambient, always-on news environments. Affective news streams blend fact, opinion, and sentiment to the point where discerning one from the other is difficult, and doing so misses the point. Characterized by premediation, affective news streams may be filled with anticipatory gestures that are not predictive of the future, but communicate a predisposition to frame it, and in doing so, lay claim to latent forms of agency that are also affective and networked. If we understand affective news streams not just as informative, but as collectively generated, pluralistic arguments on what should be news, and how news stories should be told, we may interpret affective news gestures as indicative of political statements of dissent with a mainstream news culture, and the agendas that culture cultivates. More importantly, the infusion of affect into news marks the return of affect to the paradigm of news neutrality, which often leaves citizens cynical about news and wanting more. But it also provides a way of turning affective statements of disagreement into atomized political gestures that can be networked, to piece together a contemporary understanding of the political. In this manner, affective news streams discursively render spaces where the long-disconnected publics of citizens and journalists may reconnect.

Affect drives a variety of news broadcasting and storytelling practices that infuse news reporting with intensity, thus producing affective news. For example, the breaking news ticker, now ubiquitous in TV news, is filled with intensity, expressed in anticipation of events that are in the process of happening. Its form is premediated, as it is employed to report on an event that is unfolding and has not yet been developed into a news story (Grusin 2010). News reports offered by journalists and news anchors may similarly convey a sense of intensity, especially when providing information on events constantly evolving, such as crises and emergencies, but also weather or sports updates. Affective news streams frequently populate greater narratives of suspense and curiosity, and enjoyment derived from them is often independent of the factuality of the information consumed (Knobloch et al. 2004).

Affective news streams, on the other hand, emerge out of collaboratively generated flows of information, rendered as citizens and journalists are experiencing, observing, and reporting on events in the making. They are driven by intensity and not factuality, instantaneity and not graduality. Thus, they may often be inaccurate, because they are liminal, provided we understand accuracy as structure and liminality as the transitory path to attaining accuracy. For example, in the recent Boston Marathon bombings, a variety of affective news streams generated through different platforms, including Reddit and Twitter, contained numerous reports of inaccurate information, combined with general reactions to the events, how they were being reported, and what they may have been brought on by. Read as news, these streams are factually inaccurate. Read as affective news streams, these present liminal paths to accuracy.

Because affective news streams are rendered out of subjective interpolations into a story developing about an event, they are reflective of intensity accumulated in reaction to a multitude of events, and this intensity presents their distinguishing feature. For example, affective news streams dominated the flow of news information on #egypt, as news, opinions, and reactions to the uprisings that led to the resignation of Hosni Mubarak were broadcast through the platform of Twitter (Papacharissi and de Fatima Oliveira 2012). Intensity and ambience characterized the news streams generated by tags associated with the Occupy movement on Twitter, even though they did not always produce coherent and harmonious news narratives (Meraz and Papacharissi 2013). During the 2012 US Presidential Elections, online publics were discursively rendered on Twitter, in response to statements made by the presidential candidates during the debates. Tags including #bindersfullofwomen, or #firebigbird served to organically curate affectively infused streams containing a mix of opinion, news, and general sentiment in response to issues discussed in the debates. These themes were further reproduced, remixed, and rebroadcast through other platforms, including Tumblr and a variety of meme generators, which geo-socially blended atomized takes on the news with broader and pluralized streams containing news and a variety of socially relevant information. Similarly, the hashtag #muslimrage visibly challenged a *Newsweek* magazine cover featuring the same headline, through propagating playful tweets meant to deconstruct popular stereotypes about Muslims presented in mainstream media. While #muslimrage did not contain any new news, it articulated organically populated disagreement with a dominant news frame presented in the news.

Affective news streams are characterized by instantaneity. They will contain news of the moment, subjectively determined, although this may not always present new news. News streams like #muslimrage are discursively rendered in vernaculars that are phatic and emotive, reflecting intensity of interest. Even though they may be driven by curiosity around an event, they do not necessarily procure accurate information about it, because of their liminal nature. They are generated as personal takes accumulate on what happened, might have happened, will happen, and what it means, and as such, they are characterized by futurity, sociality, and reside in the realm of the potential. The shape news takes on through these streams tends to be *affective*, the form of news storytelling *hybrid*, and the spaces rendered discursively through news storytelling frequently function as *electronic elsewheres*, or social spaces that support liminal viewpoints (Yang 2009; Berry, Kim, and Spigel 2010). Following this logic, media are not just the means for representing places that already exist, but rather, actually become the means for shaping space and producing places, which may include home, community, work, and play (Berry et al. 2010). The resulting geo-social, hybrid, and mediated environments can be understood as *elsewheres* that presence alternative viewpoints, voices, and stories. For citizens, the liminal form of space is crucial, as it permits them to access content in transition and find their own place in the story, alongside journalists, who already possess an institutionally assigned place in the story.

Digital Oralities and Literacies

In emerging traditions of journalisms, both journalists and citizens are afforded a unique place in *the story*, and news storytelling in general. News feeds collectively generated by citizens, bloggers, activists, journalists, and media outlets are premised on produsage and expose temporal and other incompatibilities between live blogging the news and reporting. Blogging and micro-blogging platforms, along with other convergent networked platforms, afford journalists neither the time to process information, nor the privilege of being the first to report it. These temporal incompatibilities are not insurmountable, and are also not entirely new, but they require acknowledging the presence of not just one, but several different paradigms of news reporting and journalism. Alternatively, we may understand these as liminal layers to a story.

News storytelling assembled through a variety of collectively operated, pluralized platforms implies a level of agency that is networked, complex, and diffused. In order to tell a story, the storyteller must make concrete decisions about how events will be presented. These decisions are collaboratively and organically made through practices of repetition and redaction that do not always produce a coherent narrative, but rather, result in parallel narratives, possessing variable levels of coherence and continuity, distinguished by their own affective imprint. For example, news streams generated through #egypt and #Jan25 effectively framed a movement as a revolution, well before it had resulted in regime reversal (e.g., Meraz and Papacharissi 2013). The more recent events of regime upheaval that occurred in Egypt during the summer of 2013 revealed the distance between the story of a revolution in the making told through social media and the limitations of regime reform that ensued. By contrast, news feeds collaboratively formed out of contributions to #ows did not affectively boost a revolution, nor did they induce regime reform. But their purpose was to provide opportunity for people to stand and be counted in disagreement with certain courses of events that led to a deep economic depression, and the digital imprint sustained by #ows fulfilled this purpose. These digital imprints, rendered as people take part in reporting and commenting on the news, form first drafts of news stories in the making.

It is often remarked that journalism presents a first rough draft of history (Graham, as quoted in Shafer 2010), and that thus, we may think of online networked platforms like Twitter as rendering a first draft of journalism (Stahl 2013). New journalisms evolve out of new places of storytelling that blend news production and consumption to produce narratives that are reflexive. Liminal spaces are where journalists and citizens meet, to collectively shape a story.

Through these processes of collaborative storytelling, claims to agency are discursive, crowdsourced to prominence, networked, and sometimes ephemeral, enabling a variety of actors to tell stories in ways that mix the conventions of news broadcasting with the phatic practices of interpersonal conversation. Drawing from Ong's (1982) work, we may begin to interpret the orality that drives this form of storytelling as digital, derivative of the blended conventions of both a primary and secondary orality. Ong (1995) distinguished between the fluidity, spontaneity, and reflexivity inherent in oral storytelling traditions, and the deliberate spontaneity of a writing and print culture, pointing to the ways in which electronic and computer-mediated texts accompany secondary orality with a secondary visualism. Ong explained that within a primary orality, the nature of the word is not visible but lives in the world of sound. Thus storytelling "comes into being in the present even though it normally may derive variously from a tradition, a past," and evolves as the voice of storytelling changes (1). By contrast, the logic of a secondary orality may mute out the voice, in favor of generating "technologized," "permanent," and thus "silent" stories that distance (2). We encounter this form of distance in the paradigm of journalistic objectivity, which requires narrators to establish objective distance from the story so as to ascertain accuracy, and thus electronically reproduce and share verified information. This distance is eliminated in the subjective form of oral storytelling, however, which affectively evolves as it circulates in the oral tradition. I suggest that online networked platforms blend interpersonal and mass storytelling practice variably, offering a reconciliation of primary and secondary orality tendencies and tensions. Where secondary orality ensured distance, digital orality affirms voice, offering a digitally enabled path into the story. Where primary orality emphasized voice, digital orality propagates voices while preserving their atomized subjectivity. A digital orality is assembled around broadcasting voice, atomized and pluralized. Affective news streams are the product of a digital orality, shaped by storytelling practices meant to give extemporaneous narrators voice and visibility within the evolving story.

NOTE

1. For more on homophily, see Lazarsfeld and Merton (1954) or McPherson, Smith-Lovin, and Cook (2001). For a more focused analysis on how homophily drives information sharing, structures of influence, and behavioral contagion or information cascades, see, for example, Aral, Muchnik, and Sundararajan (2009) or Watts (2002).

REFERENCES

Aral, Sinan, Lev Muchnik, and Arun Sundararajan. 2009. "Distinguishing Influence-Based Contagion from Homophily-Driven Diffusion in Dynamic Networks." *PNAS* 106: 21544–21549. doi:10.1073/pnas.0908800106.

Berry, Chris, So-yong Kim, and Lynn Spigel. 2010. *Electronic Elswheres: Media Technology and the Experience of Social Space*. Minneapolis: University of Minnesota Press.

Bruns, Axel. 2008. *Blogs, Wikipedia, Second Life, and Beyond. From Production to Produsage*. New York: Peter Lang.

Bruns, Axel, and Tim Highfield. 2012. "Blogs, Twitter, and Breaking News: The Produsage of Citizen Journalism." In *Produsing Theory in a Digital World: The Intersection of Audiences and Production*, edited by Rebecca Ann Lind, 15–32. New York: Peter Lang.

Burns, Alex. 2010. "Oblique Strategies for Ambient Journalism." *M/C Journal* 13 (2). http://journal.media-culture.org.au/index.php/mcjournal/article/view/230.

Chadwick, Andrew. 2011. "The Political Information Cycle in a Hybrid News System: The British Prime Minister and the 'Bullygate' Affair." *The International Journal of Press/Politics* 16 (1): 3–29. doi:10.1177/1940161210384730.

Couldry, Nick. 2000. *The Place of Media Power: Pilgrims and Witnesses of the Media Age*. London: Routledge.

Couldry, Nick. 2012. *Media, Society, World: Social Theory and Digital Media Practice*. Cambridge: Polity.

Crawford, Kate. 2009. "Following You: Disciplines of Listening in Social Media." *Continuum: Journal of Media & Cultural Studies* 23 (4): 525–535. doi:10.1080/10304310903003270.

Dahlberg, Lincoln. 2009. "Libertarian Cyber-utopianism and Globalization." In *Utopia and Globalization*, edited by Patrick Hayden and Chamsy el-Ojeili, 176–189. London: Palgrave.

Deleuze, Gillies and Felix Guattari. [1980] 1987. *A Thousand Plateaus: Capitalism and Schizophrenia*. Translated and foreword by Brian Massumi. Minneapolis: University of Minnessota Press.

du Gay, Paul, Stuart Hall, Linda Janes, Hugh Mackay, and Keith Negus. 1997. *Doing Cultural Studies: The Story of the Sony Walkman*. London: Sage.

Grusin, Richard. 2010. *Premediation: Affect and Mediality After 9/11*. London: Palgrave.

Hamdy, Naila. 2010. "Arab Media Adopt Citizen Journalism to Change the Dynamics of Conflict Coverage." *Global Media Journal: Arabian Edition* 1 (1): 3–15.

Hamdy, Naila, and Ehab H. Gomaa. 2012. "Framing the Egyptian Uprising in Arabic Language Newspapers and Social Media." *Journal of Communication* 62 (2): 195–211. doi:10.1111/j.1460-2466.2012.01637.x.

Hay, James. 2003. "Unaided Virtues: The (Neo-)Liberalization of the Domestic Sphere and the New Architecture of Community." In *Foucault, Cultural Studies, and Governmentality*, edited by Jack Bratich, Jeremy Packer, and Cameron McCarthy, 165–206. Albany: State University of New York Press.

Hermida, Alfred. 2010. "Twittering the News." *Journalism Practice* 4 (3): 297–308. doi:10.1080/17512781003640703.

Hess, Kristy. 2013. "Breaking Boundaries." *Digital Journalism* 1 (1): 48–63. doi:10.1080/21670811.2012.714933.

Howard, Phillip. 2011. *The Digital Origins of Dictatorship and Democracy: Information Technology and Poltical Islam*. London: Oxford University Press.

Jansen, Bernard J., Mimi Zhang, Kate Sobel, and Abdur Chowdhury. 2009. "Twitter Power: Tweets as Electronic Word of Mouth." *Journal of American Society for Information Science & Technology*, 60 (11): 2169–2188. doi:10.1002/asi.v60:11.

Jewitt, Robert. 2009. "Commentaries: The Trouble with Twittering: Integrating Social Media into Mainstream News." *International Journal of Media and Cultural Politics* 5 (3): 233–246. doi:10.1386/macp.5.3.233_3.

Knobloch, Silvia, Grit Patzig, Anna-Maria Mende, and Matthias Hastall. 2004. "Affective News: Effects of Discourse Structure in Narratives on Suspense, Curiosity, and Enjoyment While Reading News and Novels." *Communication Research*, 31 (3): 259–287. doi:10.1177/0093650203261517.

Lazarsfeld, Paul F., and Robert K. Merton. 1954. "Friendship as a Social Process: A Substantive and Methodological Analysis." In *Freedom and Control in Modern Society*, edited by Morroe Berger, Theodore Abel, and Charles H. Page, 18–66. New York: Van Nostrand.

Le Corbusier. 1931. *Towards a New Architecture*. New York: Dover.

Lim, Merlyna. 2012. "Clicks, Cabs, and Coffee Houses: Social Media and Oppositional Movements in Egypt 2004–2011." *Journal of Communication* 62 (2): 231–248. doi:10.1111/j.1460-2466.2012.01628.x.

Lotan, Gilad, Erhardt Graeff, Mike Ananny, Devin Gaffney, Ian Pearce, and Danah Boyd. 2011. "The Revolutions Were Tweeted: Information Flows During the 2011 Tunisian and Egyptian Revolutions." *International Journal of Communication* 5: 1375–1405.

Massey, Doreen. 1994. *Space, Place and Gender*. Cambridge: Polity.

Massumi, Brian. 2002. *Parable for the Virtual: Movement, Affect, Sensation*. Durham: Duke University Press.

McPherson, Miller, Lynn Smith-Lovin, and James M. Cook. 2001. "Birds of a Feather: Homophily in Social Networks," *Annual Review of Sociology* 27: 415–444. doi:10.1146/annurev.soc.27.1.415.

Meraz, Sharon. 2012. "The Sociality of News Sociology: Examining User Participation and News Selection Practices in Social Media News Sites. In *News with a View: Essays on the Eclipse of Objectivity in Modern Journalism*, edited by Burton Saint John III & Kristen Johnson, 78–96. Jefferson, NC: McFarland.

Meraz, Sharon, and Zizi Papacharissi. 2013. "Networked Gatekeeping and Networked Framing on #Egypt." The International Journal of Press/Politics 18 (2): 138–166. doi:10.1177/1940161212474472.

Ong, Walter. 1982. *Orality and Literacy: The Technologizing of the Word*. 2nd ed. New York: Routledge.

Ong, Walter. 1995. "Secondary Orality and Secondary Visualism." Walter J. Ong Manuscript Collection University Archives, Pius XII Memorial Library, Saint Louis University, St. Louis, MO.

Papacharissi, Zizi. 2010. *A Private Sphere*. Cambridge: Polity

Papacharissi, Zizi, and Maria de Fatima Oliveira. 2012. "Affective News and Networked Publics: The Rhythms of News Storytelling on #egypt." *Journal of Communication* 62 (2): 266–282. doi:10.1111/j.1460-2466.2012.01630.x.

Peters, Chris. 2012. "Journalism to Go: The Changing Spaces of News Consumption." *Journalism Studies* 13 (5–6): 695–705. doi:10.1080/1461670X.2012.662405.

Robinson, Sue. 2009. "'Searching for My Own Unique Place in the Story': A Comparison of Journalistic and Citizen-Produced Coverage of Hurricane Katrina's Anniversary. In *Journalism and Citizenship: New Agendas in Communication*, edited by Zizi Papacharissi, 166–188. New York: Routledge.

Schonfield, Erick. 2010. "Costolo: Twitter Now has 190 Million Users Tweeting 65 Million Times a Day." *TechCrunch*, July 8. http://techcrunch.com/2010/06/08/twitter-190-million-users/.

Sedgwick, Eve K. 2003. *Touching Feeling: Affect, Pedagogy, Performativity*. Durham: Duke University Press.

Seigworth, Gregory, and Melissa Gregg. 2010. *The Affect Theory Reader*. Durham: Duke University Press.

Shafer, Jack. 2010. "Who Said it First: Journalism is the 'First Rough Draft of History.'" *Slate*, August 30. http://www.slate.com/articles/news_and_politics/press_box/2010/08/who_said_it_first.html.

Spigel, Lynn. 1994. *Make Room for TV: Television and the Family Ideal in Postwar America*. Chicago: University of Chicago Press.

Spigel, Lynn. 2001. *Welcome to the Dreamhouse: Popular Media and Postwar Suburbs*. Durham: Duke University Press.

Stahl, Jeremy. 2013. "Thou Shalt Not Stoop to Political Point Scoring." *Slate*, April 13. http://www.slate.com/articles/technology/technology/2013/04/boston_marathon_bombing_all_the_mistakes_journalists_make_during_a_crisis.html.

Turner, Victor. 1967. *The Forest of Symbols: Aspects of Ndembu Ritual*. Ithaca: Cornell University Press.

Turner, Victor. 1974. *Dramas, Fields and Metaphors: Symbolic Action in Human Society*. Ithaca: Cornell University Press.

van Gennep, Arnold. 1909. *The Rites of Passage*. Chicago, IL: University of Chicago Press, 1960.

Vis, Farida. 2013. "Twitter as a Reporting Tool for Breaking News." *Digital Journalism* 1 (1): 27–47. doi:10.1080/21670811.2012.741316.

Watts, Duncan J. 2002. "A Simple Model of Global Cascades on Random Networks. *PNAS* 99: 5766–5771. doi:10.1073/pnas.082090499.

Westlund, Oscar. 2013. "Mobile News: A Review and Model of Journalism in an Age of Mobile Media." Digital Journalism 1 (1): 6–26. doi:10.1080/21670811.2012.740273.

Williams, Raymond. 1974. *Television, Technology and Cultural Form*. London: Routledge.

Williams, Raymond. 1983. *Towards 2000*. London: Chatto & Windus.

Yang, Guobin. 2009. *The Power of the Internet in China: Citizen Activism Online*. New York: Columbia University Press.

LOCATIVE NEWS
Mobile media, place informatics, and digital news

Gerard Goggin, Fiona Martin, and **Tim Dwyer**

Location, locality, and localism have long been important characteristics of news, but their functions have been given a dramatic twist with the advent of locative, mobile media. The capabilities of mobile media devices to determine, sense, incorporate, and conjure with the relative locations of reporting and audiences have emerged as key to alternative, small- and large-scale networked news-gathering and dissemination ventures. This paper explores the kinds of places and spaces these mobile worlds of news-making and consumption entail—and how news is being located in and through such new mobilities.

Introduction

Central to today's multiplatform, digitally networked spaces and places of news consumption are new dynamics of mobility. We say "new", because a dialectics of mobility has long been constitutive of news audiences. News involves the inclusion of the novel or newsworthy in the rituals, movements, and cycles, the habitus of everyday life. Following the emergence of popular, portable, printed news media, especially from the eighteenth century onwards, news could be consumed in a café, on public or private transport, or in a workplace or public park, as much as a household. Radio later extended these situated relationships—especially in its minaturised, battery-operated, transistor form (Arceneaux 2014); and so too eventually did television, where the receiver could move along with its audiences (Goggin 2006). The consumption of news then has long involved historically material, culturally specific, and socially coordinated relationships with time, space, and place.

The prefiguring of news use in older forms of mobility is worth remembering, as we introduce a key context for this paper: news produced for, and consumed using, mobile media devices. For some years now, surveys in many countries have shown a marked increase in mobile news consumption. Most recently a nine-country Reuters study that found 31 per cent of users had sought out news with their smartphone in the past week. In the United Kingdom and Denmark, tablet news usage had doubled in the previous 10 months, while mobile phones trumped print as the "out and about" preferred news platform (Reuters Institute 2013, 29). In the United States too, some 39 per cent of respondents in the Pew News Media Consumption survey gained news online or from a mobile device (Pew 2013). Smartphones are credited with driving the growth of mobile news, with news providers discerning marked growth in mobile device traffic (Pew 2012, 2013; Reuters Institute 2013). Both research groups concurred that news is increasingly a multi-platform endeavour, with mobiles or laptops also acting as the much vaunted "second screen", used in concert with other media (cf. Bennett and Strange 2011; Goggin 2013).

Yet despite the intense fascination among journalists, media organisations, and publics alike with developments in mobile news, there is much that remains under-researched about its sites and practices of consumption—and of co-production, a necessary corollary for our research given the increased use of mobiles for news sharing and witnessing.

Robust comparative international statistics on mobile news usage are difficult to obtain, and in any case there appear to be strong geographic, political, and cultural differences in mobile media adoption, preferences, and participation (Reuters Institute 2013, 9). Studies are only now emerging that explore cultural diversity in mobile news consumption preferences (e.g. the Open Society Foundation's *Mapping Digital Media* reports 2011–2013) and users' varied experiences of participatory environments (Väätäjä, Vaino, and Sirkkunen 2013), raising new questions about digital inclusion. A Pew Internet study, indicating that "nearly half of all American adults (47%) access at least some local news and information on their cellphone or tablet computer" (Pew 2011b), suggested users preferred "practical and real time" information on weather, local business, and restaurants, rather than general news reports. We might further ask how did cultural factors impact on use? Where, when, and why were the different genres, and news sources, important? What issues did people have finding and using news on their mobile devices?

That there is little research on the spaces and places of mobile news use is nothing surprising given the state of news media economics, but considering the financial, industrial, and cultural investments now being poured into mobile news, it is research that is badly needed—not least if we take seriously the now-fashionable proposition that digital media is nothing if not co-constructed with its audiences. Further, in an era of intensifying and competing internationalised news flows, we will argue that attention to audience mobility, localism, and place-making practices has growing policy and research significance.

In this paper we turn our attention to the innovative field of "locative" media, which some years ago was heralded by journalism educators as the future of mobile journalism (Gordon 2008). Locative news, a term now gaining currency, for instance, in the important study of the phenomenon by the Norwegian researcher Kjetil Vaage Øie (2012), refers to the possibility for news to be shaped, called up by, and curated in response to locational information about a news user in a particular place. Locational data derived from mobile devices are also key to media companies' capacity to track online news users' preferences and to deliver them targeted products, services, and advertising. However, according to the Pew Research Center, the complexities of mobile media development and delivery mean "even the weakest of the tech giants is in a far stronger financial and technological position to develop those [analytical] abilities than all but the largest news organizations" (Pew 2013, 18).

In this paper, we investigate some of these complexities, and their implications for mobile news audiences and journalism scholarship. We begin by outlining the development of locative technologies in mobile internet, and theorising their role in personalising media and mediating place. We then discuss the emergent, experimental nature of locative news and offer three case studies that illuminate the ways in which it is shaping, and being shaped by, the actions of news media producers and mobile users.

Locative Media, Mobile News, and the Making of Place

A key feature of contemporary mobile media involves their capacity to gather and represent information about the location of a device and its users, enabling, for example, the visualisation of their actions—what is often now called "locative media". Location-based technology developed on cellular mobile phones in the 1990s, being an artefact of mobile computing, software, and navigational technology, needed to identify a handset in relation to a transmitter. The potential of using such location-based information for public benefit, such as locating someone in an emergency, became the subject of telecommunications regulation—such as the US Federal Communications Commission's (FCC 2005) efforts to require mobile providers to pass on information on a mobile device's location to emergency service providers (police, fire, ambulance). Two further location technologies were incorporated into mobile phones in the 1990s and 2000s. Once global positioning technology (GPS) chips were permitted for civilian use, they were deployed in cars but also included in mobile phones—allowing developments such as wayfinding, navigation, and maps. From a different socio-technical trajectory, Wireless Internet (WiFi) transmitters were included in mobiles to allow phones to toggle between cellular mobile and wireless networks (the latter often being cheaper for users).

The combination of these three technologies now means that mobile devices harvest and store very rich information about the locations in which they are used, potentially being able to retain the entire history of such data traces. Many applications for mobile media devices, such as Google Maps, are now designed to use, analyse, refine, and benefit from such locational information gathering. They are also part of a much broader movement for the personalisation and customisation of media services, particularly sales and marketing (Yang 2013). Online "targeted display" advertisements have for some time been dynamically matched with individual consumers by combining available and aggregated information on their browsing and search habits, with demographic and geographic information (Pew 2011a). Thus mobile application programming interfaces (APIs) and "apps" (software with specialised functionality) continue to augment the functionality of small-screen mobile technologies, providing more person and place-bound news experiences.

Early experimentation in locative media development came from artistic and urban experimentation, which strongly influenced research and discussion on the topic until quite recently (Goggin 2006). What has now occurred is the coming-of-age of locative media, but not as a singular cellular-mobile-network-based system. Rather locative media is what we might term after the work of Gilles Deleuze, Bruno Latour, and others, an assemblage of overlapping systems and devices (Bennett and Healy 2009; Goggin 2009). These ecologies of locative media—fused with internet, social, and mobile media—have resulted in an arc described by Rowan Wilken as "from specialized preoccupation to mainstream fascination" (Wilken 2012), exemplified by the attention given to Google's Glass technology.

The social and cultural implications of such locative media have become the subject of important recent scholarship. Jason Farman (2012) makes a strong case for the need to pay attention to embodiment as central to the experience and affordances of locative media. In her two influential co-authored books on the topic, de Souza e Silva argues for the importance of location and location information as a key, new element of digital networks (Gordon and de Souza e Silva 2011), and explores how it creates new forms of sociability that challenge how we understand public spaces, interaction, and privacy (de Souza e Silva and Frith 2012).

We, in turn, propose that location is now a cardinal, orienting, and increasingly user-defined aspect of mobile news production and its consumption. This can be seen in at least two respects. Firstly, journalists are increasingly sensitive to ways of addressing audience interest in place, by indicating and exploiting locational information. Locative technologies, such as geospatial positioning (GPS) data and geo-tagging, have been critical to the "cartographic" turn in news, where events are mapped and user input is invited to the construction of place through images or witness accounts. In turn, audiences now expect to be able to search and aggregate news based on locational indicators and also to position themselves *vis-à-vis* events and places, via location-annotated posts to social media. The speed, scale, and complications of mobile social locative news reporting were evident following the April 2013 Boston Marathon massacre and ensuing hunt for suspects—culminating in numerous false identifications and leads.

In this paper then we will examine interest in how locative news involves interpretation of action in space and, centrally, the making and re-making of place. Our analysis is framed by Wilken and Goggin's (2012) theorisation of place, an important concept for understanding mobile technologies. They see place as relational and politically negotiated, constructed through a mix of materialities and imaginaries: location (or the "where" of journalism), locality and its social relations, and the cultural meanings associated with place (Wilken and Goggin 2012, 5). Just as media consumption and space are often "co-constitutive" (Peters 2012, 702), so are mobile, locative media, and place. Locative news is surely a new way of marshalling, mediating, and making sense of place; evidenced in the new kinds of information created through projects of emplacement, and by the movement in and through places by objects, technologies, and users. Thus understood locative news research moves beyond the narrowly technological, to encompass the significant epistemological, phenomenological, and social implications of our mobile locational encounters. The approach of this paper, then, is to explore the new mediascapes, flows, and forms of locative news, and to identify emerging directions, challenges, and opportunities for journalism scholarship. Our method is based on case studies, analysing developments in three different contexts, two country-based studies and one of a global phenomenon. Such an approach is appropriate to an emerging area, where neither the forms of news, the structures and cultures of production, nor the patterns of consumption are settled—indeed are barely tested. What characterises the present, nascent period is an unsettled, "co-creation" of locative news technologies (Banks 2013; Plattner, Meinel, and Leifer 2012)—as much by audience experimentation and involvement as industrial strategy.

Locative News

Location and concepts of the local have long been crucial to the shaping of news and its social functions (Franklin 1998). Journalists have used locational terms in headlines, for example, to signal to and connect with their imagined audiences; and, in turn, audiences have used them to recognise what is news for them, and how they might interpret it. The location of news events, or origin of a report, has historically been projected differently in different media: in print by datelines; in radio by diectic markers of presentation ("right here", "meanwhile in Sydney"); in television by a combination of captioning, voiceover, and presentational indicators; and now on the Web and mobile platforms via universal resource location (URL), geo-spatial metadata, and keyword tags. The ways locations are formulated and expressed through news have also acted as part of political discourses for building belonging in larger categories and frameworks of meaning, such as nationalism (Higgins 2004) or localism (Martin and Wilson 2002).

Newsmakers have also historically visualised locational information in stories to explain the unfolding of complex events; using maps, and from the 1800s, infographics, to illustrate how people and events move through space, over time. Geographer Mark Monmonier's classic study *Maps with the News* identifies a kind of "journalist cartography" in which "news maps not only present geographic patterns useful in understanding news reports, they are also a part of the packaging of news" (Monmonier 1989, xi). With that in mind, the visual modalities of locative representation may be key factors in analysing what engages mobile news consumers.

Indeed, the term "locative journalism" appears around 2008, following the widespread domestic uptake of geospatial mapping platforms and tools, as well as GPS-enabled iPhone 3G features and car navigation systems that enabled the visualisation of location, wayfinding, and remote place. Rich Gordon, a pioneer in location-aware journalism education, recognised that such technologies were being used, and could be deployed by journalists, "to provide geographically relevant content that enhances a participant's connection to a given place" (Gordon 2008). The rise of Web-based participatory news mapping projects, such as Everyblock, and the release of its open source code in 2009, spurred further interest in creating location-based and "hyperlocal" news services. The roughly concurrent release of graphical tagging technologies, such as quick response (QR) codes, enabled "object hyperlinking" and other recontextualisations of media and place. Mobile phone users could use their camera and an app to scan a print image (a bar code representing an encrypted Web address) to open online media content in their browsers, although the process was not always easy to manage, or reliable.

Newer augmented reality (AR) systems try to enhance locational meaning by superimposing information and narratives on users' visual field, usually through their mobile device screen but also via wearable computers. The most common form of AR, like graphical tagging, employs image recognition software to trigger wireless access to video, slideshows, or shopping platforms. Google Glass headsets, which have attracted far more attention for their privacy implications, enable users to recall and display information as an illustrative overlay on their field of vision, and to capture and upload video and sound. Thus far, however, AR remains in early stages, with Pavlik and Bridges estimating that by 2012 only 2.5 per cent of the world's leading media organisations had adopted some form, with low returns for early adopters, concern about production costs, and technological constraints (Pavlik and Bridges 2013).

Indeed, locative news is a challenging field, perhaps characteristically experimental and risky, because of its reliance on an articulation of rapidly developing technologies. One expression of this is in the privacy debates around media use of locational and personal data. While mobile users can control corporate collection of personalised location information to a degree, by disabling device and application features, they often know little about how media companies aggregate and use data about them, or how this changes over time. In response to public concerns the US Federal Trade Commission (FTC 2013) has made best practice mobile privacy disclosure recommendations to platform and operating system providers, application developers, advertising networks, analytics companies, and other third parties, including that companies will obtain express consent for data collection, use, and retention (FTC 2013). It has signalled too, a growing expectation that mobile app developers will inform users how their data are being used, and will recognise any "Do Not Track" (DNT) strategies they implement.

Despite industry concerns about the contingencies and limitations of using locative technologies, high-profile news initiatives continue to be bankrolled, most often by tech giant Google, which has driven locative media innovation. In 2011, for instance, *The New York Times*, *The Financial Times*, *Wall Street Journal*, and Canada's *National Post* network used the location-based networking platform Foursquare to distribute news (Claudia 2012). In the same year, Google announced "News Near You", a service that displays news videos from its partners within a 100-mile radius of a user's computer's internet protocol (IP) address. When users sign in and share their location, relevant news appears in their Google News feed. More presciently, the 2012 Google Now mobile app uses data collected from an individual's real-time location, calendar, Gmail, and search history to anticipate and display the information they might need at the appropriate time and place.

Academics too are exploring how location can reconfigure news and news audience interaction (Nyre et al. 2012; Øie 2012). In the LocaNews project, Norwegian researchers have imagined a radical personalisation of story delivery in dynamic relation to location:

> What would it be like if news stories constantly changed depending on the reader's physical location? ... One way to meet this demand might be to take account for the readers' location in the selection of relevant news articles to adjust news stories to specific location while at the same time allowing for continuous change in order to compensate for relocation through geographical environment. What kinds of experiences will this kind of journalism generate, and how may context intervene? And does this change the readers' social interaction with news? (Øie 2012)

Given the widespread accessibility and uptake of locative technologies, and the industrial push for targeted content delivery, we might expect large, and possibly small, news providers to be keen to incorporate such ideas, or some of the other successful initiatives discussed so far. Our sense is, however, that this is far from the case.

Rather than locative news unfolding in the strategic manner indicated by the few promising experiments that exist thus far, it is emerging more incidentally from the intersection and imbrication of other mobile media initiatives, technologies, and spatial and place-making practices. In what follows, we will develop our argument through three case studies of news audience development: multi-platform news in Hong Kong; hyperlocal news in the United Kingdom; and news media's use of global mapping technologies.

Spaces and Places of Audiences: Multi-platform News in Hong Kong

The incorporation of locative technologies into multi-platform news strategies is an emerging but important area of mobile news research. Mobile news ecologies are shaped by dynamic interrelationships between audience usage cultures, available access devices and operating systems, existing platforms and media-sharing practices. They are evolving from the convergence of mobile phone, internet, and broadcasting systems with an array of new technologies and associated social practices (Feijóo et al. 2009; Ibrus 2013). However, the links between news organisations' engagement with location in mobile media, on the one hand, and their strategic development of locative media, are not yet as straightforward, close, or intensive as one might suspect—something that can be gathered from an examination of the leading mobile internet news media company in Hong Kong.

Next Media group positions itself as a multi-product (apps and mobile websites), multi-device/operating system (iOS, Android, Windows, Blackberry), and multi-platform digital media organisation, with future development dominated by social, mobile, and locative media (or "SoMoLo"), user-generated content, and increasingly, greater personalisation of news (M. Yung, Group Chief Information Officer, Next Media Interactive, personal interview, Hong Kong, 4 March 2013). The company publishes the *Apple Daily*, which is either the second or most popular daily newspaper in Hong Kong, depending on the way online readership is factored into the figures (C. Lo, Deputy Editor-in-Chief, Apple Daily Limited, personal interview at Next Media Interactive, Hong Kong, 4 March 2013), and the leading daily in Taiwan. It also publishes the commuter *Sharp Daily* newspapers, published in both Hong Hong and Taipei; and those countries' most visited Web portals. Next Media Interactive (NMI) also offers its news to audiences as "native" apps (via apps stores), as mobile Web apps, and for mobile net browser search by way of various devices and operating systems (iOS, Android, Windows, Blackberry). In 2013, *Apple Daily*'s mobile apps were among the top downloads for iTunes and Android-platform smartphones in Hong Kong and Taiwan, and its videos were the top-ranking news downloads. Total video views on the NMI mobile channels/apps typically reach the 5 million per day mark.

Apple Daily's popularity can partly be attributed to aspects of cultural localism. Editorially it plays on its historic locale, being pro-democracy and anti-central Chinese Government (and so generally anti-Beijing), as well as being critical of pro-Communist governments in Hong Kong. Lee and Lin (2006) have argued the *Apple Daily*'s critique of the Hong Kong government is a "marketing strategy" in the context of post-colonial British rule. The *Daily* also employs extensive use of Cantonese language and an unabashedly tabloid focus on reporting crime, celebrity news, eroticism, gambling, and drug use (Lee 1997, 131).

It has gained most attention locally and internationally though for its new so-called "action news" video format and associated YouTube channel. Here real footage is supplemented by computer graphics imagery (CGI) animation, using motion capture and 3D modelling software. CGI is now a common news production technique, "typically adopted as a way to visualize an event for which there is no video footage, or when the issue reported is abstract and needs visual illustration", but NMI has developed a particularly sensationalist style of re-enactment, to the point where the company's brand survival stands or falls on its continued supply. Cheng and Lo describe it as "melodramatic emotion-laden and movie-like animation", while the *New York Times* has dubbed it "the new world of Maybe Journalism, offering a glimpse at the future of the tabloid division" (Cohen 2009). Perhaps the best-known and most popular example, which went viral internationally after its release, depicts celebrity golfer Tiger Woods' 2009 car crash, early in his adultery scandal. In a story that mixes actuality, commentary, and CGI scenes, NMI's animators controversially show Wood's now ex-wife chasing his car with a golf club, triggering his accident.

Next Media founder Jimmy Lai launched Next Media's Apple action news service in 2010, responding to audience metrics that showed Hong Kong's mobile media users were heavy online video consumers and entertainment-oriented. In order to reach commuter audiences, action news segments have been made short enough for users to watch between Hong Kong subway stations (Yung, personal interview, 4 March 2013). They engage both older audiences who are culturally attuned to traditions of cartoon-like media formats, and a younger demographic that has grown up with the post-1990s generation of Asian video animation, action films, and graphic novels, and no longer reads print news. So the popularity of the service is testimony to a nexus between editorial design, audience mobility, and cultural tastes.

In terms of developing specific locative technologies, however, Next Media's strategy is driven by international production trends, and less by news than advertising and entertainment. It has joined other print companies internationally in using mobile apps, QR code, and AR links to deliver supplementary news video and audio content, driving traffic between its print, Web, and mobile operations, but more crucially the company argues multimedial QR advertising has created opportunities to counter potential paid-for print circulation losses by offering an alternative advertising mechanism to engage with smartphone users who scan QR codes while on the move. Additionally, in keeping with its tabloid focus, Next Media's new mobile media production arm, Next Mobile, is also producing Asian-language versions of United States-based Red Robot Lab's successful location-based mobile multiplayer phone game, "Life is Crime". The gaming platform builds on the geo-social affordances pioneered by Web-based services like Foursquare, and allows the user to pretend to turn their everyday locations into a world, and battlefield, of criminal activity.

So while locative news has been envisioned as an important future dimension of news story-telling, in this case study it is a secondary concern, even for a vanguard digital media company in a burgeoning mobile market with successful app products and services, and an understanding of locative media's potential. Where then might we look for compelling trends in locative news—would the much vaunted area of "hyperlocal" news be fruitful, an area that often defines itself in contradistinction to mainstream news and that has consistently sought to base its prospects on digital innovation?

Hyperlocal News and Mobile Audiences

Hyperlocal news is an extension of journalism's long-standing focus on local and community news. Hyperlocal media focus on a narrow geographical area or set of topics seeking to find a niche, often participatory, among the service gaps left by other available media (Kurplus, Metzgar, and Rowley 2010). This includes not only traditional mainstream news but also the international technology-company providers such as Google or Yahoo, whose interest is in personalisation rather than localism. For the last decade, hyperlocal news has been associated with various online journalism experiments including "federated" websites supporting local news in a number of locations (Bruns 2009).

In a 2012 UK report exploring the current demand for hyperlocal media, innovation foundation NESTA (formerly a public-sector organisation) critically analysed the failure of early online local services to perform to scale. It noted:

> traditional media providers have found it hard to adjust their high-cost models to a sufficiently local area. Meanwhile, hyperlocal bloggers find it difficult to develop a critical mass of audience and to define the right business models to grow their offers into more sustainable services. (Radcliffe 2012, 3)

However, NESTA proposed that "location-based technologies, especially mobile devices, offer a potential revolution for very local ('hyperlocal') media that can deliver at this level of scale" (Radcliffe 2012, 3). In a follow-up report on users, NESTA argues that hyperlocal is now "of particular interest given the rapid take-up of connected devices such as smartphones and tablets, which enable citizens and audiences to consume hyperlocal media in new ways and may help to drive new business models towards long term sustainability" (NESTA 2013, 3). Commissioned research found an increased use of hyperlocal media services between 2010 and 2012 that was more prevalent among tablet, smartphone, and laptop or notebook users, compared to non-users (NESTA 2013, 26).

Overall, users' rationale for hyperlocal media consumption appeared to be more about getting functional information, such as local weather, entertainment, and venues, or breaking news (NESTA 2013, 35). Those were the most frequently cited genres, although with pronounced differences in preference across socio-economic groups (NESTA 2013, 37).

To put its work into practice, NESTA's Destination Local programme then funded 10 hyerlocal projects. One of these, the Local Edge project, was a partnership among two Edinburgh communities—Greener Leith and The Broughton Spurtle—and a developer Tigtag, to "build a platform to power a series of branded hyperlocal apps", associated with hyperlocal publishers, and run in the long term by a dedicated social enterprise (Tibbitt 2013). As instigator Ally Tibbitt describes it:

> what we're really trying to do as non-profit, volunteer led hyperlocals is to try to respond to the huge rise in mobile internet use in a way that makes local news make sense for people who are out and about in their neighbourhood with their own social reporting device in their pocket. (Tibbitt 2013)

The *Greener Leith* blog, on Tuesday 14 May 2013, for instance, featured a series of conventional local news stories, covering subjects such as failure of private landlords to return tenants' deposits or the 11 May 2013 story chronicling the efforts of St. Mary's Primary School pupils in mulching fruit trees in the Leith Links Children's Orchard (http://greenerleith.org.uk/). It also carried a story publicising and shaming drivers who double-park on Leith Walk, releasing a series of photographs posted on Twitter with the #WorstDrivers hash tag (Figure 1).

Greener Leith also provides a "news map", where most recent news updates can be viewed on a Google map image of the community area.

A far more ambitious, integrated locative news strategy may be found in another NESTA-supported hyperlocal project, the online hyperlocal magazine *Kentishtowner*, based in North London:

> Kentishtowner (est. 2010) is dedicated to cultural affairs—art, food, film, booze, community, history, music. NW5 may at the heart of what we're about, but we love the capital as a whole. We're not bound by boroughs or geography. (http://www.kentishtowner.co.uk/)

Run by two professional journalists, *Kentishtowner* describes its philosophy in these terms:

> we decided to avoid hard news—plenty of established local papers were doing a good job of that—and publish daily instead on the arts, food, history, community and people. We aspired to be a "travel guide for locals"—to help people see their neighbourhood with fresh eyes. (Emms and Kihl 2013)

Edinburgh's Worst Drivers takes on Leith Walk double parking

by Ally Tibbitt · Wednesday, 8th May, 2013 · 0 Comments

Edinburgh's Worst Drivers – the site that aims to "shame badly behaved drivers in the capital" – has turned into a bit of a social media phenomena.

This week the authors turned their fire on the irresponsible people who double park dangerously on Leith Walk, releasing a series of five photos on Twitter.

Yet more evidence that the design of Leith Walk and parking enforcement needs to be improved:

Here's are the photos from the @ediworstdrivers Twitter account:

FIGURE 1

#WorstDrivers local initiative

Rather than relying on just geo-tagging posts, they took a different route "creating map point landing pages for each and every business in our area":

> We called this section "Nearby" and it quickly developed into a unique editorially-led business directory when we realised how well these pages performed in search. We didn't want to take on the likes of Google + local pages, but know that our mixture of carefully crafted editorial and detailed local knowledge provides by far the more superior landing page for all the shops, cafés, bars, venues, restaurants and amenities in the area. (Emms and Kihl 2013)

Delivering on its founders' promise, the *Kentishtowner* offers an attractive, well-written, local news magazine, updated with stories on a daily basis. It has been featured by a range of national mainstream media, including the *Guardian* and *Sunday Times*. As the founders make clear, the venture is unabashedly commercial, in the established tradition of local newspapers. In terms of locative news, however, it partakes much more of "the rise of the local blog" (Barkham 2012) than it does of mobile news, *per se*.

In summarising our discussion of hyperlocal news experiments in the United Kingdom, it is important to recognise the difference between mobile hyperlocal concepts (like the Leith app) and Web-based ventures (such as *Kentishtowner*), following the high-profile launch and collapse of a number of flagship Web ventures, including the US start-ups *Everyblock* and *Patch*, as well as the UK *Guardian Local* (Ross 2013). Clearly some hyperlocal experiments have a strong engagement with mobile platforms and, to some extent, locational information. Yet, especially as illustrated in the current wave of UK hyperlocal sites, their capacity to expand this remains limited.

Thus far, we have discussed two contrasting examples of locative media and news from two quite distinct cultural settings. In Hong Kong, the place of interpretative communities is being creatively reimagined via innovative mobile internet news genres, formats, and technologies—but not with a focus on locative news. In Britain's hyperlocal news, locational information is an important part of news production and consumption—with the emphasis on being "local" the compelling offer of these initiatives.

In our third case study, we look directly at the impact of globally conceived and marketed geo-visualisation technologies, like Google maps, on the evolution of news mapping and sharing. Here we see locational data as sources of creativity, debate, and dispute, during a period where accepted practices are still emerging around the construction and authentication of news place.

Mobile News Audiences and Mapping Technologies

Geovisualisation tools such as online mapping and geo-tagging systems have been central to emerging trends in news, journalism, location, and locative media. Following the launch of the Google Maps API in June 2005, the BBC and Associated Press were among the first news companies to experiment with mashup maps of their news feeds, marking the nominal location of events or story origins with keyword tags and symbolic place-pins across their national territories. Since then, mapping systems have become widely incorporated into online news production.

But more significant for our purposes is the concurrent genesis of international participatory mapping projects designed to annotate, illustrate, and explicate the world's geography. From Google Earth and OpenStreetMap, to Wikimapia and Flickr, geo-referencing and interactive mapping softwares have invited user-generated, individually "asserted", and socially crafted narratives of place (Goodchild 2007) on a scale beyond the remit of most national and local media.

Social geo-mapping has become critical to user mobility and to our co-created and evolving knowledge of space and place. It has also expanded journalism's capacity to visualise the scale and scope of events, to aggregate information, recognise patterns and trace movement of subjects, objects, and trends. For example, location search apps such as Banjo, Geofeedia, and Sonar review social media feeds, indexing, aggregating, and mapping place-based, time-relevant information for journalists to review. Equally sensing technologies that monitor weather, traffic flow, animal movements, and so on, now enable always-on, mappable information-gathering projects like New York Public Radio's Cicadatracker, a data journalism initiative which has enlisted audiences in using ground temperature sensors to track and plot the hatching point of an insect with a 17-year life-cycle.

Yet while experimentation and social production have driven the first waves of locative journalism, there are now widespread concerns about the variability of mapping tools and geo-location practices that reflect growing media interest in standardising aspects of locative media production, in order to meet user expectations of accuracy and quality. Editors are now relying on locational metadata to, for example, authenticate Syrian social media videos to establish whether they are genuinely from users in that country, at the locations they purport to depict (Little 2012).

This is most obvious in the popular place-making practice of geo-referencing or "geo-tagging". This is the appending of geospatial metadata to digital media files, to indicate some aspect of location, generally the geometric coordinates where data were captured, expressed as GPS latitude and longitude. Geo-tags may also include altitude and sensor placement data, and/or semantic data: toponymic keywords including gazetted place names, postcodes, or geographic labels. The tagging process can be automated, for example where Twitter users enable coordinate tagging of their messages, or where a mobile phone GPS receiver or a wireless GPS logging device encodes exchangeable image file (EXIF) metadata in a photo or sound file. When that file is then uploaded to a media-sharing platform such as YouTube or Picasa, the system reinterprets coordinates as a place, adding a relevant label. If there are no importable metadata, tagging can also be manual, added post-capture when a file is stored or published.

As yet though, there are no media industry or public standards for geo-tagging. Manual drag and drop or "pushpin" systems rarely allow users to specify the geographic coordinates of their shot, let alone the direction of their camera or the subject of the image (Zheng, Zha, and Chua 2011). Automatic tagging systems, often used by social media-sharing communities, may allow coordinate records, but differ in their archival detail, annotation of different file types, and choice and integration of mapping software. Semantic tagging of location is even more idiosyncratic due to misspellings and reuse of place names across territories (with 1108 entries for San Francisco alone in the US GeoNet Names directory). As with social media folksonomies, user-generated locative information may be unverified, incomplete, or inconsistent (Myers 2012). These factors make machine queries of geo-tagged material unpredictable and relatively unreliable. This is an issue for locative media usability as NESTA's hyperlocal news report notes:

> accurate geotagging of content and the appropriate use of search engine optimisation are important in ensuring that relevant hyperlocal content is easy to find. To this end, we

also note the role search engines can play in ensuring that geo-tagged content is fully reflected in results. (NESTA 2013, 4)

There are also clearly significant challenges for reporters hoping to systemically find, extract, and analyse the locative information stored in participatory platforms, say for data journalism.

The quirks of mapping systems present further problems for pursuing consensual or collaborative representations of place. As Hanan Samet and colleagues note, intense competition to produce mapping software for mobile internet markets has resulted in maps that ignore many of the central principles, quality assurance policies, and standards of professional cartography, and fail to respect traditional "trade-offs between accuracy, aesthetics, and completeness" in representation (Samet, Fruin, and Nutanong 2012). Their comparative analyses of MapQuest, ESRI, and Google, Apple, Nokia, and Bing Maps found significant differences in information quality, utility, and aesthetics, some of which would negatively affect user experience, particularly on small-screen devices. The potential problems became apparent when the iPhone iOS5 replaced Google Maps with the substandard Apple Maps app, which was rushed on to the market despite developer warnings (Lowensohn 2012). Apple Maps was missing essential way-finding and location data, and displayed incorrect, erroneously placed, and out-of-date information. It not only got people lost, to the point that Australian police warned against its use (Lowe 2012), but was difficult to use in terms of data access and presentation.

Some of the challenges to participatory place-making become apparent when we examine the presentation of a new locative mashup venture like the US Climate Commons, launched in 2013 by the Earth Journalism Network, under the auspices of international non-profit Internews and with funding from Google. The Commons is a map-based participatory platform which overlays US federal data on climate change indicators, such as temperature, rainfall, and emissions, with user-contributed geo-tagged news stories about climate-related events. The project has several aims: to help North American users better understand the impacts of and responses to climate change from region to region; to aid Internews in recognising gaps or trends in coverage; and to provide analytical tools for interpreting mediated perceptions of environmental transformation (Figure 2).

Curiously, while the guide to using the Commons map (Internews 2013) provides a brief introduction for casual browsers, and more methodological detail for research analysts, at the time of writing there was no information for story contributors on identifying or locating relevant stories, and none on the moderation of submissions for relevance, timeliness, or other key criteria in evaluating characteristics and quality of journalism. The interface requires contributors to simply "submit a story" by entering the title, publication source, and URL of an online news item. Material is auto-geo-tagged by publication location. There is no capacity for semantic tagging, to add geographic data to the story record, to link related records, or for reporting incorrect geo-tagging. This process also assumes most stories are about a single place. Stories that refer to multiple places, sites remote from the publication location, different regions, the nation, or world then problematise the design convention adopted. Rather than Climate Commons delivering on its promise of climate change stories "about" a region, we will most often see stories from a regional publisher, about—well, potentially anywhere.

These features may well be amended by the time this case study is published, but it does suggest that there is a long way to go in developing user-oriented, social mapping

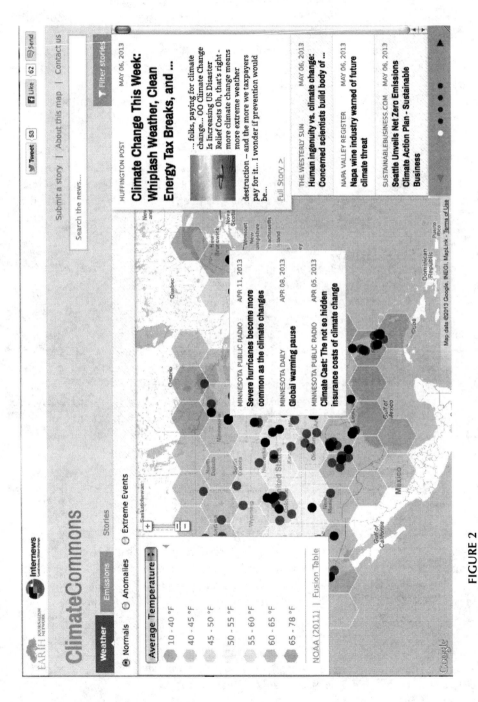

FIGURE 2
Climate Commons, temperature overlay, 8 May 2013

tools to underpin locative news. Usability, user experience, and responsive design are priorities for mobile audiences trying to navigate dynamic (zoom, click, and pan-able) four-dimensional data structures, and perform creative tasks. Attending to the spatial and locational dimensions of media environments is a new field of enquiry for journalism, and particularly important when planning interactive or participatory features that hope to represent the complexity of such mediating locations.

Conclusion

As we have outlined, it is still relatively early days in the evolution of audiences' mobile mediated worlds, their experimentation with, and domestication of, the affordances of locative technologies. Locative media is very much bound up with an acknowledgement of, engagement with, and reshaping of the places in which news consumption of audiences occurs.

Also nascent are the offerings and responses by journalists, and news and digital media organisations in locative news. We have sought to explore and emphasise the very closely linked nature of journalism and news, production and consumption, in unfolding locative news. As we have argued, development of the cultural, media, and industrial dimensions of the new kinds of place informatics and place-making practices possible with locative news has great promise.

Thus far, we find conjuring with the possibilities of locative news poses challenges on the production side. All media organisations struggle with the limitations of their content management systems and software development expertise, and with programming in open standards for mobile news—evidenced, for instance, in API problems. In its prolonged transition to digital, print media's shrinking revenues have meant there has been little capacity on the part of many news organisations to hire programmers to take advantage of the affordances and potential of mobile media technologies, such as locative media. There also remains a significant gap in understanding the specificities of how news is being produced for the internet. There are significant differences in affordances among the two broadly different, if converging, platforms: the Web (which still hosts much online news); and mobile phones and tablets (and the apps that increasingly span mobile media).

If locative news platforms are clunky and undeveloped, of course this means that any broader adoption by audiences is unlikely. Add to this the various uniquely local issues we have noted in this paper, and there is a considerable degree of divergence in locative media practice, spanning the policies of key ecosystems and data providers (such as Google and Apple), privacy issues, security issues of national government (sensitivities of maps), business models of start-ups (the case of hyperlocal mobile and online media), as well as the standards and design of visualisation mapping technologies.

These overlapping issues in the state of geo-location information ecologies of mobile media and associated technologies offer a ready explanation for the still relatively nascent state of fully fledged ubiquituous locative news. We suspect such explanations are only part of the story, however. Rather, like many other histories of new technologies, there remains a yawning chasm between, on the one hand, the social imaginaries of locative news, and, on the other hand, the materialities, path-dependency, industrial settings, and political and cultural economies of the places and spaces of mobile audiences and their unfolding futures.

FUNDING

The paper is an output of the Australian Research Council Discovery grant "Moving Media: Mobile Internet and New Policy Modes" [DP120101971].

REFERENCES

Arceneaux, Noah. 2014. "Small, Cheap, and Out of Control: Reflections on the Transistor Radio." In *Routledge Companion to Mobile Media*, edited by Gerard Goggin and Larissa Hjorth, 125–134. New York: Routledge.

Banks, John. 2013. *Co-Creating Videogames*. London: Bloomsbury.

Barkham, Patrick. 2012. "Tales of the City: The Rise of the Local Blog." *Guardian.co.uk*, March 20. http://www.guardian.co.uk/media/2012/mar/20/tales-from-city-local-blogs

Bennett, Tony, and Chris Healy, eds. 2009. "Assembling Culture." *Special Issue of Journal of Cultural Economy* 2 (1–2): 1–1. doi:10.1080/17530350903063719.

Bennett, James, and Nikki Strange, eds. 2011. *Television as Digital Media*. Durham, NC: Duke University Press.

Bruns, Axel. 2009. "News Blogs and Citizen Journalism: New Directions for E-journalism." In *e-Journalism: New Media and News Media*, edited by Kiran Prasad, 101–126. India: BR Publishing, Delhi.

Claudia, Silvia. 2012. *Why Should News Organizations Care about Location-Based Services?* http://silvaclaudia.com/2012/04/16/why-should-news-organizations-care-about-location-based-services/.

Cohen, Noam. 2009. "In Animated Videos, News and Guesswork Mix." *The New York Times*, December 5. http://www.nytimes.com/2009/12/06/business/media/06animate.html?_r=0

Emms, Stephen, and Tom Kihl. 2013. "Magazines, Mobile and Monetisation: The Kentishtowner Story So Far." *Destination Local Blog, NESTA*, April 16. http://www.nesta.org.uk/areas_of_work/creative_economy/destination_local/assets/blog_entries/magazines_mobile_and_monetisation_the_kentishtowner_story_so_far

Farman, Jason. 2012. *Mobile Interface Theory: Embodied Space and Locative Media*. New York: Routledge.

Federal Communications Commission (FCC). 2005. *Enhanced 9-1-1 – Wireless Services*. Washington, DC: FCC. http://transition.fcc.gov/pshs/services/911-services/enhanced911/

Federal Trade Commission (FTC). 2013. *Mobile Privacy Disclosures: Building Trust through Transparency*. Washington, DC: FTC. http://www.ftc.gov/os/2013/02/130201mobileprivacyreport.pdf

Feijóo, Claudio, Ioannis Maghiros, Abadie, and Gomez-Barroso Fabienne. 2009. "Exploring a Heterogeneous and Fragmented Digital Ecosystem: Mobile Content." *Telematics & Informatics* 26 (3): 282–292. doi:10.1016/j.tele.2008.11.009.

Franklin, Bob, ed. 1998. *Local Journalism and Local Media: Making the Local News*. London: Routledge.

Goggin, Gerard. 2006. *Cell Phone Culture*. London: Routledge.

Goggin Gerard. 2009. "Assembling Media Culture: The Case of Mobiles." *Journal of Cultural Economy* 2 (1): 151–167.

Goggin, Gerard. 2013. "Sport and the Rise of Mobile Media." In *Media Sport: Technology, Power and Identity in the Network Society*, edited by David Rowe and Brett Hutchins, 1–15. New York: Routledge.

Goodchild, Michael F. 2007. "Citizens as Sensors: The World of Volunteered Geography." *GeoJournal* 69 (4): 211–221. doi:10.1007/s10708-007-9111-y.

Gordon, Rich. 2008. "LoJo Lessons: Carving Paths towards the Locative Future." Readership Institute. July 2. http://www.readership.org/blog2/2008/07/lojo-lessons-carving-paths-toward.html

Gordon, Eric, and Adriana de Souza e Silva. 2011. *Net Locality: Why Location Matters in a Networked World*. New York: Wiley.

Higgins, Michael. 2004. "Putting the Nation in the News: the Role of Location Formulation in a Selection of Scottish Newspapers." *Discourse & Society* 15 (5): 633–648. doi:10.1177/0957926504045035.

Ibrus, Indrek. 2013. "Evolutionary Dynamics of the Mobile Web." *A Companion to New Media Dynamics*, edited by John Hartley, Jean Burgess, and Axel Bruns, 277–289. Malden, MA: Wiley-Blackwell.

Internews. 2013. "About this Map." *Climate Commons*. Accessed 8 May. http://climatecommons.earthjournalism.net/map/

Kurplus, David, Emily T. Metzgar, and Karen M. Rowley. 2010. "Sustaining Hyperlocal Media: In Search of Funding Models." *Journalism Studies* 11 (3): 359–376. doi:10.1080/14616700903429787.

Lee, Chin-Chuan. 1997. "Media Structure and Regime Change in Hong Kong." In *The Challenge of Hong Kong's Reintegration with China*, edited by M. Chan, 113–138. Hong Kong: Hong Kong University Press.

Lee, F., and A. Lin. 2006. "Newspaper Editorial Discourse and the Politics of Self-censorship in Hong Kong." *Discourse & Society* 17 (3): 331–358. doi:10.1177/0957926506062371.

Little, Mark. 2012. "Finding the Wisdom in the Crowd." Truth in Social Media. *Nieman Report* 66 (2): 14–17.

Lowe, Adrian. 2012. "Tourists Stranded in Searing Heat as Apple Maps Fails." *The Age*, December 10. http://www.theage.com.au/technology/technology-news/tourists-stranded-in-searing-heat-as-apple-maps-fails-20121210-2b4n8.html

Lowensohn, Josh. 2012. "Developers: We Warned Apple about iOS Maps Quality." *Cnet.com*. October 9. http://news.cnet.com/8301-13579_3-57529147-37/developers-we-warned-apple-about-ios-maps-quality/

Martin, Fiona, and Wilson Helen. 2002. "Beyond The ABC's Backyard: Radio, the Web and Australian Regional Space." *Convergence* 8 (1): 43–61.

Monmonier, Mark S. 1989. *Maps with the News: The Development of American Journalistic Cartography*. Chicago: University of Chicago Press.

Myers, Steve. 2012. "Geofeedia Helps Journalists Locate Real-Time Photos, Tweets Where News Breaks." *Poynter.org*, May 14. http://www.poynter.org/latest-news/top-stories/173764/geofeedia-helps-journalists-locate-real-time-photos-tweets-where-news-breaks/

NESTA. 2013. *UK Demand for Hyperlocal Media: Research Report*. April. http://www.nesta.org.uk/publications/reports/assets/features/uk_demand_for_hyperlocal_media

Nyre, Lars, Solveig Bjørnestad, Bjørnar Tessem, and Kjetil Vaage Øie. 2012. "Locative journalism: Designing a Location-dependent News Medium for Smartphones." *Convergence* 18 (3): 297–314.

Øie, Kjetil Vaage. 2012. "Sensing the News: User Experiences when Reading Locative News." *Future Internet* 4 (4): 161–178. doi:10.3390/fi4010161.

Pavlik, John V., and Frank Bridges. 2013. "The Emergence of Augmented Reality (AR) as a Storytelling Medium in Journalism." *Journalism & Communication Monographs* 15 (1): 4–59.

Peters, Chris. 2012. "Journalism to Go." Journalism Studies 13 (5–6): 695–705. doi:10.1080/1461670X.2012.662405.

Pew Research Centre (Pew). 2011a. Online: Key Questions Facing Digital News. *The State of the News Media 2011: An Annual Report on American Journalism*. Washington, DC: Pew Research Centre. http://stateofthemedia.org/2011/online-essay/

Pew Research Centre (Pew). 2011b. Survey: Mobile News & Paying Online. *The State of the News Media 2011: An Annual Report on American Journalism*. Washington, DC: Pew Research Centre. http://stateofthemedia.org/2011/mobile-survey/

Pew Research Centre (Pew). 2012. *The Future of Mobile News*. Washington, DC: Project for Excellence in Journalism. http://www.journalism.org/sites/journalism.org/files/Futureof-mobilenews%20_final1.pdf

Pew Research Centre (Pew). 2013. *Digital. The State of the News Media 2013: An Annual Report on American Journalism*. Washington, DC: Pew Research Centre. http://stateofthemedia.org/2013/digital-as-mobile-grows-rapidly-the-pressures-on-news-intensify/

Plattner, Hasso, Christoph Meinel, and Larry Leifer, eds. 2012. *Design Thinking Research: Studying Co-Creation in Practice*. Heidelberg: Spring.

Radcliffe, Damian. 2012. *Here and Now: UK Hyperlocal Media Today*. London: NESTA. http://www.nesta.org.uk/areas_of_work/creative_economy/destination_local/assets/features/here_and_now_uk_hyperlocal_media_today

Reuters Institute. 2013. *Digital News Report 2013: Tracking the Future of News*, edited Nic Newman and David A. L. Levy. Oxford: University of Oxford https://reutersinstitute.politics.ox.ac.uk/fileadmin/documents/Publications/Working_Papers/Digital_News_Report_2013.pdf

Ross. 2013. "*Everyblock*'s demise highlights the various strands of hyperlocal and not the failure of all." *The Journalism Notepad*, February 11. http://thejournalismnotepad.co.uk/2013/02/11/everyblocks-demise-highlights-the-various-strands-of-hyperlocal-and-not-the-failure-of-all/

Samet, Hanan, Brendan C. Fruin, and Sarana Nutanong. 2012. "Duking it out at the Smartphone Mobile App Mapping API Corral: Apple, Google, and the Competition." *Proceedings of the 1st ACM SIGSPATIAL International Workshop on Mobile Geographic Information Systems (MobiGIS 2012)*, Redondo Beach, CA, November 2012. http://www.cs.umd.edu/~hjs/pubs/dukingapi-small.pdf

de Souza e Silva, Adriana, and Jordan Firth. 2012. *Mobile Interfaces in Public Spaces: Locational Privacy, Control, and Urban Sociability*. New York: Routledge.

Tibbitt, Ally. 2013. "Getting Edinburgh Talking: There's an App for That." *Destination Local Blog*, NESTA, April 26. http://www.nesta.org.uk/areas_of_work/creative_economy/destination_local/assets/blog_entries/getting_edinburgh_talking_theres_an_app_for_that

Väätäjä, Heli, Teija Vainio, and Esa Sirkkunen. 2012. "Location-Based Crowdsourcing of Hyperlocal News: Dimensions of Participation Preferences." In *Group 12:Proceedings of the 17th ACM international conference on Supporting Group Work*, 85–94. New York: Association for Computing Machinery.

Wilken, Rowan. 2012. "Locative Media: From Specialized Preoccupation to Mainstream Fascination." *Convergence* 18 (3): 243–247.

Wilken, Rowan and Gerard Goggin. 2012. "Mobilizing Place: Conceptual Currents and Controversies." In *Mobile Technology and Place*, edited by Rowan Wilken and Gerard Goggin, 3–25. New York: Routledge.

Yang, Nu. 2013. "Make the Right Call." *Editor and Publisher*, July 35.

Zheng, Yan-Tao, Zheng-Jun Zha, and Tat-Seng Chua. 2011. "Research and Applications on Georeferenced Multimedia: A Survey." *Multimedia Tools and Applications* 51 (1): 77–98. doi:10.1007/s11042-010-0630-z.

NEWS MEDIA OLD AND NEW
Fluctuating audiences, news repertoires and locations of consumption

Kim Christian Schrøder

This article presents and discusses three different approaches to the exploration of the cross-media challenges facing news audiences, as they seek access to, navigate in and make sense of the multitude of news sources across print, broadcasting, online and mobile media platforms. From a modernized uses and gratifications perspective, based on the notion of "worthwhileness" as the determinant of people's everyday selections from the "supermarket of news", the article first reports from a longitudinal survey study in Denmark in which the author's foundational mapping of cross-media news consumption in pre-mobile 2008 is compared with replicating mappings carried out in 2011 and 2012, in a collaborative project between academics and news publishers. The analytical interest here focuses on the fluctuations between traditional news media and the surging digital news outlets of the internet and mobile devices. Secondly, the article summarizes the findings of a qualitative study of citizens' news repertoires, which was fortified with a quantitative factor analysis in order to find patterns in people's news consumption. Thirdly, findings are presented from a 2013 study that explored ubiquitous news consumption, asking respondents to specify the nexus of news platform and location of use.

Introduction

News consumption is not just something we do, it is something we do in a particular place. (Peters 2012, 697)

As a news event, the Boston Marathon bombings in April 2013 showed that a great deal of what is called "breaking news" is in the process of moving to social media platforms. It was ordinary citizen eye-witnesses who produced news by using their Facebook or Twitter accounts to immediately report on the latest developments in the chase of the suspects, while mainstream media were dependent, at least for a part of their news reporting, on what citizen journalists made available via social media. The resulting news production chain, characterized by little or no journalistic and editorial curation of the information, had consequences for the quality of the news that reached news audiences, in terms of how accurate or misleading that information was.

The Boston case demonstrates that the established patterns and routines of news consumption, including people's inclination to trust the news, are being transformed by the nexus of innovative technologies and the revolutionizing journalistic processes they afford. This nexus results in news media content which sets societal agendas and frames cultural issues in new ways for news audiences, irrespective of whether they get their news directly from social media platforms or not. It is therefore important to monitor on a continuous basis precisely what the landscape of news looks like: what technological platforms and formats are receding and emerging, and which are dominant, as well as how people are accessing, navigating in, and making sense of the landscape of news.

The monitoring of such developments in the Danish landscape of news has been among the tasks of Roskilde University's Center for Power, Media and Communication since its launch in 2012, whose current research builds on earlier audience-oriented research about the political role of the media in a mediatized society (Schrøder and Phillips 2007). In this article I present the findings of theoretical and empirical research designed to map how news audiences relate and respond to the technological and discursive affordances provided by the news media, and how they thereby assemble their news diets and news repertoires in contexts of everyday life. In turn (but not dealt with here) these changing audience practices inevitably feed back into and affect the decisions of the institutional actors in news production, as well as the political actors responsible for media policy and regulation, as they consider, respectively, the economic viability and the democratic appropriateness of the news media.

The focus of our research on the audiences of news is on how Danish citizens and consumers (in the following, for short: citizens) are navigating in today's multi-media, mediatized news landscape: What news media do they use, and for what? Metaphorically we regard the citizens as shopping in the "supermarket of news", taking news media from the shelves and putting them into their daily, weekly or monthly "shopping carts" according to what they find indispensable, necessary or enjoyable, what they have time for, what they can afford, etc.

It is the ambition of our research to build a fact base for understanding the news media–society nexus, and to feed our findings into ongoing debates about how well the news media serve Danes as resources in everyday life, including the provision of democratic prerequisites.

The article also includes a 2013 study of the location-based consumption practices in the news media landscape. The inclusion of questions about the locations of news media use in our recent research can be seen as a response to the argument, which frames this special issue, that "to tell a story of everyday life demands considering social space, and social space is increasingly inseparable from 'media space'" (Peters 2012, 697).

The Cross-media Perspective in the Age of Mediatization: Theoretical Framings

The audience research presented here is premised on the fact that audiences are "inherently cross-media" (Schrøder 2011). It is by no means a new thing that audiences compose their media diets out of a supply from different media platforms, and nor should we forget that print media like newspapers and magazines have always been pre-eminently mobile. However, with the coming of the digital age, "emerging patterns of cross-media use are far more seamless and blurred, hybrid and complex than they used to be" (Bjur et al. 2013, 15). This is so, not least because the relationship between media technologies and place has become more complex; cross-media practices may take place not by moving between different locations—each the natural habitat of one particular medium (such as radios, television sets and record players)—but instead by applying two or more analogue and/or digital media simultaneously in the same location.

Bjur et al. (2013), after reviewing a number of recent attempts to develop and operationalize new conceptual frameworks for mapping and explaining the cross-media practices of audiences, suggest that cross-media consumption can be researched from three perspectives. First, different media may distinguish themselves in terms of *functional differentiation*; this has to do with the extent to which different media complement and co-exist with each other, as when one medium specializes in fulfilling certain types of needs in order to differentiate itself from its rivals. Secondly, one can explore the ways in which people build *media repertories*, i.e. how they combine, in personal constellations of media (Couldry, Livingstone, and Markham 2007, 190–191), a variety of media technologies, media genres, and media brands or products, which jointly fulfil their everyday needs for information, diversion and sociability. Thirdly, we may adopt a situational perspective from which we study how media belong to or transcend specific socio-spatial contexts, in the form of *location ensembles* of media technologies and formats.

The empirical studies presented below cover all three perspectives, providing some preliminary insights into the diverse mechanisms of cross-media news consumption in today's news universe. First, I present longitudinal survey findings which demonstrate the consumption fluctuations over time of the different news media. Secondly, I report on a study which integrated a qualitative and a quantitative approach in order to produce a model of seven different types of news consumer, based on their differently composed news media repertoires. Thirdly, I offer findings from a survey which included questions about people's sites of news consumption inside and outside the home, as well as their preferred media platforms in the different locations.

In addition to the conceptual and empirical challenges stemming from the intensification of cross-media developments, another challenge for audience research comes from the need to situate specific media research projects in the ongoing debates about mediatization. For the last couple of decades our culture has been stepping into the era of mediatization, in which the role of the media across the range of social institutions and everyday life has grown in quantitative as well as qualitative terms (Strömbäck 2008; Hjarvard 2008; Livingstone 2009; Hepp 2013).

The empirical audience research presented in this article is conceptualized, in continuation of earlier research arguing for the need to "complexify" media–audience relations (Schrøder and Phillips 2007), as an agency-oriented antidote to the "media logic" approach to mediatization, in which "media logics" override other societal practices and actors. Following Hepp's (2013) more complex notion of "cultures of mediatization", the processes and "logics" of mediatization should not just be explored at the level of social institution, but also in the everyday processes through which people encounter, acquire and make sense of the media in their dual appearance as technologies and multimodal discourses: "It is not a simple matter of a … logic of production, for example, having an impact upon the logics of use and so upon people's everyday lives. The situation is much more complex, involving the mediation of different logics, a plurality of logics" (Hepp 2013, 35).

What we might call "audience logics" play a prominent role in such a plurality of logics and can be conceptualized by reference to the notion of "worthwhileness" (for a fuller description, see Schrøder and Larsen 2010). Not intended for rigorous empirical operationalization, the argument is that in order to become adopted into an individual's news media repertoire, a news medium must be experienced by this individual as subjectively worthwhile. Worthwhileness is a multidimensional phenomenon consisting of at least seven dimensions. These dimensions, acquired by individuals as part of their media socialization, enter into what we may call the "worthwhileness equation", which determines why some news media and not others are chosen to become parts of an individual's news media repertoire.

The seven worthwhileness dimensions can be briefly described as follows:

1. *Time spent*: A news medium must be worth the time spent. Some news media are experienced as so important that you take the time necessary to use them, others are worthwhile "by default", i.e. they are used when temporarily convenient in time pockets in the course of everyday life.
2. *Public connection*: Deriving from research by Couldry, Livingstone, and Markham (2007, 3) and defined as news content which brings "an orientation to a public world where matters of shared concern are ... addressed", I define public connection as the "content dimension" of worthwhileness. I have: (a) broadened the concept to include any news content which helps maintain relations to one's networks and the wider society; and (b) I distinguish between "democratic worthwhileness" (content that caters to the citizen identity) and "everyday worthwhileness" (content that links you to personal networks).
3. *Normative pressures*: Your use of a news medium or not depends to some extent on whether it is "*comme il faut*" or "*media non grata*" among your significant others.
4. *Participatory potential*: For some people, the affordance of participation matters in a news medium, i.e. whether you can be (inter)active by sending a link to a friend, "like" on social media, contribute your own user-generated content, etc.
5. *Price*: A news medium must be affordable, and worth the price.
6. *Technological appeal*: The technological smartness of a device may be an independent asset for some users, notably for early adopters of new media technologies or software, but this also encompasses the convenience of the remote control for using Text TV, or the material appeal of a magazine's glossiness.
7. *Situational fit*: Last but not least, a news medium must be suitable for the time and place of its use, the way radio fits in with driving a car, or a newspaper is appropriate on a commuter train.

As stated above, the worthwhileness dimensions have not been operationalized rigorously for empirical research, but they all served as a guiding back curtain during the qualitative interviews, and some of them have close parallels in some of the questions that were asked in the survey: for instance, we asked which news media respondents had used during the past week (i.e. found worthwhile); which they found most indispensable (most worthwhile); which participatory activities they had engaged in (i.e. participatory potential), and so forth.

Fluctuating News Audiences
Methodological Challenges of Longitudinal Research

The surveys of news media use have been conducted in a longitudinal perspective. The particular mapping of any one year is interesting in itself, but the ability to compare developments in news consumption over a span of years is even more valuable.

However, the implementation of a longitudinal survey must be accompanied with an important caveat, as the opposing considerations of replicability of the questionnaire, on the one hand, and the questionnaire's meaningfulness for respondents, on the other, lead to an unavoidable paradox: due to the rapidly changing media-technological scenarios, if the same wording was used for the questionnaire in 2012 as in 2008, respondents would be likely to experience a lack of fit between the questions and their lived reality of media devices. By contrast, if the wording of the questions is changed, the last study will not count as an exact replication of the first one.

We have tried to solve this problem by making some minimal adjustments to the wordings used in the questionnaire, seeing these adjustments not as obstacles to replication, but as ways *to ensure the "sameness" of the questions as experienced by the respondents*. Accommodating the fact that increasingly TV news can be watched on other devices than a TV set, we opted for the primacy of technological platforms and changed the 2008 wording "news on TV" to the 2012 wording "news on a TV set", and similarly for radio news. Allowing for print media to be accessed on several technological platforms, we changed the 2008 wording "national morning newspapers" to the 2012 wording "national morning newspapers on paper". Knowing that people may go online from several technological devices, we changed the 2008 wording "news on the internet" to "news on a computer (desktop or laptop)". In order to accommodate the role played by mobile devices, we added questions about news on a tablet and on social media (non-existent as news sources in 2008) to supplement our question about news on mobile phones (to which we added "or smartphones").

Consequently, the findings presented for the years 2008, 2011 and 2012 are not strictly commensurable, but arguably this is the best we can do under the circumstances if we wish to undertake longitudinal comparisons of news media use.

Mapping the Landscapes of News Media Worthwhileness, 2008–2012

The survey was administered to different, representative samples of just over 1000 Danes over 18 years of age in 2008, 2011 and 2012 in the month of November. The findings presented here are national averages without demographic details. The results are significant at the 95 per cent level, except that the order of two media separated by less than 3 per cent in the tables/figures could be the reverse.

Figure 1 shows a snapshot of the Danes' news media consumption in 2012—what could be called the balance of power between the preferred news media of the national audience.[1] TV is the most widely used news medium (84 per cent),[2] with radio news (68 per cent) and news on a computer (67 per cent) fighting head-to-head for second place. Surprisingly, perhaps, Text-TV is in sixth place, used by 45 per cent, ahead of both news on a mobile phone (39 per cent) and news from social media like Facebook and Twitter (36 per cent). The latter figure does not show people's use of social media as such, but is a genuine expression of people's use of social media for news, as the questionnaire specified the "use of social media for news as you know it from other news media". The emergence of social media as news providers appears to show, as Hermida et al. (2012, 818) found in Canada, that "a significant number of social media users tend to rely on the people around them to tell them what they need to know rather than relying solely on institutional media". Strikingly, the national daily, once a principal bastion of democratic citizenship, follows in ninth place with a mere 34 per cent having used a printed national newspaper during the past week. News on a tablet device is emerging in the supermarket of news in 15th place with a 22 per cent following, after being available in Denmark for

2012: Danes' use of news media
"have used past week"

Medium	%
TV news	~85%
Radio news	~70%
Computer news	~68%
Local weekly	~52%
TV current affairs	~50%
Text TV	~45%
Mobile news	~38%
Social media	~35%
National daily	~32%
Radio current affairs	~32%
Local daily	~28%
Free daily	~27%
Computer news int.	~25%
Magazines	~24%
Teblet news	~22%
Professional magazine	~18%
Tabloid newspaper	~17%
TV news int.	~12%
Blog	~8%
Mp3	~3%

FIGURE 1
Worthwhileness of news sources, 2012: Danish news users' ranking of 20 news media and news formats (for all categories examples were provided for respondents)

less than two years. Notably, on a weekly basis almost 24 per cent of the Danes are oriented towards online international news sources on computer screens.

The turbulence that characterizes the audience's cross-media news landscape is evident from Figure 2, which traces the fluctuations over a period of just four years, 2008–2012. Small declines characterize both TV news, news on a computer, local weeklies and Text-TV, while radio news seems more stable; national daily newspapers and free urban dailies took a fall from 2008 to 2011, but appear to have stabilized in 2012. A couple of news media have grown in importance for audiences, notably mobile phones, whose breakthrough as news media occurred between 2008 and 2011 and then continued to grow, but also news from social media and tablet news which have grown by 8 points and 16 points, respectively, from 2011 to 2012.

Anticipating some of the arguments below, it seems that most of these fluctuations have less to do with changing needs for specific kinds of content than with the spread of increasingly more flexible and convenient means of accessing this content. In terms of the theoretical framework on which our research is based, therefore, the fluctuations appear to be driven especially by the technological and situational kinds of worthwhileness, which in turn have consequences for other worthwhileness dimensions, notably the dimension of time. As an example, if you have accessed "overview" news on a portable device during the day (during breaks at work or during transport), and if you have participated as a "producer" in the sharing of news on social media mobile platforms, you will return home equipped with a substantial amount of the information you need in order to maintain your networks of public connection. This will tend to lower your need to spend time on acquiring news of the "overview" type on a computer or on Text-TV, while you may still want to satisfy your need for depth and background news (see Figure 4 below), and the ritual of watching TV news will still seem natural for many.

The added value of the longitudinal perspective also appears in the ability to discern downward and upward trends, and thereby to assess the potential implications of shifting

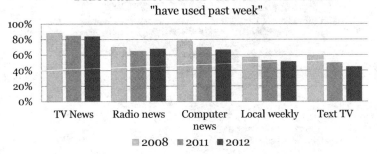

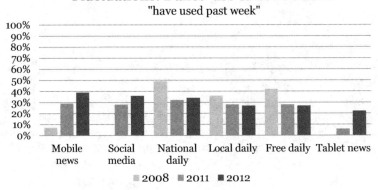

FIGURE 2
The fluctuating worthwhileness of primary news sources, 2008–2012. Question: "Which of these news media do you find most indispensable?"

patterns of use for different social groups. As an example, another analysis of news consumption in Denmark in 2012, which only surveyed this year, proclaimed that among young people "Facebook is losing out as a news medium", finding comfort in the finding that "television and radio news are still the most popular sources of news among the 16–25 year-olds" (*metroXpress*, December 20, 2012). Without sharing that study's implicit concern over the dubious democratic potential of social media, our longitudinal study offers a corrective: just tracing the role of social media for young people's news consumption from 2011 to 2012, it is clear that social media are far from "losing out"; rather we are in the middle of a surge, as news from social media increased from 43 to 53 per cent among the 15–35 age group. We shall then have to look to other kinds of research to inform us about the balance of enlightenment and entertainment resulting from this form of news consumption.

The findings for "most worthwhile" news medium (Figure 3) show that social media have not yet affected people's sense of the different news media's importance. While TV news (from 39 to 31 per cent) is not as indispensable as it used to be, news on a computer and on radio maintain their rankings, while national dailies have stabilized their ranking after taking a severe fall from 2008 to 2011 (from 15 to 7 per cent). News on a mobile phone is gaining steadily in importance (from 3 to 7 per cent), while some might be democratically concerned that the flexible but superficial news format of Text-TV maintains its status as most indispensable for 5 per cent of the population.

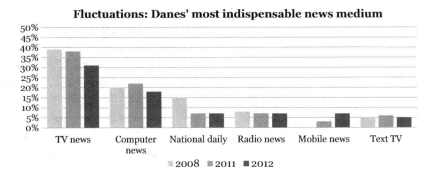

FIGURE 3
The most worthwhile news media: fluctuations, 2008–2012

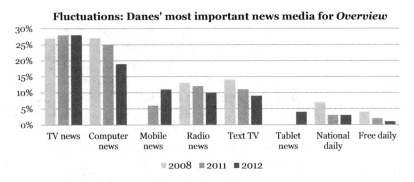

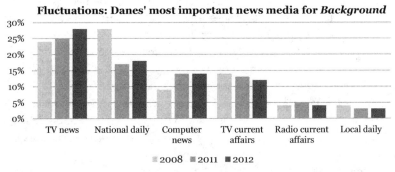

FIGURE 4
The most important news media for "overview" and "background": fluctuations, 2008–2012

The surveys distinguish between two functionalities of news, as we presume that most people have a need both for monitoring on a continuous basis what is on the news agenda and for going into depth with selected issue- or incident-based stories, seeking background information about them. As Figure 4 shows, TV news is perceived by a large group to be the most worthwhile news medium for both overview and background (28 per cent for both functions), and to have become more important for background news since 2008. Not surprisingly, the overview function is increasingly served by mobile platforms (mobile phones 11 per cent, tablets 4 per cent), which allow for anytime/anywhere news updates, in contrast to the stationary Text-TV and the situationally less versatile radio news (down from 14 to 9 per cent).

The figures confirm that the daily newspaper had long lost its historical dominance in the overview function in 2008 (7 per cent), only to decline even further in 2012 (3 per cent). For background information, while taking a severe beating from 2008 to 2012 (from 28 to 17 per cent), the national daily (together with the local daily) seems to have stabilized in 2012, while news on a computer (often provided by the exact same news organizations) has become the source of depth information for more people (from 9 to 14 per cent). It will be the task of qualitative research to probe further into to what extent background news in a newspaper is different from that on a computer, as online news, in addition to the compilation of more story facets on the immediate page, affords access through internal and external links to an almost infinite archive of previous news reports and source documents.

The online technologies increasingly afford citizens the possibility of accessing audiovisual news anywhere within the domestic space, as well as outside the home depending on the availability of wifi and/or cellular connectivity. In order to explore in a preliminary way the freedom from location enabled by different technologies, our survey asked respondents to indicate their TV viewing on computers and mobile phones.

It is still a small, but growing number of people who watch TV on a computer on a daily basis: 17 per cent watch TV on their computer every day (especially the 55+ age group), and 9 per cent do so on their smartphone (especially the 15–35 age group) (Figure 5). Interestingly, many more people have acquired *some* experience with this mode of watching: the number of people who had never done this on a computer decreased from 45 to 37 per cent from 2011 to 2012, while the corresponding figures for mobiles phones were 84 to 67 per cent. Those who have become comfortable with these technologies and have adopted this practice at least on a weekly basis in 2012 amount to 29 per cent (computer) and 14 per cent (smartphone). We thus seem to have moved beyond the stage when, in terms of Rogers's (2003) stages of the diffusion of innovations, this mode of news acquisition was used only by "innovators" (the first 2.5 per cent of adopters) and "early adopters" (the next 13.5 per cent). In other words, the curve of wide adoption by the "early majority" and the "late majority" is likely to increase sharply over the coming years, with clear implications for people's use of news media across the terrain of everyday life, inside and outside the home.

For some news consumers it is the possibility to participate actively in the dissemination, criticism and production of news which attracts them to the news media which afford this kind of "participatory worthwhileness".

While it is clearly what Picone (2007) calls "lean back" forms of interactivity which still dominate the picture in 2012, in the form of taking part in voting (30 per cent) or sending a news link to a friend (20 per cent) (Figure 6), the more "lean forward" oriented kind of participation, in which users produce their own textual input to the news process, such as commenting on an article (9 per cent), sending email to a journalist (4 per cent) and participating in a debate (7 per cent), are still only used by a minority, although this is growing. The growth in "commenting on an article" comes especially from the 35–54 age group, whereas "sending a news link to a friend" derives mainly from the 15–34 age group.

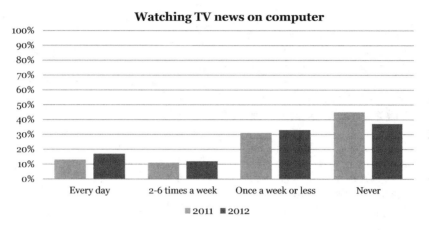

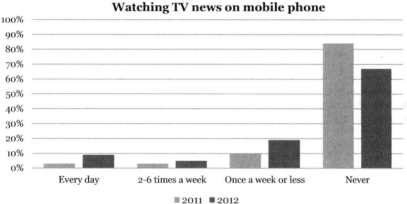

FIGURE 5
Watching TV news on a computer or mobile phone, 2011–2012

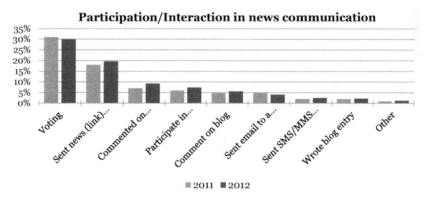

FIGURE 6
Participation in news communication, 2011–2012

The longitudinal survey from 2008 to 2012, in sum, enables us to track significant developments in the landscapes of news consumption, with the following landmarks:

- There has been a breakthrough for mobile technologies as news platforms, due to the rise of smartphones, tablets and social media.
- There has been a dramatic drop in the use of national daily newspapers in print, also in their former stronghold as providers of background/depth information.
- TV news is unrivalled as the most important news medium in Denmark, across the two functions and across age groups. The emergence of mobile devices and social media has so far had only a moderate impact on the use of traditional media.[3]
- Online news on computers and mobile devices has established itself as a significant news provider across demographic groups. For the overview function, the aggregate of online news on computers and mobile devices surpasses TV news.
- It has become common to watch TV news on computers; a considerable number of people have familiarized themselves with watching TV news on a mobile device.
- The amount of people using some interactive affordances of news media has almost doubled from 24 to 43 per cent.

The sense-making aspects of these developments—for instance how worthwhileness motivations cause different groups of people to compile their cross-media news repertoires—is an aspect which we have also explored, in the form of an integrated qualitative/quantitative study.

Mapping Citizen's News Repertoires

In addition to mapping statistically what people take from the shelves of "the supermarket of news", we have also explored the composition of the newswares which individual citizens take into their shopping carts, in order to map the cross-media news repertoires which individuals draw on as resources for everyday enlightenment and entertainment. These repertoire mappings have been reported on in detail elsewhere (Schrøder and Kobbernagel 2010), so here I shall merely summarize the findings, in order to invoke one more component towards understanding the complexity of news media consumption.[4]

The fieldwork on which this research draws, carried out in 2009, was qualitative. With 35 informants we conducted long individual interviews inspired both by the traditional depth interview of the "a-day-in-the-life" type, and the think-aloud format. To this qualitative format we added a quantitative translation device in the form of a Q-methodological task, in which informants sorted 25 cards, each with one news platform or format written on it, on a pyramidal grid that registered each news medium's relative importance (worthwhileness) in the informant's everyday life. Subsequently, these 25 card configurations were factor analysed in order to fortify the process of analytical generalization of the qualitative data (Schrøder 2012).

As shown in Table 1, the 35 Danish informants can be divided into seven types of news consumers, who differ with respect to the constellation of news media to which they assign greatest importance to everyday life. For each user type, the typology shown here lists the top-five news media which characterize the individuals who are constituted as a user group by the factor analysis, out of the total of 25 news media which all informants ranked.

It is clear, without going into details, that the seven user types are distinguished by clearly different patterns of news media use. It is also clear, however, that in contrast to news typologies from other countries (for instance, the United States, see Pew Research

TABLE 1
Typology of cross-media news consumption, Denmark, 2009 (Schrøder and Kobbernagel 2010)

	The traditional, versatile news user	The "popular" digital news user	The depth digital news user	The light newspaper reader	The heavy newspaper reader	The news update addict	The regional omnivore
1	Prime-time Danish TV news	Social net media	Danish internet news sites	Prime-time Danish TV news	National mainstream newspapers	24-hour TV news	Prime-time Danish TV news
2	National mainstream newspapers	Danish internet news sites	Social net media	Tabloid newspapers	Prime-time Danish TV news	Prime-time Danish TV news	Local/regional dailies
3	Radio news (before 9 am)	Prime-time Danish TV news	Prime-time Danish TV news	Free daily newspapers	Text-TV	Text-TV	"Serious" current affairs TV
4	"Serious" current affairs TV	"Entertaining" current affairs TV	Internet: culture sites	Danish internet news sites	Danish internet news sites	Danish internet news sites	Family and women's magazines
5	Danish internet news sites	Free daily newspapers	Free daily newspapers	"Entertaining" current affairs TV	National niche newspapers	Social net media	Danish internet news sites

Center 2008), the Danish typology is also fairly homogeneous in the sense that all seven types have "mainstream TV" (no doubt due to the strong role of public service channels) and "internet news sites" among the top five. All the groups thus use a mixture of traditional and new sources of news, a finding which is compatible with the survey findings reported above. In light of the breakthrough for the location-transcending mobile news platforms since this study was done in 2009, it is likely that by 2014 these platforms will have moved into a stronger position across the seven typologies.

Before turning to our study of the locations of news consumption, let us dwell for a moment on the possible democratic implications of these findings about the Danes' cross-media news consumption (for a similar discussion based on previous research, see Schrøder and Phillips 2007). We may ask whether these levels and mixtures of news media qualify Danish citizens as well-informed, resourceful and competent citizens? Begging the question of how to define such a model citizen (but see Schudson 1998; Barnhurst 2003), it is clear that in order to address the issue of such a citizen's media portfolio with any degree of certainty, we would need to consult a long range of research drawn from the collected efforts of political scientists and communication scholars (Keane 1991; Gamson 1992; Schudson 1998). However, we may venture some preliminary reflections on the basis of the above empirical findings, starting with a counter question: What would the news repertoire of a competent citizen look like?

The traditional answer to this question has been that the daily newspaper is a *sine qua non* of informed citizenship; a recent Danish study of five national newspapers thus argued that the decline of this medium to its present level of usage may lead to a democratic deficit that poses a serious challenge to the democratic health of the country (Lund 2013). From this perspective, it is a bad sign that only three of the seven groups have the national or regional daily among the top-five news media, and that so few respondents in the longitudinal survey use this news source for the acquisition of overview and background.

However, the fact that all seven groups draw significantly on public service TV news points in the opposite direction, as other research has documented that citizens of countries with strong public service news media possess higher levels of public knowledge (Curran et al. 2009, 2013). Similarly, all groups have online news sources among the top five, and a substantial portion of this news comes out of the very same publishing houses whose print media are being deselected by the citizens. Recent cross-national comparative research documents that the loyalty of Danish citizens to established news brands is considerable compared to the citizens' online news preferences of many other countries (e.g. the United States and Italy), where online aggregators and online indigenous news media play a more prominent role (Reuters Institute Digital News Report 2013).

Finally, the prominent role of mobile platforms and social media would appear to indicate that the Danes possess considerable digital literacies, which are increasingly becoming a prerequisite of democratic citizenship, as well as civic agency in general, in the years to come (Lunt et al. 2014).

Locations of News Consumption

Chris Peters (2012, 698) observes, following Soja (1996), that research into the practices of everyday life should comprise, in addition to the situatedness in "historicality" and "sociality", the "spatiality" of human life. We have recently completed empirical research through which we hope to contribute at least an embryonic glimpse of the reciprocal and mutually constitutive relationship between news consumption and place: news consumption co-shapes—along with a multitude of other processes that are more indigenous and often more vital to everyday life—our construction and maintenance of social-communicative space, and conversely different places influence how we consume and negotiate the news.[5]

The "Total" column of Table 2 shows that in spite of the explosive growth in the ownership of mobile media technologies, most of our news consumption still takes place in the home where, in the communal space of the living room or the kitchen, we watch TV news, listen to radio news or read news on our computer (71 per cent), or use one of these devices in a room of our own (41 per cent). If we look at the eight locations pair-wise, 90 per cent report getting their news at home, 36 per cent get it at work or a place of study, and 38 per cent during public or individual transport (these aggregate figures are not reported in the table).

Read horizontally, starting from the locations, the rank orders and percentages show how the eight different situationally inscribed locations afford the use of some news platforms rather than others: both in the communal and the personal rooms in the home, TV news and news on a computer are dominant (but in reverse order), with radio news in a clear third place. At work, the computer dominates over radio news; but arguably these figures refer to different situational circumstances: people use different news media in the

TABLE 2
News media use in different locations, Denmark, 2013[a]

	Total[b]	TV news	News on a computer	Print news	News on a mobile phone	Radio news	News on a tablet
At home: communal space (living room, kitchen, etc.)	71	1 (87)	2 (52)	4 (32)	5 (24)	3 (40)	6 (19)
At home: personal space (own room, bedroom, etc.)	41	2 (54)	1 (59)	6 (16)	4 (27)	3 (29)	5 (19)
At work (office, shop, factory, etc.)	31	5 (7)	1 (75)	4 (16)	3 (24)	2 (33)	6 (5)
At a place of study	6	NA	1 (78)	3 (14)	2 (35)	5 (5)	4 (7)
Whilst travelling/commuting on public transport	9	6 (7)	4 (13)	2 (33)	1 (63)	3 (14)	5 (13)
Whilst travelling/commuting in car, bicycle or other personal transport	28	NA	NA	NA	2 (10)	1 (94)	NA
Whilst out and about generally (e.g. mobile, internet café)	6	6 (6)	2 (16)	3 (13)	1 (85)	5 (6)	4 (11)
Other people's homes	5	1 (79)	3 (36)	6 (16)	2 (39)	4 (27)	5 (21)

Question: Where were you when you looked at/listened to the news during the last couple of days? (Please list the three most important locations).
[a]Figures show the ranks of different media use in a location and, in parentheses, the percentage of users in each situation. NA indicates a percentage <2.
[b]"Total" shows the percentage of the total sample ($N = 2024$) who used news in each location.

work spaces of the office (news on a computer) as compared with the work spaces of building sites and shops (radio as a back curtain accompaniment through the day).

The differences in news consumption during public and individual transport demonstrate particularly clearly how a location's situational and technological frames determine news consumption. In the car and on a bike, radio news rules supreme, and four news platforms are non-existent, while the commuters in trains and buses predominantly check the news on mobile phones, with the printed newspaper in second place. In a parallel study in the United Kingdom, the technological conditioning was particularly decisive: commuters in the London area used printed newspapers much more than commuters in other regions due (in addition to the wide supply of print titles) to the fact that mobile signals are unreliable in the London Underground system.

Read vertically, starting from the news platforms, the distribution of first and second ranks in the table shows which media fit into the various situations most smoothly. We easily fit TV news into the communal spaces of the home, as something we can share, while news on a computer is a situationally more versatile news medium, which fits easily into situations in which mentally and perhaps also physically we occupy an individual space: in our own room, at the office desk or in a place of study.

Print news is used in many different locations, but the low volume of use is limited by the fact that many do not any more have a printed news medium at their disposal. Mobile news fits into the situations in which we are literally most mobile: "out and about" and when we are commuting. Tablets are still not widely owned and have not yet found their proper role among the different news platforms, but the figures appear to indicate that it is mostly used at home. In future research we hope to explore how tablet computers become integrated into people's everyday life when market saturation has increased. Radio news fits eminently into those situations where our eyes and hands are not free to operate other news media, such as driving a car and biking. The rankings of the different news media show that, generally speaking, news on a computer and mobile news are the most situationally versatile news media. However, it is also striking that radio news occupies a middle rank in many locations. Given that through the day many popular radio channels bring a mixture of music, news and current affairs, these middle rankings should alert us to the possibility that radio is an important—although inconspicuous and inadvertent—resource for people's awareness of democratically important information.

Our study does not tell us *when* the Danes use the news media. But the differences in *where* they use them (at home/at work/transport) and *how* they use them (overview/background and on which platforms) appear to indicate that it is only a minority who seek continuous news updates. This is supported by the findings of the Reuters Institute Digital News Report (2013) study, where only 26 per cent of the respondents can be categorized as "News lovers" (extremely interested in news, which they access several times a day). Irrespective of the fact that digital platforms have become an integrated element in most people's news routines, affording news anytime, anywhere, the majority continue to get their staple of news a few times a day from a limited number of news sources, primarily the different types of content offered by the two public service broadcasters and the digital news menus of the national newspapers.

To this may be added the observation that the mobile (anywhere, anytime) technologies afford an increase in the kind of news consumption deriving from what we called (above) "worthwhileness by default", in which news is consumed in more or less coincidental time pockets, leading to a haphazard, or serendipitous, news acquisition of the headline/"overview" type.

In more general terms, the reliance, in getting news, on multipurpose devices (desktop and laptop computers, smartphones, tablets), which provide immediate points of entry to a vast range of informative and entertaining pursuits, may have ambiguous consequences: on the one hand, news consumption on these devices may entail a less immersive form of news acquisition, in which the temptation of other content offers and activities may produce more superficial and briefer journeys into the landscapes of news. On the other hand, the lure of news may vie successfully, in domestic as well as work environments, for our extended attention as attractive avenues to valuable information or simply as displacement activities for the seeming drudgery of more demanding chores and obligations.

Towards More Complex Insights?

The kinds of research drawn on in this article, for the attainment of insights based on qualitative as well as quantitative methods, provide valuable information about the way citizens and consumers are navigating in today's mediatized cultures, and should be replicated and adapted in the interest of scholars, news producers and policy-makers alike.

In the spirit of methodological pluralism (Schrøder et al. 2012), there are potentially numerous paths that researchers could follow in order to map the temporal–locational ecology of media consumption. One promising avenue of research appears to be the multidimensional scaling approach used by Cédric Courtois, which analyses the complex triple constellations of audience uses of media as texts/content/genres, media as analogue and digital technologies, and media as social and spatial contexts (Courtois 2012b, 729f).

One serious future challenge for the study of the places and spaces of (news) media use derives from the difficulty of—ethnographically—tracing the footsteps of individuals as they traverse the terrain of everyday life. This is a much greater challenge in today's multiplatform landscape than when James Lull (1980) sent student assistants into the home of 200 American families in order to map the social uses of television, a study which claimed that its intervention into the home was not experienced as intrusive by the informant families. Nevertheless, this challenge has been taken up by Taneja et al. (2012) who, in order to overcome the limitations of self-reports, used a fieldwork methodology in which individual media users were shadowed in a real-time chronology, across the contexts of everyday life.

While their method is bold, and while they may underestimate the consequences of their intrusiveness, their findings appear not to grasp the real complexity of cross-media audience practices, as their four location-based media packages are connected to just a handful of media in each location. Still important "old" media like print and radio are not included in the analysis.

The multimethod path taken by Vittadini and Pasquali (2014) may offer greater potential, as they explore the merits of online ethnographies in which they observe media use with a technique of "virtual shadowing". Similarly, Jensen and Sørensen (2014) argue in favour of a multimethod strategy to explore online social media use through a triangulating mixture of questionnaire-based surveys, classical focus groups and ethnographic observation of selected informants' actual online practices.

Courtois, finally, warns against any illusion that heavily technology-dependent empirical tools, such as portable people meters or geo-locational logging, are necessary in order to obtain insights into cross-media use in the digital age. Sometimes methodological simplicity can be a virtue: "We think it relatively more efficient to focus on … a considerable amount of domestic face-to-face interviews" (Courtois 2012a, 9/12).

At this point in time, however, the best methodological recommendation for obtaining explanatory insights about the temporal–locational ecology of media use appears to be the old dictum to let a thousand flowers bloom.

FUNDING

The 2012 and 2013 research on which this article is based was made possible by funding from Roskilde University's research initiative (2012–2014) "Power, Media and Communication".

NOTES

1. The questionnaire presented a list of 20 news media and formats and asked: "Which news media have you used (viewed, listened to, read) over the past week?" The figures say nothing about the amount of time spent on the news media.
2. Similarly, Papathanassopoulos et al. (2013, 12), in their 11-nation study, find that "TV remains the most popular choice for news in all countries of our research".

3. This finding is confirmed by Hermida et al. (2012, 820) in Canada. See also Nielsen and Schrøder (2014).
4. The concept of "repertoire" is used in different ways in the literature: Hasebrink and Popp (2006) define a "media repertoire" as an individual's entire portfolio, or cluster, of media selected for consumption in everyday life across spatio-temporal settings. A media repertoire is thus a package of media "combined into a comprehensive pattern of media use", which is "characteristic for individual users" (Bjur et al. 2013, 28). For Taneja et al. (2012), a media repertoire is a location or situation-bound media ensemble which an individual may, and normally will, adopt when entering that location/situation. Consequently, a repertoire according to Hasebrink and Popp inevitably comprises a multitude of media used fleetingly or massively by an individual, while a repertoire according to Taneja et al. only includes a limited selection of four or five media, which "belong" in a specific location/situation (such as home, work, while commuting, etc.). Our research follows the definition of Hasebrink and Popp.
5. The research into the locations of news media consumption comes out of a 2013 survey of news consumption in nine countries. Roskilde University's Centre for Power, Media and Communication co-funded this study, which is directed by The Reuters Institute for the Study of Journalism, University of Oxford. The survey was carried out by YouGov in February 2012 with a sample in Denmark of 1024 respondents. The full report of the nine-country study, and all data materials, is available on www.digitalnewsreport.org. While the bulk of the study was carried out in all nine countries, the study of the places of news consumption was carried out in two countries: Denmark and the United Kingdom.

REFERENCES

Barnhurst, Kevin. 2003. "Subjective States: Narratives of Citizenship among Young Europeans." *Multilingua* 22: 133–168.

Bjur, Jakob, Kim Christian Schrøder, Uwe Hasebrink, Cédric Courtois, Hanna Adoni, and Hillel Nossek. 2013. "Cross-media Use. Unfolding Complexities in Contemporary Audiencehood." In *Transformations: Shifting Audience Positions in Late Modernity*, edited by Nico Carpentier, Kim Christian Schrøder, and Lawrie Hallett, 15–29. New York: Routledge.

Couldry, Nick, Sonia Livingstone, and Tim Markham. 2007. *Media Consumption and Public Engagement. Beyond the Presumption of Attention*. Basingstoke: Palgrave Macmillan.

Courtois, Cédric. 2012a. "The Triple Articulation of Audiovisual Media Technologies in the Age of Convergence." Phd diss., University of Ghent, Belgium.

Courtois, Cédric. 2012b. "When Two Worlds Meet: An Inter-paradigmatic Mixed Method Approach to Convergent Audiovisual Media Consumption." *Participations* 9 (2): 716–742.

Curran, James, Anker Brink Lund, Shanto Iyengar, and Inka Salovaara-Moring. 2009. "Media System, Public Knowledge and Democracy: A Comparative Study." *European Journal of Communication* 24 (5): 5–26. doi:10.1177/0267323108098943.

Curran, James, Sharon Cohen, Stuart Soroka, Zira Hichy, Toril Aalberg, Kaori Hayashi, Shanto Iyengar, et al. 2013. "Media System, Public Knowledge and Political Engagement: An 11-nation Study." Paper presented at the International Communication Association conference, London, June 17–21.

Gamson, William. 1992. *Talking Politics*. Cambridge: Cambridge University Press.

Hasebrink, Uwe, and Jutta Popp. 2006. "Media Repertoires as a Result of Selective Media Use. A Conceptual Approach to the Analysis of Patterns of Exposure." *Communications* 31 (3): 369–387. doi:10.1515/COMMUN.2006.023.

Hepp, Andreas. 2013. *Cultures of Mediatization*. Cambridge: Polity Press.

Hermida, Alfred, Fred Fletcher, Darryl Korell, and Donna Logan. 2012. "Share, Like, Recommend." *Journalism Studies* 13 (5–6): 815–824. doi:10.1080/1461670X.2012.664430.

Hjarvard, Stig. 2008. "The Mediatization of Society: A Theory of the Media as Agents of Social and Cultural change." *Nordicom Review* 29 (2): 105–134.

Jensen, Jakob Linaa, and Anne Scott Sørensen. 2014. "Analyzing Online Social Networks from a User Perspective: A Quantitative-Qualitative Framework." In *Audience Research Methodologies: Between Innovation and Consolidation*, edited by Geoffroy Patriarche, Helena Bilandzic, Jakob Linaa Jensen, and Jelena Jurisic, 144–159. New York: Routledge.

Keane, John. 1991. *The Media and Democracy*. Cambridge: Polity Press.

Livingstone, Sonia. 2009. "On the Mediation of Everything." *Journal of Communication* 59 (1): 1–18. doi:10.1111/j.1460-2466.2008.01401.x.

Lull, James. 1980. "The Social Uses of Television." *Human Communication Research* 6: 197–209. doi:10.1111/j.1468-2958.1980.tb00140.x.

Lund, Anker Brink. 2013. *Mangfoldighed i dansk dagspresse – et publicistisk serviceeftersyn* [Diversity in the Danish Daily Press – a Publicist Service Check]. Frederiksberg: Center for Civilsamfundsstudier.

Lunt, Peter, Anne Kaun, Pille Pruulmann-Vengerfeldt, Birgit Stark, and Liesbet Van Zoonen. 2014. "The Mediation of Civic Participation: Diverse Forms of Political Agency in a Multimedia Age." In *Audience Transformations*, edited by Nico Carpentier, Kim C. Schrøder, and Lawrie Hallett, 142–156. New York: Routledge.

Nielsen, Rasmus Kleis, and Kim Christian Schrøder. 2014. "The Relative Importance of Social Media for Accessing Finding, and Engaging with News: An Eight-country Cross-media Comparison." *Digital Journalism*. doi:10.1080/21670811.2013.872420.

Papathanassopoulos, Stylianos, Sharon Cohen, James Curran, Toril Aalberg, David Rowe, Paul Jones, Hernando Rojas, and Rod Tiffen. 2013. "Online Threat, but Television Is Still Dominant." *Journalism Practice* 1–15. http://dx.doi.org/10.1080/17512786.2012.761324.

Peters, Chris. 2012. "Journalism to Go. The Changing Spaces of News Consumption." *Journalism Studies* 13 (5–6): 695–705. doi:10.1080/1461670X.2012.662405.

Pew Research Center. 2008. *Audience Segments in a Changing News Environment: Key News Audiences Now Bland Online and Traditional Sources*. Washington, DC: Pew Research Center for the People and the Press.

Picone, Ike. 2007. "Conceptualising Online News Use." *Observatorio* 3: 93–114.

Reuters Institute Digital News Report. 2013. *Reuters Instute for the Study of Journalism*. University of Oxford. www.reutersdigitalreport.org.

Rogers, Everett M. 2003. *Diffusion of Innovations*. 5th ed. New York: Free Press.

Schrøder, Kim Christian. 2011. "Audiences Are Inherently Cross-Media: Audience Studies and the Cross-Media Challenge." *Communication Management Quarterly* 18 (6): 5–27.

Schrøder, Kim Christian. 2012. "Methodological Pluralism as a Vehicle of Qualitative Generalization." *Participations. Journal of Audience and Reception Studies* 9 (2): 798–825.

Schrøder, Kim Christian, and Bent Steeg Larsen. 2010. "The Shifting Cross-Media News Landscape: Challenges for News Producers." *Journalism Studies* 11 (4): 524–534. doi:10.1080/14616701003638392.

Schrøder, Kim Christian, and Christian Kobbernagel. 2010. "Towards a Typology of Cross-Media News Consumption: A Qualitative-Quantitative Synthesis." *Northern Lights. Yearbook of Film and Media Studies* 8 (1): 115–137. Bristol: Intellect Press. doi:10.1177/0163443707081693.

Schrøder, Kim Christian, and Louise Phillips. 2007. "Complexifying Media Power: A Study of the Interplay between Media and Audience Discourses on Politics." *Media, Culture & Society* 29 (6): 890–915. doi:10.1177/0163443707081693.

Schrøder, Kim Christian, Uwe Hasebrink, Sascha Hölig, and Martin Barker. 2012. "Introduction. Exploring the Methodological Synergies of Multimethod Audience Research." *Participations. Journal of Audience and Reception Studies* 9 (2): 643–647.

Schudson, Michael. 1998. *The Good Citizen: A History of American Civic Life*. Cambridge, MA: Harvard University Press.

Soja, Edward. 1996. *Thirdspace: Journeys to Los Angeles and Other Real-and-Imagines Places*. Oxford: Blackwell.

Strömbäck, Jesper. 2008. "Four Phases of Mediatization: An Analysis of the Mediatization of Politics." *The International Journal of Press/Politics* 13 (3): 228–246. doi:10.1177/1940161208319097.

Taneja, Harsh, James G. Webster, Edward C. Malthouse, and Thomas B. Ksiazek. 2012. "Media Consumption across Platforms: Identifying User-Defined Repertoires." *New Media and Society* 14 (6): 951–968. doi:10.1177/1461444811436146.

Vittadini, Nicoletta, and Francesca Pasquali. 2013. "Virtual Shadowing. Online Ethnographies and Social Networking Studies." In *Audience Research Methodologies: Between Innovation and Consolidation*, edited by Geoffroy Patriarche, Helena Bilandzic, Jakob Linaa Jensen, and Jelena Jurisic, 160–173. London: Routledge.

NEWS MEDIA CONSUMPTION IN THE TRANSMEDIA AGE
Amalgamations, orientations and geo-social structuration

André Jansson and Johan Lindell

Technological convergence and altered dynamics of content circulation, what is here referred to as "transmedia textures", change the ways in which news is consumed. This is in regard to both how individuals navigate and orient themselves through representational spaces and flows, and how their media practices amalgamate with other activities in everyday life. The aim of this study is to explore how altered dynamics of amalgamation are related to various news media orientations and how these relationships correspond to forces of structuration. The study applies a communication geographical analytical framework and combines quantitative and qualitative interview data from Sweden. The empirical data illustrate how the spatial practice of news consumption changes into an increasingly amalgamated, mobile practice. Transmedia textures flourish within geo-social settings marked by relatively affluent, mobile lifestyles and cosmopolitan news orientations. However, it is also shown that transmedia textures, due to the forces of geo-social structuration, sustain sedentary lifestyles, corresponding to more locally oriented news media practices.

Introduction

Today the lives of the globe's citizens are wrapped around a seemingly endless encounter with material and symbolic modes of communication. Newspapers are read on buses and trains, car radios are tuned to the morning news, joggers listen to talking books while exercising and people make love in front of the television. The mediated experience of modernity is one of "a whirling phantasmagoria" (McLuhan 1951, v). (Stevenson 2010, 22)

Along with other forms of media content, news today tends to flow smoothly between different types of platforms, as well as between users. News outlets distribute their material through multiple channels, and media users may access news material by means of different platforms, from different places and while on the move. News consumption is now "unfettered by wires and cables", freed from previously quite well-restricted, space–time constraints (Hemment 2005, 32), and news is accessed in the "interstices" of the scheduled and routinized activities throughout the course of the day (Dimmick, Feaster, and Hoplamazian 2010). Altogether, technological convergence and altered dynamics of content circulation change the ways in which news is consumed, in terms of how individuals navigate and *orient* themselves through representational spaces and flows, and how their media practices *amalgamate* with other activities in everyday life. What we are witnessing is thus more than a technological and representational transition; it is a multi-layered spatial transition that can be described as a shift from *mass media textures* to *transmedia textures* (Jansson 2013a).

As the opening quote indicates, media practices have a rather long history of amalgamating with various forms of spatial practice. Also the consumption of mass media such as newspapers and radio news often entails the combination of virtual and corporeal mobility (Urry 2007). The paradigmatic shift from mass media textures to transmedia textures (which also manifests itself through the materialization of various "hybridized" textures), however, implies that virtual and corporeal mobilities are combined in increasingly diversified and open-ended ways as media users may access any virtual space (including "news spaces") from any geographical location through their miniaturized transmedia technologies. Such a shift, and its potential consequences for the practice of news consumption, we argue, is in need of further scrutiny. This study sets out to shed empirical light on some of the potential novelties (as well as continuities) pertaining to the "places and spaces" of contemporary news consumption—a topic that to date has not been sufficiently attended to in the field of journalism studies, as noted by Peters (2012).

Not many studies have explored how the altered dynamics of amalgamation are related to various news media orientations and how these relationships correspond to forces of structuration (Giddens 1984). The aim of our study is to do this via two analytical steps. Firstly, we investigate how transmedia textures materialize through concrete practices of media use, in general, and news media consumption, in particular. We use both qualitative and quantitative interview data (gathered through ongoing Swedish research projects) to highlight how mobile news consumption amalgamates with different types of spatial practice, and how such patterns unfold in different social and geographical spheres of society. This means that we are interested in news consumption as a site of *geo-social structuration*, constituted through socially stratified modes of appropriation and orientation. Not only are the expanding opportunities for consuming and circulating news while on the move unevenly distributed in social and geographical space (due to the level of various technological resources); the media practices as such, and the ways in which they are carried out *in space*, contribute to the social classification of media users and their lifestyles.

Secondly, we explore how the (mobile) enactment of transmedia textures is related to orientations within the representational realm. Here, we are interested in the distinction between "local" and "cosmopolitan" outlooks, since they constitute opposing spatial orientations in relation to the news flow (see Merton [1949] 1968). Through our empirical data we are able to highlight historical continuities in terms of structuration, implying that the occupation of more privileged social positions and urban residency correspond to orientations towards the "extra-local world". Whereas such news orientations partly resonate with transmedia textural practices, they are not fostered by technological alterations. Rather, the composite patterns can be understood as extensions of social pre-dispositions rooted in habitus (Bourdieu [1979] 1984), and are thus integral to the structuration process.

Before presenting the analyses, we introduce our analytical framework, which is derived partly from the interdisciplinary field of communication geography, partly from

Giddensian sociology of structuration. In relation to the analytical framework, we also discuss previous studies conducted within our subject area. Thereafter, we present our empirical study, and discuss the quality of our data.

Communication Geography, Structuration and News Consumption

The relationship between space and (mediated) communication is multidimensional, and has become increasingly ambiguous due to altered technological conditions. Phenomena such as interactivity, convergence and automated surveillance tend to blur spatial boundaries, and problematize what used to be relatively fixed relationships between different channels, sites and actors of communication (such as sender versus receiver). During the last decade, such ambiguities have generated a growing interest in spatial issues among media and communication scholars (see Couldry and McCarthy 2004; Falkheimer and Jansson 2006), and a corresponding interest in the media among geographers (see Adams 2009).

This has ultimately led to the establishment of an interdisciplinary field of communication geography. In a recent article, elaborating Adams' (2009) earlier theorizations, Adams and Jansson (2012) map out the epistemological field of communication geography according to a quadrant model (Table 1). The vertical dimension represents variations pertaining to *geographical scale*, distinguishing the general ("macro") properties of *space* from the social specificity of *place*. The horizontal dimension depicts the space–communication nexus; the interchangeable relationship of space/place and communication as either *container* or *content*. Altogether, the model pinpoints four communication geographical fields of inquiry: *representations*, *textures*, *connections* and *structures*. Whereas the boundaries between these realms might be contested through empirical research, they provide relevant starting points for explorations of the space–communication nexus at different scales.

In our ambition to study media practices as a generative part of spatial production (geographically and socially) our study relates to the "micro" level of the model. Firstly, our study deals with *textural amalgamations*. Texture refers to the symbolic-material processes and arrangements through which communication and space co-constitute one another. They are made up of material objects and resources for communication, as well as the very communicative flows and dynamics that define certain places in social and cultural terms (Jansson 2007). This means that the dominant forms of media that saturate society at the structural level ("communication in spaces") also affect the very experience and sensory "feel" of ordinary, mundane places. For example, whereas the introduction of

TABLE 1
Applied conceptual framework for research in communication geography (after Adams 2009; Adams and Jansson 2012)

Geographical scale	Space–communication nexus	
	"Communication as container"	"Communication as content"
"Macro"	Connections (spaces in communication)	Structures (communication in spaces)
"Micro"	Representations (places in communication) *Orientations of news consumption*	Textures (communication in places) *Amalgamations of news consumption*

such mass media technologies as radio and television was paralleled by a shift in sociality, involving for example certain forms of scheduled togetherness, modes of talk and domestic design (see Williams 1974; Morley 1986; Spigel 1992), something similar is happening today. More and more spatial practices are either substituted for (as in the cases of banking or postal services) or amalgamating with the usage of transmedia technologies (see Schulz 2004).

The term "transmedia" is inspired by Jenkins's (2006) work on "transmedia storytelling" and refers to the increasingly inter-connected and open-ended circulation of media content between various platforms, where social agents are increasingly involved in the production of flows. Compared to mass media textures, transmedia textures are marked by integration and flexibility, meaning that different platforms are connected to one another in a seamless manner that also makes each separate technology relatively flexible. As Madianou and Miller (2013) discuss in their account of "polymedia", in integrated and flexible media environments individual choices of platform depend more on moral, emotive and situational circumstances than on mere functionality. In the case of news consumption, this means that there are a plethora of channels and forms available for receiving news, some of which are more or less adapted to personal preferences (e.g. areas of interest and modes of delivery). Ordinary users may thus move in and out of news flows via a variety of entrance points, forming liquid patterns of consumption. These processes not only give rise to new compositions and experiences of news materials as such, but are also part of the ongoing texturation of everyday life.

Secondly, in furthering our understanding of news media usages as spatial practices taking place in a changing media landscape, the study focuses on how different groups *orient* themselves in relation to various "places in communication", that is, *representations* of/from different geo-social regions. Here, we start out from Merton's ([1949] 1968) classical distinction between "locals" and "cosmopolitans", that is, between those who are primarily interested in familiar places and events, and those who orient themselves towards the "extra-local", often international, realm of, for example, politics and current affairs. This basic distinction, it must be noted, does not advance any sophisticated approach to cosmopolitan*ism*, however. It does not make any claims in terms of the ethical standards guiding different subjects in local or cosmopolitan directions (see e.g. Chouliaraki 2006; Madianou 2013), but rather distinguishes between different scopes of engagement and potential action. As several scholars have subsequently pointed out, cosmopolitan news orientations (following Merton) often correspond to the possession of greater amounts of capital and thus to greater capacity to influence social processes also in local settings (see Gans 1962). In recent years this has been discussed particularly in relation to urban gentrification, where emerging lifestyles tend to integrate a desire to sense the "'action/pulse/rhythm/opportunities' of the global at the scale of the local" (Rofe 2003, 2520). This transformational condition, through which urbanism is culturally re-encoded and socially reconstituted through the spatial praxis of mobile middle-class populations associated with the service and information economy (Zukin 1982; Featherstone 1991), is also a condition of intense symbolic mediation (through the circulation of various news media as well as popular culture, marketing, fashion, and so forth).

Our interest in relating an analysis of local versus cosmopolitan news orientations to the growing prominence of transmedia textures in everyday life is thus a way of providing an updated account of "geo-social" structuration processes. Giddens (1984) defines structuration as the ongoing reproduction, and successive negotiation, of structures of power and dominance in society through everyday practices. A key advantage of the Giddensian approach to structuration is that it encourages us to think about practices as mutually forming and formed through intersectional structures (involving such dimensions as class, gender, ethnicity and infrastructural conditions). Structure is thus integral to practice so conceived. This also involves practices of spatial production; the construction of territories and boundaries of belonging and control through which orders of social space are projected on to symbolic-material geographies (from the domestic sphere to geo-political space). Similar points have been made by Bourdieu, who sees the practical dispositions of *habitus* as an important mechanism of geo-social segregation and distinction, whereby social structures are "translated, with more or less distortion, into physical space, in the form of a certain arrangement of agents and properties" (Bourdieu [1997] 2000, 134). Both Giddens and Bourdieu provide important tools for linking communication geographical issues to broader concerns with social space and power. More concretely, they help us to interpret how contemporary patterns of media amalgamation and orientation are related to the geo-social "arrangement of agents and properties".

Based on what we know from studies of earlier media transformations (technological and institutional), and about the distribution of local and cosmopolitan orientations in social space, our hypothesis is that the "transmedia shift", or "transmediatization" (for a broader discussion of this concept, see Jansson 2013a), foremost implies sharper differentiations within general structuration processes. This hypothesis can be grounded in four observations. Firstly, the diffusion of innovations tends to follow a socio-economic logic where people with much economic and educational capital are better equipped and often more interested in adopting new innovations (Rogers [1962] 2010).

Secondly, earlier analyses of how the differentiation of television programming has affected viewing patterns (e.g. in Sweden) have consistently shown that broader repertoires of choice sustain further specialization on behalf of audiences (see Reimer 1994; Bjur 2009). This is also to say that the divisions between different types of news consumers, as well as between news consumers and "non-news consumers", tend to expand when people have more to choose from (see Strömbäck, Djerf-Pierre, and Shehata 2012).

Thirdly, and related to the previous point, the very technological affordances of new media have historically tended to lead in contradictory directions. As Tomlinson (2001) points out in relation to the issue of "mediated cosmopolitanism", the very same technological affordances that enable media users to expand their views towards *cosmos* and the distant other (if they have any such ambitions) are the affordances that may tie people closer to the *hearth*. "Technologies of cosmos" and "technologies of the hearth" may thus be one and the same thing. This condition is likely to become even more relevant in times of multi-functional transmedia forms, which may sustain social cohesion at the local level as well as extended global networks (see also Silverstone 2007; Ling 2008).

Finally, when it comes to local versus cosmopolitan news orientations, empirical analyses from Sweden have shown that "the local" constitutes a kind of common denominator among news media audiences, while interests in "extra-local", national and international news are further stratified in social space (see Nilsson and Weibull 2010; Lindell and Jansson 2012; Weibull 2012). These patterns also resonate with empirical analyses holding that cosmopolitan value orientations—understood as a form of "global openness"—are often nurtured through the interplay between educational capital, international mobility and news media consumption (see Phillips and Smith 2008; Lindell 2012).

Empirical Data

In order to accomplish our aim we have combined analyses of two sources of data. The first source is a representative SOM survey (Society, Opinion, Media) conducted in the region of Värmland (Sweden) in autumn 2010. Bordering to Norway, Värmland is located in mid-western Sweden. As with many provincial regions in Sweden, Värmland is experiencing an ongoing urbanization process wherein rural inhabitants increasingly move to the residence city Karlstad or larger nodes such as Stockholm, Oslo and Gothenburg (Nilsson, Aronsson, and Norell 2012). Starting on 24 September 2010, the questionnaire was distributed to a total of 2000 people between the ages of 16 and 85 over the course of 20 weeks. The answering rate was 56 per cent (1120 respondents). The questionnaire contained a broad variety of questions dealing with opinions, attitudes and habits related to, for example, lifestyle and politics, and also included a set of background variables. Our focus here is on two separate areas: firstly, the consumption of news via mobile media devices, and secondly, geographical orientations within news flows. The first area, which provides a general indication of what groups consume news on the move, thus allegedly enacting transmedia textures, is covered through a question dealing with how often respondents read news from two of the main online news sources, *Aftonbladet* and *Expressen* (also well-established Swedish tabloids) on their mobile devices. The second area, which relates to the issue of local versus cosmopolitan orientations, is covered through a question about how important respondents find news from different regions of Värmland, as well as certain extra-regional centres (Stockholm, Oslo and Göteborg). In order to understand how these phenomena relate to various processes of geo-social structuration, they are analysed in relation to various demographic variables.

We hold that these questions maintain valid information about the issues scrutinized here. However, certain limitations must be mentioned in both areas. Firstly, it would have been valuable to include a greater variety of news sources and platforms for providing a better take on transmedia textures. Appropriations of certain brands are socially and culturally structured/structuring practices as such. Secondly, as for the question of news orientations, it would have been beneficial to include also more distant (worldwide) places for reaching more distinct indications of cosmopolitan outlooks. Still, by way of constituting indicators of "extended frames of reference", our variables and subsequent analyses capture the "extra-local" in the Merton ([1949] 1968) sense of the word.

Our second data source consists of qualitative interviews gathered within the research project "Secure Spaces: Media, Consumption and Social Surveillance". The project revolved ultimately around issues of mediated surveillance, privacy and social control. However, the rich empirical material, consisting of 36 qualitative interviews from three different settings—a relatively sedentary Swedish small-town area; suburban migrant communities of Turkish and Kurdish origin; globally mobile dwellers in inner-city Stockholm—also covers questions of everyday (media) practices and experiences in a mediatized society. They thus illuminate textural conditions as well as orientations within the news flow with a particular focus on new (trans)media technologies. For the purpose of the present analysis, we have incorporated findings from the interviews conducted in small-town contexts (winter 2010–2011) and inner-city Stockholm (spring 2012). From these contexts we gather vivid illustrations of what the transition from mass media to transmedia textures might imply in social and spatial terms.

It must be stressed here, of course, that the transmedia shift must also be interpreted in relation to factors other than residential conditions. Nevertheless, the general comparison between provincial and urban settings helps us clarify the geo-socially structured implications of technological shifts, in general, and the extended differentiation of news consumption, in particular.

News and Spatial Practice: Textural Amalgamations

At the general level, analysing the data from the 2010 SOM survey, it must be noted that news consumption via mobile devices is still a relatively restricted phenomenon: while mobile devices present new modes of news consumption they are mainly conceived of as interpersonal communication devices (Westlund 2010). In a preceding analysis of the same data, Karlsson (2012) found that only 4 per cent of the population in Värmland used a mobile device for accessing any of the news services offered by *Expressen* or *Aftonbladet* on a regular basis (at least three times a week). This can be compared with 6 per cent of the US sample accessing news through a mobile device on a daily basis in 2010 (Chyi and Chadha 2012). Furthermore, these digital practices are socially stratified, implying that younger people with higher education and more privileged social positions are at the forefront when it comes to appropriating them into their lifestyles. Men are also more inclined to consume news through mobile devices than women (Karlsson 2012).

These patterns of structuration can be further illuminated through an analysis of how mobile news consumption correlates with different types of international mobility (Table 2). The correlation is particularly significant with regards to work-related international mobility, suggesting that the new, liquefied mode of news consumption might even be considered a distinctive marker among "globals" (Elliott and Urry 2010), for whom miniaturized media are indispensable resources for keeping track of the world both privately and professionally.

Our qualitative material from inner-city Stockholm contains several interviews with individuals whose lifestyles represent these distinctive patterns of open-ended news media consumption. To these individuals the continuous enactment and reproduction of transmedia textures become tantamount to a life "in media" (Deuze 2011). During an ordinary day, involving urban mobility between different sites of work and leisure,

TABLE 2
Correlations between mobile news consumption and different forms of international mobility

	Mobile news consumption	Leisure-related international mobility	Work-related international mobility
Mobile news consumption	1 (889)	0.10** (856)	0.23*** (857)
Leisure-related international mobility	0.10** (856)	1 (1051)	0.16*** (1041)
Work-related international mobility	0.23*** (857)	0.16*** (1041)	1 (1049)

Measurements indicate strength in correlation between variables (Pearson's r). N values are given in parentheses.
The variable "Mobile news consumption" is an index (Cronbach's alpha = 0.63) created from two separate variables measuring the extent to which respondents read the two biggest evening papers in Sweden (*Expressen*, *Aftonbladet*) on their mobile devices.
Source: SOM survey conducted in Värmland in 2010.
*$p \leq 0.05$, **$p \leq 0.01$, ***$p \leq 0.001$.

practices are typically accompanied by several digital platforms, whose affordances are applied alternately according to situational, moral and emotional convenience. These activity streams tend to get routinized according to established fixtures of circulation, such as the workplace or particular means of transport, but also involve respresentational flows that transcend the boundaries of individual technologies. This interchangeability of platforms (in relative terms) marks out the properties of transmedia textures and corresponds to Madianou and Miller's (2012) characterization "polymedia". At the same time, as we can tell from the broader picture of our project, the geo-social framework of our inner-city interviews represents conditions where the expansion of such textures is most intense. Clearly, the movement of "transmediatization" both responds to and reinforces certain types of lifestyles and life conditions to a greater extent than others, in particular those marked by fluid boundaries between work and leisure, and high levels of everyday mobility between social regions. Here, as described by one of our respondents, a 42-year-old male university teacher, news consumption interweaves with other media practices in a relatively seamless manner:

> Respondent 1: I use my iPhone for news and for listening to music, SMS and such, then I have a stationary PC at work … I have internet at home, on phone and on the computer.
>
> Interviewer: What media do you consider most important?
>
> Respondent 1: I think the telephone is also a computer, sometimes I sit with both, it depends on when. The phone's great when you're waiting or on the train, you can't really take out the laptop when you have 13 minutes to kill, but when I'm at work and I have the computer it becomes a phone again. I might watch Play [Swedish public broadcaster's online, on-demand TV service] on the computer then on the phone if I go somewhere. The same things are always available in principle. I have the iCloud now so it should be more integrated.

The integrated and flexible nature of transmedia textures, which enables media users to switch easily between different platforms, also implies that the loyalty to certain genres, brands and sources might get reinforced. As Karlsson (2012) notes in his analysis of mobile news consumption, mobile applications and news websites have a tendency to strengthen each other as platforms of circulation (when the logic of convergence is played out within certain segments of the market), whereas the printed version of newspapers remains outside this synergetic relationship. A similar condition regards "traditional", stationary television, partly belonging to the sediments of mass media textures. This is not to say that these technologies lose their social significance; for example, the "liveness" of television is still a significant source of attraction, entertaining various forms of social communion. Many other types of contents, however, such as regular news-casts, easily "migrate" to online platforms and Play channels that can be accessed according to convenience.

Mode of access then largely becomes a question of *what kinds of platforms and what types of content most conveniently amalgamate with what types of socio-spatial practice*. The rise of "transmediatization" leads to an explosion of new amalgamations (Schulz 2004), where the circulation of news material (institutionally as well as privately generated) is just one of many parts integral to the texturation process. The following quote, taken from an interview with a 45-year-old woman working as an educationalist at a family advice centre in central Stockholm, reveals a relatively "news saturated", and transmediatized, everyday routine:

Respondent 2: I usually read *DN* or *SVD* [Swedish newspapers, on paper and online], I switch, I usually go on the computer at work. I look at things that interest me, everything from booking training or recipes, mostly finding out things, looking for information. On the way home from work I usually read the evening *Aftonbladet* on my phone.

Interviewer: What about TV?

Respondent 2: Very little, just the few things I'm interested in. I can use SVT Play if there's something I want to watch. Also Metro on the metro...

Interviewer: How do you use your mobile phone?

Respondent 2: I call of course, I use it for crosswords, for looking things up, I SMS a lot, check the news, check directions, not so much email, just to check it but I prefer the computer for that. It's so small and I see so badly.

However, even though transmedia textures seem perfectly suited for mobile lifestyles as they unfold in high-technologized urban environments, they may also accommodate more sedentarist orientations and routines. From previous analyses of our provincial interviews (Jansson 2013b) we know that the very same platforms, precisely *because of* their flexibility and inter-connectivity, may contribute to the enclosure of pre-established social communities, notably the household unit. Most of our small-town respondents were locally rooted people, belonging (to a varying degree) to the "late majority" of media adopters, implying that transmedia technologies (especially laptops and smartphones) were common possessions, but often appropriated due to institutional imperatives and the socially imposed need to conform to material standards. The mobile device, for example, was in most cases understood as the single most indispensable example of media technology, not only because of its flexibility, but perhaps more prominently for security reasons and for keeping in touch with family members.

These centripetal dynamics also imply that the symbolic contexts and flows within which news contents are consumed follow classificatory schemes that are culturally less distinctive (in the Bourdieusian sense; see Bourdieu [1979] 1984) compared to the above examples. One of our respondents in the small-town sample, a 41-year-old female social worker, describes how her online routines follow a spatialized pattern where status updates on Facebook constitute the symbolic epicentre:

Respondent 3: Facebook is the page I always return to. When I start up I immediately go to Facebook and read until the end of the first page. And then I go somewhere else and do something else, to *Aftonbladet* or *Expressen*, for example ... But then I spin back to Facebook, and see "hmm, two new updates", and then one has to check them out.

The distinctions between urban and provincial life-contexts, and between different social groups, must not be over-generalized. Still, it is less likely that this description would have appeared among more well-educated, urban subjects. Our main point has thus been to illuminate the ways in which the enactment and production of transmedia textures ultimately lead in different directions as these ongoing everyday practices are part of geo-social structuration. This also affects news consumption. One the one hand, as we have seen, there are general textural assets that enable news contents to circulate in increasingly open-ended ways. On the other hand, the degree to which news is actually being consumed and circulated in such ways, and the type of cultural repertoires is becomes part of, follow quite familiar patterns of structuration. This begs us to look closer into the question of local versus cosmopolitan news orientations.

"Locals", "Cosmopolitans" and Geo-social Structuration

In this section our focus shifts from a perspective concerned with *communication in place*, that is, how "the place" of news consumption is re-negotiated as a result of the textural shift from mass media textures to transmedia textures, to a perspective oriented to understanding the relevancy of various *places in communication*. In this study, such an analytical shift involves the ambition to discern how various news orientations are dispersed in geo-social space. More specifically, it involves asking the news consumers to estimate the importance of news depicting different geographical regions, ranging from different sub-regions in Värmland to the residence city of Karlstad to the "extra-local" cities of Gothenburg, Stockholm and Oslo.

Following Merton ([1949] 1968), the level of engagement with representations of more distant, "extra-local" places—the embodiment of an "extended frame of reference" ([1949] 1968, 446)—is here understood as a fragment of a much more encompassing and aspirational cosmopolitan disposition (see e.g. Beck 2006; Kendall, Woodward, and Skrbis 2009). The main question here, then, concerns the extent to which different news orientations pertain to certain geo-social spheres in society, such as area of residency, gender, education and subjective class. Is there, in the midst of overall changes regarding news consumption as a spatial practice, continuity regarding the ways in which actors from different social and geographical spheres in society orient themselves in relation to news from various places?

As illustrated above, compared to the mass media textures dominating the time when Merton ([1949] 1968) introduced his distinction between "cosmopolitan" and "local" news orientations, contemporary transmedia textures are much different and set in motion new modalities and spatialities of news consumption. This does not mean that one should assume that this, largely technological, change turns wider structuration processes and logics of social reproduction on their heads. As observed above, different groups enact transmedia textures in different ways; consuming news on the move emerges, for example, as a marker among "globals" (see Elliott and Urry 2010). In our epistemological shift to "places in communication", thus, we hypothesize "continuity" and a general reproduction of Merton's ([1949] 1968) findings. More specifically, we expect an "extra-local" news orientation to belong to a certain geo-social region; the highly educated, highly mobile urban people. Such a preconception—that news habits and orientations are part of a wider disposition and life biography, linked to habitus (Bourdieu [1979] 1984)—is further illustrated in both Park's and Merton's comments:

> The man in the small city reads the metropolitan in preference to the local paper. But the farmer, it seems, still gets his news from the same market in which he buys his groceries. The more mobile city man travels farther and has a wider horizon, a different focus of attention, and, characteristically, reads a metropolitan paper. (Park 1929, 75)

> [Cosmopolitans] devote themselves more fully to the kind of vicarious experience set forth in journals, whereas the locals are more immediately concerned with direct interpersonal relations. The one tends to read about the great world outside, the other,

TABLE 3
Factor analysis of news orientations: "cosmopolitans" and "locals"

	"Locals"	"Cosmopolitans"
Northern Värmland	0.85	0.13
Eastern Värmland	0.85	0.19
Western Värmland	0.78	0.22
Karlstad area	0.50	0.37
Gothenburg	0.27	0.88
Stockholm	0.19	0.90
Oslo	0.17	0.77
Explained variance (%)	51	18

Principal component analysis with Varimax rotation. The numbers indicate strength (Pearson's r) of each indicator to the factor. Values have been rounded to two decimals. "Explained variance" refers to the share of the variance between the variables that is explained by each dimension ("locals", "cosmopolitans").

to act in the little world inside. Their reading practices reflect their ways of life. (Merton [1949] 1968, 460–461)

Here, principal component analysis indicates that, indeed, there emerge two types of news orientations amongst Värmland's news consumers (Table 3). On the one hand, there are those who navigate through the flow of news according to a local orientation and thus primarily find their context of living and the surrounding region to be the most relevant places in the news flow. These are Merton's "locals". On the other hand, there are those navigated by an "extra-local" orientation and who accordingly find Gothenburg, Stockholm and Oslo the more relevant places to be informed and updated about. These are Merton's "cosmopolitans". Karlstad, the residence town of the region Värmland, is found relevant within both types of orientations (Table 3). This tells us that even in a contemporary globalized, (trans)mediatized landscape, the relevance structures pertaining to Merton's sociology of news consumption remain intact in a regional Swedish context.

But according to what patterns are these news orientations geo-socially structured? To put it bluntly, who are the "cosmopolitans" and who are the "locals"? In Table 4, a regression analysis displays the role of age, education, gender, subjective class, residency, mobile news consumption and international mobility in cultivating an "extra-local" news orientation. The role of "high education", "woman" and "urban residency" (Karlstad) all play statistically significant ($p \leq 0.05$) roles. This suggests that the archetypical consumer of the "extra-local" is a highly educated woman living in an urban area (Karlstad).

The fact that level of education and urban residency play important roles in structuring news orientations points to the significance of relevance structures, or "frames of reference", in processes of social reproduction. Against the background of the increasing amount of research emphasizing the connection between various forms of "extra-local" affiliations and cultural capital (Weenink 2008; Phillips and Smith 2008; Lindell 2012), our present findings are hardly surprising. Our qualitative interviews from inner-city Stockholm may also allow us to extrapolate and elaborate the quantitative findings into a more vivid picture. These interviews illuminate the ways in which transmedia textures, when embedded in more affluent social structures, hold the potential to reinforce cosmopolitan outlooks in new ways. Our interview with the university teacher quoted above, whose professional habitus paired with immigrant background (Spanish father) generate a rather distinctive form of cosmopolitanism, testifies to the ease with which

TABLE 4
Regression analysis: predictors of cosmopolitan news orientations

	Merton's "cosmopolitans"	
	Model 1	Model 2
Age 30–49 (ref. 16–29, 50–64, 65–85)	0.16* (0.08)	0.08 (0.08)
Level of education "high" (ref. "low", "mid-low", "mid-high")	0.35*** (0.09)	0.35*** (0.10)
Woman (ref. man)	0.30*** (0.07)	0.38*** (0.08)
High white-collar worker (ref. farmer, worker, white-collar worker, entrepreneur)	0.20 (0.14)	0.16 (0.16)
Entrepreneur (ref. farmer, worker, white-collar worker, high white-collar worker)	0.23 (0.13)	0.18 (0.15)
Living in Karlstad (ref. rural area, smaller town, commune town)	0.35*** (0.08)	0.36*** (0.09)
Mobile news consumption (ref. "never")		0.15 (0.11)
International work mobility (ref. "never")		0.20 (0.12)
International leisure mobility (ref. "never")		0.04 (0.08)
Constant	−0.41	−0.49
R_{adj}^2	0.09	0.10
N	778	663

Values are non-standardized coefficients with standard deviations in parentheses. The dependent variable "Merton's cosmopolitans" is a factor variable derived from the principal component analysis (see Table 3). Values are rounded up to two decimals.
Source: SOM survey conducted in Värmland in 2010.
*$p \leq 0.05$, **$p \leq 0.01$, ***$p \leq 0.001$.

those who have both technological assets and cultural competence may navigate the world online, making it part of the ordinary world-at-hand:

> Respondent 1: I often check BBC, CNN, then I often use Google translate for Russian news, Spanish *El Pais*, especially for politics, changes in governments, the crisis in Greek newspapers, I've been following how their newspapers angle things. I've started using the old service Kiosken where you can update newspapers from around the world. I'm interested in different alternatives.
>
> Interviewer: Is it mostly national or international news?
>
> Respondent 1: 50/50 Swedish and foreign news, perhaps less Swedish, more like 40/60 ... You need to see things from different sides so I don't believe in any single source, I think it's all angled, but I usually go to that country's newspapers if something happens there, then check the tabloids, the serious media, links to blogs and commentators, I speak to people I know who come from that country, I get a picture from all of them to get a complex picture, but I also realize if I'm not from that country I don't get all the references so I don't trust any source over others.

Furthermore, the significance of gender, the fact that women are the ones more likely to label the "extra-local" representations important, is particularly interesting as it goes against traditional, often patriarchal, descriptions of the cosmopolitan as an *homme du monde* ("man of the world") (Tomlinson 1999). Simultaneously, however, this further confirms the findings of Merton's Rovere study where cosmopolitan *women* emerged as those who approached the news as serving the function of a "transmission-belt for the diffusion of 'culture' from the outside world" (Merton [1949] 1968, 461). In a Värmland context, this must also be understood in relation to the fact that women have been more inclined to create mobile, extra-regional life biographies, while men to a greater extent remain loyal to the local, provincial context (Lindell and Jansson 2012). This, in turn, is significant of a broader structural transformation of Swedish society, where women to a greater extent than men pursue higher levels of education and thus orient themselves towards metropolitan areas (Utbildningsstatistisk årsbok 2013 2012).

Moreover, and somewhat to our surprise, we observe how different types of international mobilities (work- or leisure-related) do not significantly relate to extra-local news orientations. At face value, this underlines Beck's (2002, 19) argument that one can have "roots and wings at the same time" and that various forms of "imaginative travel" (Szerszynski and Urry 2002) pertaining to news consumption allow people to develop concerns for distant places regardless of their corporeal fixity in space. To this it should be noted that the areas included in the news valuing are part of the national, "greater society" and as such it does not ask respondents to value the relevancy of geo-social regions outside the nation (with the exception of Oslo, Norway). While not visually displayed here, it is also worth noting that our data suggest that mobile news consumption is related to *both* the local and the cosmopolitan orientations. We may thus conclude that the inclination to consume news through mobile devices corresponds to a general interest in news, which may be local as well as cosmopolitan in nature.

One important reason why cosmopolitan orientations are not more strongly related to mobile news consumption than local orientations is that the interest in new technological devices, and thus the propensity to naturalize transmedia textures, is more articulated among men and among class fractions in possession of economic rather than cultural capital. Cosmopolitan news orientations are thus very likely to be found among individuals, especially women, working within those cultural sectors of society where new technological innovations are appropriated (if they are) with a certain degree of scepticism or reluctance. The following media routines, described by a 42-year-old female architect living in central Stockholm, provide an illustration of what we may call "resistant cosmopolitanism":

> Respondent 4: At 8 pm I watch the news and then a film, I have routines. I never watch American films, they're uninteresting, I watch a lot of German and British TV shows and films. German programmes that are local, I have all the German channels, I very rarely watch the Swedish channels, mostly German and British, but most German. There I have my routines.
>
> Interviewer: How do you use social media?
>
> Respondent 4: Facebook very little.
>
> Interviewer: Do you have a profile?
>
> Respondent 4: No. Actually I have a profile but I never use it or put out anything. I use email of course. No other really, much less than most people.
>
> Interviewer: Do you use any other social media?
>
> Respondent 4: Which could that be? No.
>
> Interviewer: How do you use your mobile phone?
>
> Respondent 4: I have a regular mobile still, I don't want an iPhone, I only use it to speak with my daughter, so we can move around as we want.

This quote identifies an interesting site of resistance to transmedia textures, linked to the cultural desire for maintaining clear boundaries in terms of time, space and social relations. From such a perspective, which may also be linked to anti-materialist criticisms to the incorporation of commercial technologies in the lifeworld, the integrated and system-dependent nature of transmedia technologies constitutes a threat to individual autonomy and established criteria of cultural quality (such as "originality"). Here, the cosmopolitan mode of news consumption thus corresponds to the use of well-established quality media, such as particular newspapers, talk-radio channels and TV channels, rather than networked platforms. The defence of these media, and their authority as trustworthy news sources, provides an important complementary picture of the inbuilt social tensions of geo-social structuration.

Concluding Discussion: Geo-social Structuration of/through Contemporary News Consumption

News consumers of today potentially move further and further from being a homogeneous, spatially fixed mass audience into becoming a myriad of dispersed individual connoisseurs, picking and choosing between an increasing number of technological and symbolical news platforms designed under the leitmotifs of space, speed and convenience (Peters 2012, 699–700; see also Westlund 2013). We are witnessing a paradigmatic transition as to the ways in which news is consumed; the spatial practice of news consumption is changing into an increasingly amalgamated, mobile practice (see Hemment 2005; Dimmick, Feaster, and Hoplamazian 2010).

At the same time, however, the expansion of transmedia textures, and thus the alteration of news practices, is geo-socially *structured* and *structuring*. As we have shown, transmedia textures flourish above all within geo-social settings marked by relatively affluent, mobile lifestyles. However, there are no technologically inbuilt factors that propel this type of spatial practice or indisputably foster certain, ephemeral modes of news consumption: technological advancements, in terms of how we *could* consume news, "do not necessarily generate immediate adoption" (Westlund 2010, 105). Our empirical analyses suggest that transmedia textures may also (in other geo-social spaces) sustain the close bonds and local moorings of sedentary lifestyles, which in turn correspond to more centripetal dynamics of news media practices.

Furthermore, as to the question of how news media users value proximity *contra* distance in a potentially global flow of information, we have concluded that traditional patterns are largely reproduced. To "world culture", Hannerz (1990, 237) reminds us, there are two ways to relate: "there are cosmopolitans, and there are locals". Indeed, the results presented in this regard support the argument that this distinction would actually hold true, and that as to the phenomenon of news consumption, there are structural continuities in the midst of technological change. One important exception can be noted, however; in the contemporary Swedish setting women are the ones who, to a greater extent, display an orientation towards the "extra-local world". This finding signifies a larger shift in the geo-social structuration of the post-industrialized Swedish society where women generally possess greater amounts of cultural capital and reach higher education levels (Utbildningsstatistisk årsbok 2013, 2012). To a great degree this condition translates into extended transmedia connectivities. But it is also among culturally rich groups that one can identify a stream of resistance against further (trans)mediatization.

TABLE 5
Relations between amalgamations and orientations

	Transmedia amalgamations *low*	Transmedia amalgamations *high*
Merton's "cosmopolitan" news orientation	"Resistant Cosmopolitans"—mass media textures of cosmos	"Connected Cosmopolitans"—transmedia textures of cosmos
Merton's "local" news orientation	"Resistant Locals"—mass media textures of the hearth	"Connected Locals"—transmedia textures of the hearth

It is possible to organize these findings into a two-dimensional model that displays the relationship between amalgamations (textural dimension) and orientations (representational dimension) (Table 5). The model visualizes, firstly, that the transmedia shift propels forms of enactment that point towards either cosmos or the hearth depending on geo-social conditions. At the one extreme we can identify a category of "Connected Cosmopolitans", largely represented by well-educated urban groupings leading mobile lifestyles. These are often depicted as being at the forefront of both technological innovation and social change. Still, just as significant a development is the establishment of "transmedia textures of the hearth" among groupings that rather prioritize locally oriented news—"Connected Locals". These are more often located in provincial areas and typically consist of men with less cultural capital but a general interest in new technology.

Secondly, the model identifies the above-mentioned distinction between "Connected Cosmopolitans" and "Resistant Cosmopolitans", where the latter grouping, largely due to their possession of cultural capital and (supposedly) more anti-materialist values, remains sceptical to the dependencies and open-ended amalgamations sustained by transmedia technologies.

Finally, but not least, the model pinpoints a category of "Resistant Locals", referring to those groupings that are locally oriented in their news consumption, but not inclined to appropriate and use new transmedia technologies. Whereas this ideal type remains at odds with the social transitions associated with (trans)mediatization and cosmopolitanization, our empirical analysis suggests that it probably represents the broadest strata of the population. Local news orientations still maintain a stronghold among groups with lower levels of education, among the working classes and in provincial areas—again testifying to the (reproductive) significance of media practices within geo-social structuration. Likewise, when it comes to the usage of mobile devices and other transmedia technologies of communication for news consumption, such practices are still the preserve of a relatively affluent and numerically small group of the population. In spite of the coming of the "transmedia age", the social pervasiveness of mass media textures must not be under-estimated.

ACKNOWLEDGEMENTS

The authors want to thank Michael Karlsson and Michael Krona for valuable comments on earlier versions of this manuscript.

FUNDING

The analyses of the 2010 SOM data were enabled through a research grant from the Ander Foundation, Karlstad, Sweden. The project "Secure Spaces: Media, Consumption and Everyday Life" was conducted by Professor André Jansson (Karlstad University) and Professor Miyase Christensen (Stockholm University), from 2009 to 2012, and was funded through a grant from the independent research foundation Riksbankens Jubileumsfond, Sweden [grant number P2008-0667:1].

REFERENCES

Adams, Paul C. 2009. *Geographies of Media and Communication*. Malden, MA: Wiley-Blackwell.

Adams, Paul C., and André Jansson. 2012. "Communication Geography: A Bridge between Disciplines." *Communication Theory* 22 (3): 299–318. doi:10.1111/j.1468-2885.2012.01406.x.

Beck, Ulrich. 2002. "The Cosmopolitan Society and its' Enemies." *Theory, Culture & Society* 19 (1–2): 17–44. doi:10.1177/026327640201900101.

Beck, Ulrich. 2006. *Cosmopolitan Vision*. Cambridge: Polity Press.

Bjur, Jakob. 2009. "Transforming Audiences: Patterns of Individualization in Television Viewing." PhD thesis, Department of Journalism, Media and Communication, University of Gothenburg.

Bourdieu, Pierre. [1979] 1984. *Distinction: A Social Critique of the Judgment of Taste*. Translated by Richard Nice. London: Routledge.

Bourdieu, Pierre. [1997] 2000. *Pascalian Meditations*. London: Polity Press.

Chouliaraki, Lilie. 2006. *The Spectatorship of Suffering*. London: Sage.

Chyi, Hsiang I., and Monica Chadha. 2012. "News on New Devices." *Journalism Practice* 6 (4): 431–449. doi:10.1080/17512786.2011.629125.

Couldry, Nick, and Anna McCarthy, eds. 2004. *Media Space: Place, Scale and Culture in a Media Age*. London: Routledge.

Deuze, Mark. 2011. "Media Life." *Media, Culture & Society* 33 (1): 137–148. doi:10.1177/0163443710386518.

Dimmick, John, John C. Feaster, and Gregory J. Hoplamazian. 2010. "News in the Interstices: The Niches of Mobile Media in Space and Time." *New Media & Society* 13 (1): 23–39. doi:10.1177/1461444810363452.

Elliott, Anthony, and John Urry. 2010. *Mobile Lives*. London: Routledge.

Falkheimer, Jesper, and André Jansson, eds. 2006. *Geographies of Communication: The Spatial Turn in Media Studies*. Göteborg: Nordicom/Göteborg University.

Featherstone, Mike. 1991. *Postmodernism and Consumer Culture*. London: Sage.

Gans, Herbert J. 1962. *The Urban Villagers*. New York: The Free Press.

Giddens, Anthony. 1984. *The Constitution of Society*. Cambridge: Polity.

Hannerz, Ulf. 1990. "Cosmopolitans and Locals in World Culture." *Theory, Culture & Society* 7 (2): 237–251. doi:10.1177/026327690007002014.

Hemment, Drew. 2005. "The Mobile Effect." *Convergence* 11 (2): 32–40.

Jansson, André. 2007. "Texture: A Key Concept for Communication Geography." *European Journal of Cultural Studies* 10 (2): 185–202. doi:10.1177/1367549407075904.

Jansson, André. 2013a. "Mediatization and Social Space: Reconstructing Mediatization for the Transmedia Age." *Communication Theory* 23 (3): 279–296. doi:10.1111/comt.12015.

Jansson, André. 2013b. "Textures of Interveillance: A Socio-Material Approach to the Integration of Transmedia Technologies in Domestic Life." In *Media, Surveillance and Identity: Social*

Perspectives, edited by André Jansson and Miyase Christensen, 145–162. New York: Peter Lang.

Jenkins, Henry. 2006. *Convergence Culture: Where Old and New Media Collide*. New York: New York University Press.

Karlsson, Michael. 2012. "Värmläningars Nyhetskonsumtion via Mobiltelefon [Mobile News Consumption in Värmland]." In *Värmländska Landskap: Politik, Ekonomi, Samhälle, Kultur, Medier*, edited by Lennart Nilsson, Lars Aronsson, and P.-O. Norell, 447–457. Göteborg: SOM-Institutet, Karlstad University Press.

Kendall, Gavin, Ian Woodward, and Zlatko Skrbis. 2009. *The Sociology of Cosmopolitanism: Globalization, Identity, Culture & Government*. New York: Palgrave McMillan.

Lindell, Johan. 2012. "Beyond 'Distant Suffering' and Pity-Compelled Cosmopolitanism: Examining the Relation between the Consumption of Ordinary News, General Media Consumption and Cosmopolitan Outlooks in Scandinavia." *Observatorio* (OBS*) 6 (1): 47–62.

Lindell, Johan, and André Jansson. 2012. "Nyhetsvärdering, Omvärldsorientering och Regional Identitet [News Values, Orientations and Regional Identities]." In *Värmländska Landskap: Politik, Ekonomi, Samhälle, Kultur, Medier*, edited by Lennart Nilsson, Lars Aronsson, and P.-O. Norell, 457–470. Göteborg: SOM-Institutet, Karlstad University Press.

Ling, Rich. 2008. *New Tech, New Ties: How Mobile Communication is Reshaping Social Cohesion*. Cambridge, MA: MIT Press.

Madianou, Mirca. 2013. "Humanitarian Campaigns in Social Media: Networked Architecture and Polymedia Events." *Journalism Studies* 14 (2): 249–266. doi:10.1080/1461670X.2012.718558.

Madianou, Mirca, and Daniel Miller. 2013. "Polymedia: Towards a New Theory of Digital Media in Interpersonal Communication." *International Journal of Cultural Studies*, 16 (2): 169–187. doi:10.1177/1367877912452486.

Merton, Robert. [1949] 1968. *Social Theory and Social Structure*. New York: Free Press.

Morley, David. 1986. *Family Television: Cultural Power and Domestic Leisure*. London: Comedia.

Nilsson, Åsa, and Lennart Weibull. 2010. "Vad Händer med Läsningen av den Stora Morgontidningen i den Nya Medievärlden? [What Happens to Newspaper Readership in the New Media Landscape?]" In *En Region Blir Till*, edited by Lennart Nilsson, 345–376. Göteborg: SOM-institutet.

Nilsson, Lennart, Lars Aronsson, and P. O. Norell. 2012. "Värmländska Landskap [The Landscapes of Värmland]." In *Värmländska Landskap: Politik, Ekonomi, Samhälle, Kultur, Medier*, edited by Lennart Nilsson, Lars Aronsson, and P.-O. Norell, 9–21. Göteborg: SOM-Institutet, Karlstad University Press.

Park, Robert E. 1929. "Urbanization as Measured by Newspaper Circulation." *American Journal of Sociology* 35 (1): 60–79. doi:10.1086/214918.

Peters, Chris. 2012. "Journalism to Go: The Changing Spaces of News Consumption." *Journalism Studies* 13 (5–6): 695–705. doi:10.1080/1461670X.2012.662405.

Phillips, Timothy, and Philip Smith. 2008. "Cosmopolitan Beliefs and Cosmopolitan Practices: An Empirical Investigation." *Journal of Sociology* 44 (4): 391–399. doi:10.1177/1440783308097128.

Reimer, Bo. 1994. *The Most Common of Practices: On Mass Media Use in Late Modernity*. Göteborg: JMG.

Rogers, Everett M. [1962] 2010. *Diffusion of Innovations*. New York: The Free Press.

Rofe, Matthew W. 2003. "'I Want to be Global': Theorising the Gentrifying Class as an Emergent Elite Global Community." *Urban Studies* 40 (12): 2511–2526. doi:10.1080/0042098032000136183.

Schulz, Winifried. 2004. "Reconstructing Mediatization as an Analytical Concept." *European Journal of Communication* 19 (1): 87–101. doi:10.1177/0267323104040696.

Silverstone, Roger. 2007. *Media and Morality: On the Rise of the Mediapolis*. Cambridge: Polity Press.

Spigel, Lynn. 1992. *Make Room for TV: Television and the Family Ideal in Postwar America*. Chicago: University of Chicago Press.

Stevenson, Nick. 2010. "Marshall McLuhan and Media and Cultural Studies." In *Transforming McLuhan: Cultural, Critical and Postmodern Perspectives*, edited by Paul Grosswiler, 17–36. New York: Peter Lang.

Strömbäck, Jesper, Monika Djerf-Pierre, and Adam Shehata. 2012. "The Dynamics of Political Interest and News Media Consumption: A Longitudinal Perspective." *International Journal of Public Opinion Research* 25 (4): 414–435.

Szerszynski, Bronislaw, and John Urry. 2002. "Cultures of Cosmopolitanism." *The Sociological Review* 50 (4): 461–481. doi:10.1111/1467-954X.00394.

Tomlinson, John. 2001. "Instant Access: Some Cultural Implications of 'Globalising' Technologies." *Global Media Cultures Working Paper No. 13*. University of Copenhagen.

Tomlinson, John. 1999. *Globalization and Culture*. Cambridge: Polity Press.

Urry, John. 2007. *Mobilities*. Cambridge: Polity Press.

Utbildningsstatistik årsbok 2013 [The Educational Statistics Yearbook 2013]. 2012. Stockholm: Statistiska Centralbyrån (SCB)/Statistics Sweden.

Weenink, Don. 2008. "Cosmopolitanism as a Form of Capital: Parents Preparing their Children for a Globalizing World." *Sociology* 42 (6): 1089–1106. doi:10.1177/0038038508096935.

Weibull, Lennart. 2012. "Den Lokala Morgontidningen Igår, Idag och Imorgon." In *Värmländska Landskap: Politik, Ekonomi, Samhälle, Kultur, Medier*, edited by Lennart Nilsson, Lars Aronsson, and P.-O. Norell, 405–432. Göteborg: SOM-Institutet, Karlstad University Press.

Westlund, Oscar. 2010. "New(s) Functions for the Mobile: A Cross-cultural Study." *New Media & Society* 12 (1): 91–108. doi:10.1177/1461444809355116.

Westlund, Oscar. 2013. "Mobile News: A Review and Model of Journalism in an Age of Mobile Media." *Digital Journalism* 1 (1): 6–26. doi:10.1080/21670811.2012.740273.

Williams, Raymond. 1974. *Television: Technology and Cultural Form*. London: Fontana.

Zukin, Sharon. 1982. *Loft Living: Culture and Capital in Urban Change*. Baltimore: Johns Hopkins University Press.

NEWS IN THE COMMUNITY?
Investigating emerging inter-local spaces of news production/consumption

Luke Dickens, Nick Couldry, and **Aristea Fotopoulou**

This article examines the emergence of new, inter-local spaces of news production and consumption, drawing on extensive fieldwork and interviews with community reporters trained by a community reporter organisation based in the north of England. Practices of news production and content generation are focused on people's own communities and they are underpinned by an ethos of production, which is grounded in a critical consumption of news and collective processes of skill acquisition. Through an analysis of motivations and practices, we account for the values that sustain community reporter communities and discuss how such practices, while emerging from the place of local community, also extend across wider communities of interest. It is suggested that an evolving practice of skill sharing and mutual recognition could potentially stimulate the regrowth of democratic values.

Introduction

New practices of news production/consumption (Bruns 2005) are emerging in the digital age as the resources for, and entry barriers to, content production have changed radically. While much work has been done on mainstream news institutions' treatment of user-generated content (Örnebring 2009; Wardle and Williams 2010), such work has prioritised "former" audiences' activities (Rosen 2006) directed *back towards* mainstream journalism. But what if such activities are often directed elsewhere, for example within people's own communities or networked spaces that link up community reporters (CRs) across multiple locations? This article will investigate such new spaces of news circulation, drawing on interviews with CRs trained by, or networked with People's Voice Media (henceforth PVM), a CR organisation based in the north of England whose aim is to become a "Reuters of the Community".[1]

We are interested in how this new landscape of news production/consumption works from the perspective of community-based actors seeking to forge an alternative model of news, one in which community voice is more heavily weighted (see also BESPOKE 2011). News production/consumption—indeed all media production/consumption—has a material geography, much neglected in mainstream media studies.[2] Yet geography, at least urban geography, was at the heart of one of the earliest newspaper studies (Park [1925] 1967), which understood the early US newspaper industry as a response to changes in the lifeworld's *spatial* configuration as people moved from villages to cities: if "local news is the very stuff that democracy is made of" (Park [1925] 1967, 85), then the local news element even in broader news production should not be neglected.

Accordingly, it is important to understand better how community news producers/ consumers conceive their media-related practice. This article draws on interviews among PVM's network of reporters about their production *and* consumption practices. The resulting picture does not resolve into either a centralised valorisation of "user-generated content" or into a decentred hyperlocalism (Radcliffe 2012). Instead we encountered a more complex relationship whereby local stories are produced and linked within an inter-local exchange; yet it is often audiences' feelings of *not* being recognised in national news agendas that drives them to generate *and consume* news stories more locally.

We conducted our fieldwork during rapid, even destructive change in the distribution of local government resources and nationally funded income. The multi-billion pound cuts announced in the 2010 emergency budget statements set in motion a restructuring of local governance. In particular, the Localism Act (2011), reduced disability services, employment services and housing benefits.[3] Meanwhile, regional funding sources for civil society organisations like PVM were severely cut. Both PVM and its CRs were experiencing acute financial pressure when we worked with them.

Independently, changes in the landscape of news production impacted negatively on local democracy (Goldsmiths Leverhulme Media Research Centre 2010), with rival news providers emerging in potential response to these changes (see "Research Context" below). Their diverse strategies of content production reflect a wider, unresolved debate about what "news" is for, where and by whom it should be produced and consumed, and whether our inherited philosophies of journalism can address current challenges and opportunities. Will flows of significant information ("news stories") be radically reconfigured in the digital age (Rantanen 2009; Peters and Broersma 2012), generating a differently structured "mediaspace" (Couldry and McCarthy 2004)? It helps here to remember what Lefebvre saw as the dialectical nature of all spatial practices (Lefebvre 1991, 18): even if capitalism operates through an "abstract space" (for money and resource transmission), new "social spaces" can still emerge through local action, for example a space of CR practice (Jackson 1994). Throughout we must attend to the highly particular processes by which "locality" is produced, both in news practice (Kirby 1989) and more generally (Appadurai 1995). That means basing our inquiry in the values and practices of actual CRs. We need to be sensitive both to changing production practices and the grounding of those changes in a dissatisfaction with national media's historic neglect of many localities.

After reviewing relevant literature and a contextual note, we explore in sequence the resources, news conceptions and networked spaces of community reporting, reflecting finally on the potential democratic values they imply.

Community Reporting, Place and Media Literacy

The optimism surrounding new digital journalistic practices has been heavily criticised. Van Dijck and Nieborg (2009) urge critical awareness of peer-production trends in business models of the digital economy and Web 2.0, advising against terms such as "produsage" and "co-creation" and asserting that this business-generated "new digital infrastructure has come to govern our mediascape as well as our social lives" (870). Similarly, Rebillard and Touboul (2010) have challenged "Web 2.0" promissory narratives in relation to journalism and participatory culture. Our study, however, concerns members of a specific community, not anonymous users or "crowds", exploring how they understand their content-generation practices, which are certainly not solicited by corporate media, and their own visions about what constitutes news and participation in news production.

Our article is not concerned with participation directly in mainstream journalism. Such "participatory journalism" potentially enables citizens to be active in the collection and dissemination of news (Bowman and Willis 2003). However, Wardle and Williams (2010) note that although audience comments, footage, experiences and stories are collected by the BBC, the structural roles of BBC news journalists have not been challenged by these practices: "journalists have remained journalists and audiences have remained audiences" (Wardle and Williams 2010, 792). Similarly, in an analysis of user-generated tabloid content for *The Sun*, Örnebring argued these practices do not signify a power shift between producer and consumer; indeed, users were encouraged to produce content oriented to their personal and everyday life, rather than to have any direct involvement in news selection.

Unlike participatory journalism, citizen journalism seeks to transfer power and responsibility from journalists to individuals or community groups. Indymedia, as a distinct, radical model of journalistic practices (Platon and Deuze 2003), is the most cited example. Other models, such as "hyperlocal" media, seek to address the decline of traditional news media industries (Picard 2003; 2008) and to introduce a community orientation to news media operations (Howley 2010). Hyperlocal media have been described as "a hybrid of civic, community, statewide public affairs, and alternative newspaper movements combined with the interactive and broadcast abilities accompanying Web 2.0" (Metzgar, Kurpius, and Rowley 2011, 774). However, Metzgar, Kurpius, and Rowley (2011, 779), in their analysis of US-based hyperlocal media, note a difference between civic journalism and hyperlocal media: by providing local information, civic journalism enables citizens to act in their own communities, whereas hyperlocal media operations and their editorial choices are largely driven by market criteria.

The question of what "community" is served by such journalism is complex. John Dewey wrote about the relationship between issues of concern and publics, arguing that issues make publics. While this raises broader questions of visibility (Marres 2007), more important here is how shared concerns are debated and resolved in everyday social spaces, and not just the spaces prescribed for political deliberation or speech (Couldry 2010). Rodriguez (2011, 24) similarly has defined "citizens' media" as "the media citizens use to activate communication processes that shape their local communities". Additionally, in an ethnically diverse community in Los Angeles county, Chen et al. (2012) analysed the relationship between local storytelling and civic engagement: when local stories are missing from mainstream media, or existing publications fail to talk about the collective problems of a specific community or neighbourhood, Web-based storytelling platforms can enhance civic engagement and inter-group interaction. We too found that the absence of a media platform to express shared local concerns was an impetus for community reporting. Spaces of social co-operation and mutual recognition are potentially created when news production operates within specific communities.

Such practices, and their underlying values, are critical to the emergence of a different geographical configuration of news production and consumption. Rantanen (2009), in her analysis of localisation and places in news, has noted how news-flow studies have largely ignored questions of "where" and "when", prioritising the analysis of news content. Yet news plays a significant role in constructing our experiences of place: "belonging has no meaning unless news offers readers a point of identification" (Rantanen

2009, 80). As we see later, it is local points of reference that for CRs create such opportunities for identification, and news about such reference points emerges itself from local practices of skill-building and mutual recognition.

What CRs bring to news generation has implications for debates on media literacy. In their review for the UK regulator Ofcom, Livingstone, Van Couvering, and Thumim (2008, 46) note the importance of content creation for media literacy, but identify two research gaps: the relationships between amateur production and the creative industries; and how "an experience of production encourages a critical understanding of media products". This article begins to address both gaps, while also linking to international debates on how narrative exchange contributes to wider civic engagement (Bennett 2008; Rheingold 2008).

Research Context and Methodology

Empirically, this paper draws on personal accounts recorded through in-depth, semi-structured interviews with 12 self-selecting CRs reached through an open call sent through the PVM mailing list. The semi-structured interviews were conducted in February and March 2013, and were part of an 18-month participatory action research study with PVM whose full details are not relevant here (see www.storycircle.co.uk). The group consisted of eight women and four men, aged between 20 and 63 years, and living in Salford, Greater Manchester; Toxteth, Liverpool; Brighton on England's south coast; and the Blaenau Gwent region of South Wales. For each location, CRs were linked to a corresponding partner agency: PVM in Salford, Toxteth TV in Toxteth, Three Valleys TV in Blaenau Gwent and the Sussex Community Internet Project in Brighton. Our sample captured the heterogeneity of individual CRs and their localities that are missed in hyperbolic narratives about "here comes everybody" (Shirky 2007). All accounts have been anonymised.

PVM, a social enterprise based in Salford, aims "to support people to have a voice … and describe their own reality" and "contribute to raising community and individual aspiration". A core part of this vision is PVM's Community Reporter programme, which prioritises the production of "community reporting" for *community* empowerment (Watton 2009), rather than individualised production by "citizen journalists" hoping to break into the mainstream (Wilson 2012).

PVM operates a "social licensing" franchise model that enables other community groups to purchase CR training packages, receive accreditation and participate in a dedicated online network of reporters and content.[4] While originating in the North West, this network spread across other UK areas, and in early 2012 was formalised through a national Institute of Community Reporters.[5] To date, PVM has supported approximately 1000 people through their Community Reporter programme, bringing community perspectives to bear on local housing policy, schooling and public space.[6]

PVM is one of many similar organisations focused on local news production/consumption emerging within a rapidly restructuring media landscape. Several small, "hyperlocal" groups have begun to develop their own training and support for local people: for example, the Community Media Training School run by Citizenseye in Leicester, or the Community Correspondents programme by South Leeds Life.[7] At a national level, several initiatives have developed platforms to draw together networks of community-level reporters: notably, the Media Trust's "Newsnet" service (now called "Newswire") or GlobalNet21's "citizen zone", as well as the UK government-endorsed Your

Square Mile.[8] The United States has a more advanced hyperlocal sector (Kurpius, Metzgar, and Rowley 2010; Metzgar, Kurpius, and Rowley 2011), while several services host community-reported content internationally, including Global Voices and WeAreChange.[9]

The "Community Reporter": Motivations, Relationships and Skills

Backgrounds and Motivations

While community media has a longer and broader history (Rodriguez 2001; Fuller 2006), the CRs embodied in the United Kingdom's fast-changing digital news landscape comprise a diverse range of people. Some have a relevant professional background (community work, media education) while others have found CR training and practice meaningful at a decisive point in their lives. It is important to have a sense of CRs' underlying motivations to acquire skills and to get involved, if we are to understand where the potential transformation of locality through community reporting comes from.

Some saw the roots of their current CR practice well before recent debates about "prosumers" (Bruns 2005). Maggie, a retired teacher with mobility problems, had organised community projects for capturing local stories:

> I think I've always been, without realising, a community reporter ... I was doing other sorts of community reporting without being recognised as a community reporter.

Being a CR then is not a given, but an emergent identity. It involves a need to address the challenging material circumstances of people's lives by giving an account of what is happening around them. This need starts a positive process for those who might otherwise have been locked into inactivity: meeting people and gaining more confidence; employment and skill acquisition; and getting recognition for one's skills and abilities.

Unsurprisingly, when asked what CR practice meant to them, interviewees often replied in almost evangelical terms: "it's a passion, not a penance" (Maggie); or "being a community reporter means everything to me!" (Lynda, an unemployed middle-aged woman). Similarly, Terry explained that:

> I'm disabled ... but it's given me a whole new meaning in life, the whole community media has.

Even where CRs and CR trainers had passed through media professions, they contrasted mainstream journalism and community reporting. Carly, one of the media-trained CRs we interviewed described the difference in ethical terms:

> I'm trained in media anyway, and I've been teaching digital media production at all different levels for years, the [CR] training for me was more about the community reporter ethos.

For her, identifying as a CR results from the belief that news about local communities should be produced in ways that relate explicitly to the specific communities from which that news emerges. Is this the beginning of a practical response to the challenges of today's underfunded journalism environment?

Relationships

For our participants, membership in a community of shared news production values helped reshape their wider experience of community and locality. Indeed, practices of community reporting always involved entering into a wider "community of practice" involving mutual recognition of each other's everyday skills and abilities (Wenger 1998). One key form of interaction between CRs, shaping how specific communities of reporters established localised bonds, was the "meet-up". Meet-ups facilitated mutual recognition and information/skill exchange between CRs:

> We discuss what we can, we look at various things that we're doing, seeing if we can leverage that, and ... we look at what's happening in the town and make sure that we're covering it. (Terry)

Some groups came together around specific interests or local issues (youth groups, housing associations, disability groups), while others took a more general interest in their neighbourhoods. In the everyday spaces of the "meet-up" (held in community centres, church halls and freely available meeting rooms), CRs chatted, over tea and coffee, about local issues and their own media practices with other similarly inclined local people. In the absence, generally, of significant material reward, these interactions fostered a clear but necessary sense of solidarity:

> it was one of the best decisions I've ever made, because I made so many friends. And *I mean beyond friends if that makes sense*, people that are there for me, that have been supportive, and if I've said I've got this problem or that problem, or I've got this idea, I've got that idea, I only have to click my fingers and it's there, the help is there. (Lynda, emphasis added)

This community was for Lynda grounded in a practice of care for particular people and places, enacted through a practice of active listening (Dreher 2010):

> [T]o me through the eye of a camera is the way forward because what [reporters are] seeing through the lens of a camera or through their own eyes can be shared ... through other people.

Such active listening, being grounded in a relationship of care for a local community, goes beyond the position of the "prosumer" (the consumer who also sometimes produces for him- or herself), implying a different relation to journalist practice and democratic norms. As discussed next, training was an important way in which CRs developed such shared practices.

Training and Skills

Local CR groups' informal meet-ups often complemented explicit packages of training offered by PVM through its Institute of Community Reporters initiative. This training involved a combination of basic technical and social competencies, using accessible technologies and software and encouraging in people the confidence to tell their own stories about issues that affected them, rather than turn them into professional journalists.

PVM training emphasises the experiential use of technologies such as flip-cams. For many, it was an opportunity to learn basic editorial skills and shape media content into recognisable stories:

I had a cine-camera, a DVD recorder thing, and I didn't really know how to use it. I knew how to point it, I knew how to record things, but I didn't know how to get the film off it on to a computer and play with it. And once I did that I got the bug. (Trevor)

The training emphasis remained on the quality of narrative exchange, not on producing professional media outputs: "we're not all trying to be Steven Spielbergs, but everyone's got their own way of putting stuff across" (Keith).

Others that undertook CR training saw it as a practice that addressed accessibility and adult media literacy issues. As Sandra, a trainer, explained:

working with the housing group, especially with it being older people ... people that don't normally have access to computers haven't got the basic, basic skills, and part of the training was assuming that they don't have that, and they don't.

CR training can challenge digital divides and literacies (Livingstone and Helsper 2007) by helping CRs develop the technical *and* social skills of storytelling. The training process was central in creating a culture of skill and knowledge sharing for CRs, and lies at the heart of this distinctive space of news production/consumption.

PVM's own accreditation of these skills involved a micro-culture of esteem and recognition, which was ratified with a "Community Reporter" badge. As Gary Copitch, CEO of PVM explained:

The Institute of Community Reporters is about individuals ... We thought it's about time to give recognition to people ... The badge gives people credibility.

CRs echoed this sense of validation in their own pursuit of meaningful stories:

I've got my badge now, so when I ask questions, I'm a community reporter, it backs me up. It opens doors ... it gives you a bit more confidence when you go up to somebody and say, put the badge in their face, "I've got a badge!" (Sandra)

Yet the CR community of practice, while often closely focused on a bounded locality, was also cut across by wider communities of interest that could *transcend locality* and create a broader sense of belonging to something more significant (see subsequent section, "The Networked Spaces of Community Reporting"). Thus for Carly, the practical media training served to build solidarity within her local meet-up group and, simultaneously, with a national "movement":

when I'm training ... you're part of something larger than just that project, it's a movement, and I think that gives it more credibility, and I think it makes you feel like you're more a part of something. You're not just, "Oh I've just been trained on a flip camera."

As discussed next, practices of news production and consumption between CRs created a space where positive stories about their communities could be voiced both within and beyond their immediate localities. In this way, CRs gained some sense of control and empowerment over their own issues across a range of scales.

A Distinct Mode of News Production/Consumption?

When interviewees spoke about the news media they consumed, they often noted occasions where mainstream news did not provide them with points of identification.

Our CR sample were generally active and regular consumers of a variety of news (local/national; radio, TV, internet, less so newspapers). Most reporters showed a strong sense of dissatisfaction with mainstream news, primarily for its sensationalist focus on "all those poor people shooting each other and ripping each other off and selling each other drugs ... looking for the juicy stuff that makes headlines and the front page" (Keith). This critical stance towards mainstream news often pushed them towards local news:

> I wouldn't waste my money [on mainstream newspapers]. *The Sun* is always behind anyway, it's always late with the news and as I say, the newspapers are basically the same as the TV, propaganda. (Lynda)

Dissatisfaction with the mainstream media was a key motivation for seeking new types of news to consume and for producing news themselves on initially a local scale. When CRs could not find points of identification in the mainstream news, they created their own opportunities for identification:

> I was sick of being lied to by the mainstream media and I just wanted to do things that I want to be involved in and that interest myself, which I know myself will interest other people ... don't hate the media, be the media. (Lynda)

Lynda contrasted her discontent with mainstream news directly to her own journalistic instinct for newstelling as "truth":

> I never leave home without my camera ... [T]hat's me now, more in your face. I'm not frightened of interviewing anybody or poking my lens at anybody ... I just cover the truth.

Similarly, Sandra expressed a desire to go beyond the news she consumed by making the news herself within a profoundly local context:

> You realise a lot of things go on behind the scenes, which no one knows about, so it's not reported in the local paper, it's not reported on the local radio, or any local media, it just happens you overhear a conversation ... I go hunting then!

This *counter*-media practice finds its initial focus around the notion of "positive news" which needs careful unpacking.

"Positive News"

The need for "more positive" news to counter the relentless cycle of murders, wars, scandal and government wrangling has been a commonplace of news debate in Britain since the 1990s.[10] CRs' language appears to repeat this commonplace, but with the difference that, from the perspective of particular communities (often significantly disadvantaged), they want to correct what they see as specific misrepresentations:

> people always think of the Toxteth riots, which was 1981; do you know what I mean? It's like, "Move on." ... [laughs] there's been so many positive things ...that have happened in Toxteth over the last 30 years ... it just changes people's perceptions hopefully, that's what Community Reporters does of a place. (Safi)

Far from a naive celebration of the parochial that rejects any links to political contention, when reporters explained to us what they meant by "positive" news, they made clear links to significant and contentious issues:

> I think [it is] stories that look at local issues, but also look to *give people a voice about how they could have solutions from within the community*. For example we've done some reports on the welfare reforms and how they impact on tenants and certain associations, and how they impact on people with disabilities and stuff ... coming from that is a voice of people's fear and anxiety, but there's also through the consultation, *people are suggesting things that could be done to help in their situation*, ... in terms of what the community could do to support the community. (Carly, emphasis added)

If what matters is linking local issues to local action, CRs can be positive agents of news production, taking advantage of the new intersections between consumption and production and escaping the stereotype of the "reactive" citizen that mainstream British media generally present (Lewis, Inthorn, and Wahl-Jorgensen 2005).

PVM had a policy of avoiding explicit political references, within a wider strategy to elicit more positive news, but struggled at times to differentiate between the narrowly partisan and the more constructive ways in which CRs might address the implications of political decisions. However, Lynda noted:

> The world isn't just rosy coloured glasses, people need to see beyond the box and know what's happening beyond the box, you know give the glasses a wipe, it isn't all like, local garden fete, or you know somebody's done this that's good. There is bad things out there that need bringing to light, you know, crime. Like the local council, they commit crime every day, every week, every year, by pulling down property, stocks of housing.

The specific news values that underlie CRs' understandings of stories are examined next.

What Constitutes a "News" Story?

Local practices of mutual recognition played an important role in how CRs produced *and* consumed news:

> I found what [we] were doing was looking for the stories, the unremarkable, remarkable stories, if that makes sense ... the more I got into it the more I understood that my background as a sales engineer in sales for 20-odd years, although being business-to-business, was not that different from reporting; ask questions, get answers, just being nosey really ... And as unremarkable as anybody can be to the naked eye, you don't know what's going on behind that façade. (Trevor)

Indeed, what *counted* as a news story was guided by values of mutual recognition between CRs:

> there's a story in everything, ... you spend a lot of time ... getting the trainee reporters to see that ... *if it's important to them, then it's a story, it's an issue* ... you see it almost through their eyes ... it makes you see things all around. (Becky, emphasis added)

> stories dealt with a variety of themes: stories in terms of disability, human rights stories, anything that affects people and harms them, we need to cover and report about, and also even things like parking issues, you know? I think one of our biggest programmes last year was one about parking issues. (Maggie)

This identification of local impact often cuts across different groups, helping bind them through mutual recognition. For instance, stories about "wet leaves" on the pavement impacting blind or partially sighted people related to wider issues faced by the elderly as well. In addition to such bridging effects, stories also helped transcend scale. As became evident from our interviews, community reporting as a news production practice helped citizens to engage with concerns about the localised impact of national cuts on housing, health and wellbeing from within their communities. In this way, the practice repositions CRs' sense of local belonging within a potentially national space of comparison: "it's not just Toxteth; it's everywhere ... where the community reporters exist" (Sefi).

Community reporting brings a concern with local change to a new audience, opening up community-level engagement with the implications of such changes, that is, as "issues" of common concern which for John Dewey are an important part of the democratic process (Dewey 1954). Thus, one CR:

> noticed that the church she went to as a child was for sale, which upset her so she went off to find out where the congregation was now, why they'd left that building and she's making a film about that ... normally she might just go home and tell her mum, now she can make a film about it to try and engage the community. (Emma)

Making news changes the starting-point from which one consumes what others produce, providing a new reference point for assessing the selection choices that may underlie mainstream production. As Mark explained:

> since I've done some community reporting, I look more closely to see if there's any hidden details, I look more deeply, thinking: has this been changed to make somewhere look really good or really bad?

We now turn to the emerging inter-local geographies involved in CR.

The Networked Spaces of Community Reporting

Local News from the Inside

There is a strong link between CRs' distinctive sense of what is news, whether as consumers or producers, and their sense of being positioned within a local community. The embedding of CRs in their own communities broadens the types and depth of story that they can tell.

> Because I'm from the borough I kind of know my audience, I know what the locals want, what they're about. It's quite a wide range I'd say from elderly people down to children. When you're surrounded by the people I think you know what they want. (Hannah)

Hopefully, this meaning-context affects also how local audiences react to this new type of local news. Certainly, some CRs reflected on this greater richness as an antidote to the increasingly frantic "churnalism" (Davies 2007), in other words the recycling of stories in mainstream news media, even where it respects citizen journalists:

> I'm really here on the ground ... community reporting is from people who are on the ground, in other words are *with* the sources ... Which I think is the big difference between community reporting and citizen journalism ... in citizen journalism ... they're working in many cases with just what they've read in other newspapers, in the main

newspapers ... We're there, we see what's going on around us, and we do know what's going on and we can tell the story. (Terry, emphasis added)

This is not just about stealing a lead on mainstream news, but connecting the production and consumption of news through tacit understandings of the issues that affect local people in their everyday lives.

Indeed, being a CR seems to *change* how locality is understood, and in the process build a different material geography of news production/consumption. CRs feel that "outsiders" lack a more balanced understanding of everyday life in their locality, leading to misrepresentation. Misrepresentations of localities by incoming journalists can have lasting material impacts on people's lives (Champagne 1999), and CRs interviewed from Salford or Toxteth routinely referred to the consequences of their localities' negative media image.

It is from the position of being "not ... an outsider coming in to [report] [but] an *actual* member of the community" (Mark, emphasis added) that CRs understand their production/consumption. As Keith explains:

It means that we're not laying there being fed all this crap by people like the BBC, ITV, Sky, where they dive on the worst of an area. It's like "Moss Side this" or whatever it is, "Nottingham is the gun capital"; we're the people who are actually living within it and it will give us our own perspectives.

Some saw their community reporting as an active strategy for "trying to change perceptions of what people think of an area ... because it's not all bad news" (Keith), both externally and internally. For instance, PVM noted:

our main problem is not people's perceptions outside, it's people's perceptions inside ... mainstream media are looking in all the time, even the local newspaper now ... it is about giving voice to people *within* the community. (emphasis added)

Safi's account is given against the explicit background of the decline of local news infrastructure (in Toxteth, the closure of *The Post* and *The Mersey Mart*):

Toxteth has got a reputation on it, and very much unfounded, but it's ... Toxteth community reporters who can tell the positivity of what's going on ... it lets people know the real deal. (Safi)

For CRs, the need to respond to misrepresentation of *their* locality was often intensely linked to class position, with the strongest connection between locality and negativity being in the working-class areas of Toxteth, Salford and the Welsh valleys. We see in these sentiments the contemporary traces of a longer history of critical local commentary outside the journalistic mainstream. Raymond Williams (1983) discussed the campaigning style of William Cobbett in his "Rural Rides" during the nineteenth century— an approach defined by "social and political argument combined with observation of how people lived" (O'Connor 2006, 37)—and the continuity with working-class journalists in the early twentieth century. Yet being a community insider need not be merely a hyperlocal practice, and is imagined by Lynda and Terry to transcend particular locations:

I take my community reporting very serious, I like to go to different locations, ... I get involved in lots of aspects of my community really and in other cities, I go beyond my own area. (Lynda)

> I am disabled and I write from the disability point of view as well, and I'm involved over at [town] with a group ... when we think of community reporting, you're not just reporting from communities geographically, we're reporting from communities of interest. (Terry)

If "communities of interest" which are located in different parts of the United Kingdom can emerge through the practice of CR, this suggests the beginnings of a differently configured infrastructure for local news.

Emerging Inter-localities

So far the local focus of news production/consumption "from the inside" might seem bound within a local, perhaps "hyperlocal", model of news. Yet something distinctive was PVM's role in establishing *inter*-connections between locally orientated CR groups. These efforts to build a national infrastructure are best understood as ways to put local practices into productive *exchange* with other localities, rather than simply aggregating local voices on a national scale (citizen journalism), or focusing solely on local voices (hyperlocal news). The local is not superseded, but becomes differently connected, within a national space of comparison. Although building an effective online network platform has proved challenging for PVM, we focus here on an emerging connection between different localities which we term here "inter-local".

Such an inter-local dialogic space emerges through the ways that CRs *feel* connected, through shared training approaches, reporting practices and a wider ethos. As Hannah suggested, "even without meeting them you can connect with them because we're doing the same thing for all the same reasons". Moreover, Hannah felt that the dedicated CR Web platform had "given us a platform by which all of us, all of these news groups and website groups and bloggers all around the country, can get together". Indeed, while there are of course well-known social media platforms that enable mass narrative exchange, use of those spaces may be less important than a *dedicated* Web space that preserves a sense of community voice while also bringing it into contact with distant others. Indeed, the Institute of Community Reporters website space was felt to facilitate multiple connectivities and possibilities for community news production/consumption:

> It means that I am connecting my community, and my community is of interest, with the media, and by media now, I mean the whole internet, knowing what sites are available to promote my community, my communities. (Terry)

These inter-connections could be both national and local without being limited to either:

> in the network then it is national, 'cause we'll read stuff from people down in say London or Bristol or whatever and they'll read our stuff ... I don't think there'd be that much different between us apart from some silly accents! ... Bypassing all of the big media crap and all telling each of our own stories. (Keith)

Local communities of practice intersect with wider communities of interest, when CRs can share experiences relating to local knowledge *and* local action. Lynda provided an example:

> There was an item a while back ... that if you were on benefit ... you could get a discount [on your energy bills]. I live in Manchester, and I passed that information on to

Yorkshire, and several people contacted their suppliers and were absolutely over the moon ... because it's out in the wilds, it's in the countryside, where I contacted, they had no idea that this was available, to help them with their winter fuel bills and stuff.

Similarly, Mark gave an example of inter-local exchange around his interests as a youth worker, and how such understandings had further supported his own practices:

I've spoken to someone from the next-door city ... to get some inside information about what ... the youth scene is like over in Manchester ... since the council completely got rid of their youth service ... This person I knew who was involved as a community reporter that had had some youth background work, so I spoke to them ... it put into contrast just how lucky we are in the area where we live, compared to just down the road ... it was useful as well in case the eventuality does come round that the same will happen in the area where I live.

In parallel with appreciating the value in sharing community-level news across localities, Safi was convinced that sharing production techniques linked up people from different localities, creating mutual recognition and an inter-local appreciation of community news:

they're knowing us, we're knowing them, whereas a few months ago, we weren't aware of each other, so hopefully ... that skill-sharing can expand maybe. What might be good, even getting somebody from a different locality, like someone from Manchester coming to Liverpool, someone from Liverpool going to Manchester, various ways of sharing skills with people.

While CR news reaching mass audiences was discussed only as a remote possibility, reaching communities of interest in other locations was feasible. Keith talked about a film he had produced about a local music venue:

it was the story of the very first Northern Soul café/bar, called the Twisted Wheel Club ... you just won't understand how much of an influence it had on the whole scene of soul up in the north ... The film has had interest to be shown all over the world, we're talking from like Hollywood, Indonesia ... lots of soul clubs all over the world, Australia, wherever.

In the reflections of the CRs we interviewed, there emerged traces of something more than a simple promotionalism: an ethics of *listening* and narrative exchange that was not opposed to mainstream journalism but suggested a distinctive approach based in mutual recognition (Honneth 2007). We end our discussion with Hazel's emphatic sense of what exchanging news means to her:

I love passing on news ... about what's happened in the community. And I love hearing people's opinions and I love the opportunity of being able to, not changing their minds, but give them a different point of view for them to look at, you know, "Wow, wow I never even thought of that" ... I actually listen to what other people have to say. (Hazel)

To make this exchange between CRs a viable and sustained practice, the development of a stronger digital infrastructure remains necessary. So far, the uneven distribution of government funding has meant that this aspect of inter-local dialogue has not been prioritised. While spaces of inter-local dialogue are emerging in offline meet-ups and between communities of interest, online platforms which effectively accommodate and strengthen these dialogic exchanges also need to be developed along the lines suggested by PVM. The design of such platforms needs to take account of the locally grounded dynamics of news production and consumption.

Conclusion

Participating in the production of news can enhance people's sense of each other's perspectives on the world: not necessarily conflicting with the philosophy of large-scale news production, such participation deserves to be considered as an alternative starting-point for news production/consumption at a time of huge uncertainty for traditional models of journalism. The CRs we interviewed are more than individual "prosumers" (people who both produce and consume): they have an ethos of production that is *grounded* in a critical consumption of news and an evolving practice of skill-sharing and mutual recognition. The collapse of local journalism bites deeply in disadvantaged localities such as those from where our reporter sample often came: there the CR ethos may be more than individual passion or self-expression and closer to the necessary response to an absence of collective voice. This practice starts out very often from the place of local community, but as we have shown, extends to wider communities of interest, and generates an interest in inter-local news sharing between CR groups. Such a practice contains at least the seeds of a different news infrastructure.

We recognise, however, that distribution is a key aspect in any new model of news production/consumption. The network of reporters we interviewed largely relied on PVM's existing distribution platform—the Institute of Community Reporters website—which at the point of writing was redesigning its interface, in consultation with us as part of our action research. The website was being redesigned to incorporate functions that would allow reporters to connect with one another, and audiences to provide comments or other forms of feedback. For this reason, our detailed discussion is here limited to practices of production and consumption, and only touches on new possibilities of distribution.

The embedding of such practices of news consumption/production in wider communities of practice cannot be captured by generalised critiques of social media (Van Dijck 2009), nor is it satisfactorily dismissed by claims that what is needed today is more local news of the very same type whose economic model is now under threat (Goldsmiths Leverhulme Media Research Centre 2010). Admittedly, the economic model for extending and sustaining community reporting is so far equally unclear, and some forms of initial subsidy are clearly needed.

Debate about such new forms of news subsidy should be informed by an understanding of the values that can emerge in CR communities: values of voice, listening and recognition (Honneth 2007; Couldry 2010; Dreher 2010). Could such emergent values themselves be the seeds of the "free social enquiry" that John Dewey (1954, 163–180) once saw as necessary to stimulate the regrowth of democracy itself?

ACKNOWLEDGEMENTS

This paper was produced thanks to the generosity and insights of staff and community reporters at People's Voice Media, Salford, UK. We would also like to thank Chris Peters and the anonymous reviewers for comments on earlier drafts of this paper. The research from which this paper draws was part of a wider, multi-strand action research project led by Goldsmiths, University of London (see http://www.storycircle.co.uk) within the Framework for Innovation and Research in MediaCity consortium (see http://www.firm-innovation.net).

FUNDING

This work was supported by the UK's Engineering and Physical Research Sciences Council [grant number EP/H003738/1].

NOTES

1. See http://peoplesvoicemedia.co.uk/.
2. For specific examples of this neglected geography, see Brooker-Gross (1983), Boyd-Barrett and Rantanen (1998), Dencik (2013) and Rodgers, Barnett, and Cochrane (2009). More generally, see Couldry (2000) and Adams (2009).
3. See http://www.hm-treasury.gov.uk/2010_june_budget.htm), the Localism Act (2011) (http://www.legislation.gov.uk/ukpga/2011/20/contents/enacted) and the Welfare Reform Act (2012) (http://www.legislation.gov.uk/ukpga/2012/5/contents/enacted).
4. See http://www.communityreporter.co.uk.
5. See http://blog.peoplesvoicemedia.co.uk/2012/04/19/launch-of-the-institute-of-community-reporters/.
6. From http://peoplesvoicemedia.co.uk/case-studies.
7. See http://www.citizenseye.org/training-school/, http://www.southleedslife.com/communityreporters/and the monthly *Port Talbot Magnet* (www.lnpt.org).
8. See http://www.mediatrust.org/get-support/community-newswire-1/, http://21st-century network.com/blog/ and http://www.yoursquaremile.co.uk/.
9. See http://globalvoicesonline.org/.
10. Broadcaster, Martyn Lewis, initiated debate on the need for "good news" in 1993. See http://www.independent.co.uk/voices/not-my-idea-of-good-news-at-the-end-of-a-week-of-horrifying-events-martyn-lewis-bbc-presenter-argues-for-a-change-in-news-values-1457539.html and http://www.independent.co.uk/voices/profile-sweetie-among-cynics-martyn-lewis-top-in-a-tough-profession-he-campaigns-for-good-news-and-writes-about-cats-so-why-are-the-claws-out-for-him-by-geraldine-bedell-2320494.html. See also http://positivenews.org.uk/.

REFERENCES

Adams, Paul C. 2009. *Geographies of Media and Communication*. Chichester: Wiley-Blackwell.
Appadurai, Arjun. 1995. "The Production of Locality." In *Counterworks*, edited by Richard Fardon, 204–225. London: Routledge.
Bennett, Lance W. 2008. "Changing Citizenship in a Digital Age." In *Civic Life Online: Learning How Digital Media Can Engage Youth*, edited by Lance W. Bennett, 1–24. Cambridge, MA: MIT.
BESPOKE. 2011. *Insight Journalism as a Catalyst for Community Innovation and Engagement*. London: V&A.
Boyd-Barrett, Oliver, and Terhi Rantanen. 1998. *The Globalization of News*. London: Sage.

Bowman, Shayne, and Chris Willis. 2003. "We Media: How Audiences Are Shaping the Future of News and Information." The Media Center at The American Press Institute. Accessed February 20, 2013. http://www.mediacenter.org/mediacenter/research/wemedia/

Brooker-Gross, Susan R. 1983. "Spatial Aspects of Newsworthiness." *Geografiska Annaler, Series B, Human Geography* 65B: 1–9.

Bruns, Axel. 2005. *Gatewatching*. New York: P. Lang.

Champagne, Patrick. 1999. "The View from the Media." In *The Weight of the World*, Pierre Bourdieu, 46–59. Stanford, CA: Stanford University Press.

Chen, Nien-Tsu N., Fan Dong, Sandra J. Ball-Rokeach, Michael Parks, and Jin Huang. 2012. "Building a New Media Platform for Local Storytelling and Civic Engagement in Ethnically Diverse Neighborhoods." *New Media and Society* 14 (6): 931–950. doi:10.1177/1461444 811435640.

Couldry, Nick. 2000. *The Place of Media Power*. London: Routledge.

Couldry, Nick. 2010. *Why Voice Matters*. London: Sage.

Couldry, Nick and Anna McCarthy. 2004. *Mediaspace*. London: Routledge.

Davies, Nick. 2007. *Flat Earth News*. London: Chatto and Windus.

Dencik, Lina. 2013. "Alternative News Sites and the Complexities of 'Space'." *New Media and Society* 15: 1207–1223. doi:10.1177/1461444812471812.

Dewey, John. 1954. *The Public and its Problems*. Chicago: Gateway.

Dreher, Tanja. 2010. "Speaking up or Being Heard? Community Media Interventions and the Politics of Listening." *Media Culture & Society* 32 (1): 85–103. doi:10.1177/0163443709350099.

Fuller, Linda. 2006. *Community Media*. Palgrave: MacMillan.

Goldsmiths Leverhulme Media Research Centre. 2010. "Meeting the News Needs of Local Communities." Accessed August 2, 2012. www.mediatrust.org.

Honneth, Axel. 2007. *Disrespect*. London: Sage.

Howley, Kevin. 2010. *Understanding Community Media*. Los Angeles, CA: Sage.

Jackson, John Brinckerhoff. 1994. *A Sense of Place, A Sense of Time*. New Haven, CT: Yale University Press.

Kirby, Andrew. 1989 "A Sense of Place." *Critical Studies in Mass Communication* 6 (3): 322–325. doi:10.1080/15295038909366756.

Kurpius David D., Emily Metzgar, and Karen Rowley. 2010. "Sustaining Hyperlocal Media: In Search of Funding Models." *Journalism Studies* 11 (3): 359–376. doi:10.1080/146167 00903429787.

Lefebvre, Henri. 1991. *The Production of Space*. Oxford: Blackwell.

Lewis, Justin, Sanna Inthorn, and Karin Wahl-Jorgensen. 2005. *Citizens or Consumers? What the Media Tell Us About Political Participation*. Maidenhead: Open University Press.

Livingstone, Sonia, and Ellen Helsper. 2007. "Gradations in Digital Inclusion: Children, Young People and the Digital Divide." *New Media & Society* 9 (4): 671–696. doi:10.1177/1461444807080335.

Livingstone, Sonia, Elizabeth Van Couvering, and Nancy Thumim. 2008. *Adult Media Literacy*. London: Ofcom.

Marres, Noortje. 2007. "The Issues Deserve More Credit: Pragmatist Contributions to the Study of Public Involvement in Controversy." *Social Studies of Science* 37 (5): 759–780. doi:10.1177/0306312706077367.

Metzgar, Emily, David Kurpius, and Karen Rowley. 2011 "Defining Hyperlocal Media: Proposing a Framework for Discussion." *New Media & Society* 13 (5): 772–787. doi:10.1177/1461444810385095.

O'Connor, Alan. 2006. *Raymond Williams*. Lanham, MD: Rowman & Littlefield.

Örnebring, Henrik. 2009. "The Consumer as Producer – of What?: User-generated Tabloid Content in the The Sun (UK) and Aftonbladet (Sweden)." *The Future of Newspapers*. 142–156.

Park, Robert E. [1925] 1967. "The Natural History of the Newspaper." In *The City*, edited by Robert Ezra Park, E. W. Burgess, and Roderick Duncan McKenzie, 80–98. Chicago, IL: University of Chicago Press.

Peters, Chris, and Marcel Broersma. 2012. *Rethinking Journalism*. London: Routledge.

Picard, Robert G. 2003. "Cash Cows or Entrecôte: Publishing Companies and Disruptive Technologies." *Trends in Communication* 11 (2): 127–136. doi:10.1207/S15427439TC1102_04.

Picard, Robert G. 2008. "Shifts in Newspaper Advertising Expenditures and their Implications for the Future of Newspapers." *Journalism Studies* 9 (5): 704–716. doi:10.1080/14616700802207649.

Platon, Sarah, and Mark Deuze. 2003. "Indymedia Journalism: A Radical Way of Making, Selecting and Sharing News?" *Journalism* 4 (3): 336–355. doi:10.1177/14648849030043005.

Radcliffe, Damian. 2012. *Here and Now: UK Hyperlocal Media Today*. London: NESTA.

Rantanen, Terhi. 2009. *When News was New*. Chichester: Wiley-Blackwell.

Rebillard, Franck, and Annelise Touboul. 2010. "Promises Unfulfilled? 'Journalism 2.0', User Participation and Editorial Policy on Newspaper Websites." *Media, Culture and Society* 32 (2): 323–334. doi:10.1177/0163443709356142.

Rheingold, Howard. 2008. "Using Participatory Media and Public Voice to Encourage Civic Engagement." In *Civic Life Online: Learning How Digital Media Can Engage Youth*, edited by Lance W. Bennett, 97–118. Cambridge, MA: MIT.

Rodríguez, Clemencia. 2001. *Fissures in the Mediascape*. Cresskill, NJ: Hampton Press.

Rodríguez, Clemencia. 2011. *Citizens' Media against Armed Conflict*. Minneapolis, MN: University of Minnesota Press.

Rodgers, Scott, Clive Barnett, and Alan Cochrane. 2009. "Mediating Urban Politics." *International Journal of Urban and Regional Research* 33 (1): 246–249. doi:10.1111/j.1468-2427.2009.00845.x.

Rosen, Jay. 2006. "The People Formerly Known as the Audience." Accessed August 2, 2012. http://journalism.nyu.edu/pubzone/weblongs/pressthink/2006/06/27/ppl_frmr_p.html

Shirky, Clay. 2007. *Here Comes Everybody*. London: Penguin.

Van Dijck, José. 2009. "Users like you? Theorising Agency in User-generated Content." *Media Culture & Society* 31 (1): 41–58. doi:10.1177/0163443708098245.

Van Dijck, José, and David Nieborg. 2009. "Wikinomics and Its Discontents: A Critical Analysis of Web 2.0 Business Manifestos." *New Media & Society* 11 (5): 855–874. doi:10.1177/1461444809105356.

Wardle, Claire, and Andrew Williams. 2010. "Beyond User-generated Content: A Production Study Examining the Ways in which UGC is Used at the BBC." *Media, Culture and Society* 32 (5): 781–799. doi:10.1177/0163443710373953.

Watton, Eileen. 2009. "'The Contribution of Social Media to Community Empowerment and Regeneration': An Investigation of Peoples Voice Media's Community Reporters Programme." Salford: A report for PVM, University of Salford.

Wenger, Etienne. 1998. *Communities of Practice*. Cambridge: Cambridge University Press.
Williams, Raymond. 1983. *Cobbett*. Oxford: Oxford University Press.
Wilson, Teresa. 2012. *Community Reporting and Citizen Journalism*. Manchester: People's Voice Media, Institute of Community Reporters.

CITIZENS OF NOWHERE LAND
Youth and news consumption in Europe

Shakuntala Banaji and Bart Cammaerts

Injunctions for young people to participate in democratic life become more emphatic as voting rates in Western democracies decline and a growing disenchantment with traditional political life becomes apparent. In this context, city spaces and private property have been central to representations of the public sphere in which young people enact their participation. Crucially, young people have frequently been framed within televised spaces either as belligerent intruders or as a feral underclass. Theoretically, given the emphasis on information seeking, trust and news consumption as one of the cornerstones of civic life, the links between citizens' political, social and spatial positioning in relation to news products is of crucial importance. Via an analysis of experiences of news by diverse young citizens, the article decentres the technologies of watching or reading news and repositions the relationships between political news seeking, trust in journalism, meaning-making and socio-economic status within a framework of local experiences of politics and civic life. Crucially, it sheds light on the question of how groups of excluded youth conceptualise their own status in relation to the state, the nation and news media, and their critical comments about representation.

Introduction

A set of assumptions—from the neutrality of press and broadcast news to the centrality of news viewing in shaping civic values—tend to structure much research involving young people, news and political knowledge. Several of these assumptions involve notions of linear causality which place youth who neither seek nor consume news, or who do so in a highly critical manner, in deficit as citizens. Take, for instance, the idea that the consumption of print news presages more informed citizenship (Graber 1988; Chaffee and Yang 1990; Putnam 2001); or the conclusion that higher levels of trust in the polity and in the news media are linked to greater participation in adulthood (discussed by Amadeo, Torney-Purta, and Barber [2004] in their circle paper on youth and trust); or again, the belief that the news media, like the family and the school, are vehicles for positive (adult-approved) political socialisation. A few studies engage critically with these common assumptions, drawing attention to complicating factors such as young people's representation by the news (Wayne et al. 2008), their representation in politics or their involvement in the production of news or political stories (Buckingham 2000). Further research (Couldry, Livingstone, and Markham 2007; Carter 2008; Olsson and Dahlgren 2010) approaches these topics from the intersection of news reception, the social contexts of youth, and the embedding of politico-civic beliefs and identities via everyday contexts. This latter confluence of the everyday social and spatial contexts in which young people live and from which they develop their views on news, politics and citizenship, is the one at which our research departs in asking:

RQ1: How do life experiences, particularly spatial experiences of social disadvantage, exclusion or privilege inflect young people's material and symbolic news consumption patterns and their interpretations of mediated politics?

RQ2: How are young people's experiences of news—both spatial and interpretive—connected to their levels of trust in or critique of media and political institutions?

In answering these research questions, this article draws on original data gathered by the authors and their colleagues during two cross-national projects on young people, civic participation and media in Europe, which took place in the years 2006–2009 and 2011–2012. Before we delve into methodology and data, however, we theorise further the material and spatial aspects of news consumption and youth citizenship, and the link between these realms and wider issues of social class, technological access, civic mobilisation and media representation.

Youth, Spaces and Citizenship

One of the most important spaces where young people "learn" about citizenship, democracy and politics is the educational system. Gutmann (1987, 287) even goes as far as to claim that "'political education'—the cultivation of the virtues, knowledge and skills necessary for political participation—has moral primacy over other purposes of public education in a democratic society". Notwithstanding the personal relationships of care and mentoring which develop between many teachers and young people, the school remains a highly ideological space, primarily focused on the socialisation of young people through subtle and unsubtle disciplinary techniques. Although there have been attempts in some countries to liberalise a citizenship curriculum, noted educationists have argued that many schools damage young people's citizenship and life chances, leaving them scarred by psychic or physical violence and/or failing to provide them with the basic resources to construct and inhabit a peaceful, democratic society (Harber 2004, 2008).

School is by no means the only space where lessons about democracy and dutiful citizenship are learnt. Churches, the family, political parties, old social movements such as trade unions and communication systems have all been identified as spaces through which social values and beliefs convenient to ruling elites are reproduced, but also as spaces where (class) struggle may be situated (Althusser 1971, 143–147; Pateman 1972). In other words, these institutions and spaces can be also reclaimed or contested. Civic spaces and collectivities such as community centres, youth movements or new social movements have gained importance in terms of young people's democratic learning (Thomas 1994; Roker, Player, and Coleman 1999; Alexander 2008; Ginwright and Cammarota 2007; Valentine and Skelton 2007).

All this speaks to a common critique voiced in the late 1980s, which to an extent is being addressed in scholarship today, namely the undervaluation of everyday contexts in relation to democracy, participation, and the building of civic values and cultures (Pateman 1989; de Certeau 1988). de Certeau's work is particularly interesting in this regard as he argues that the mundane and the everyday play a pivotal role in the various practices and performances (or strategies and tactics) that we develop to comply and to resist. In line with this framework, Catherine Alexander's (2008, 182–185) work with deprived youth in Northern England speaks poignantly to the importance of everyday class politics and locality in the development of youth civic identities. Young people from different class backgrounds have differential access to, and expectations of, both immediate physical localities and the notional spaces of politics and civic life such as news rooms or parliament.

When scrutinised through the lens of age, the linking of democratic culture to the everyday lives of young people reveals further problematics. Hava Gordon's (2010, 5–7) work with young activists mobilising for social movements inside and outside schools demonstrates palpably that "age is an axis of inequality", not just a "socially constructed" or "biological category". Age is also linked, she argues, to greater or lesser access to public and private space and, in particular, to space that is unsurveilled (by adults as well as the state). The overlap between age and social class can thus be seen as a key axis of power in both geographical and political spaces of agenda setting, representation and news consumption.

If we conceptualise representation as the depiction of, giving voice to or advocacy on behalf of individuals and social groups, age and class are linked to differential access to and power within the representational space of conventional news. At the intersection of age, class and gender, young women's citizenship is often constructed as being bound within "safe" domestic spaces and offline spaces more than young men's; and, for working-class youth in under-funded schools, access to places of discussion, news interchange, mobilisation and conflict are extremely circumscribed. Saliently, Gordon's work emphasises the centrality of mainstream media representations of young people as "citizens-in-waiting", and in particular the impact of news attention for youth protests on young people. Her data suggest that young activists learn that to get coverage for their causes in the mainstream national news, they should disguise, curtail or simplify aspects of their struggles for social change (Gordon 2010, 160–162). As we show in our discussions of data, some youth experience increasing levels of political efficacy via enhanced access to news-making and consumption through technology, and state representatives. Others are deprived of control over their daily activities within physical spaces/localities and over media representations of their actions, localities and identities. While it seems almost banal to suggest that with distance and exclusion may come greater scope for cynicism, avoidance and critique, paying attention to such contingencies as homelessness, addiction, incarceration and constant misrepresentation or political activism leads to greater understanding of the divergent circumstances in which political and civic efficacy are rooted, and against the backdrop of which news narratives unfurl. At the heart of these discussions lies the notion that "citizenship" is experienced differentially based on factors such as age, education, gender and social class.

Of course, citizenship is a highly normative concept that is often used to denote the nature of the relationship between individuals and the state, the latter being understood as geographically bounded. So, while citizenship traditionally refers to a set of rights and obligations (Esping-Andersen 1990; Etzioni 1993), it is as much about enforcing boundaries, and thus a device for continuing exclusion of "The Other" and a denial of difference. Citizens are allocated specific rights and prerogatives by the state which "others"—i.e. foreigners, migrants, prisoners, etc.—may not have. In response to processes of globalisation, regional integration (i.e. the European Union), the emergence of international information and communication networks, increased degrees of mobility amongst some classes, and new migration patterns amongst others, traditional nation state-bounded notions of citizenship have been challenged at a variety of levels giving rise to notions of what is sometimes called "unbounded" citizenship (Cammaerts 2007, 2). Illustrative in this regard is the emergence of phrases such as cultural citizenship, ecological citizenship, netizenship, transnational citizenship or cosmopolitan citizenship (van Steenbergen 1994; Bauböck 1994; Hauben 1995; Hartley 1999), all transcending the individual and collective rights focus inherent to conceptualisations of "bounded" nation state citizenship. Hermes (1998, 159) speaks to this shift when she redefines citizenship as:

> sets (plural) of practices that constitute individuals as competent members of sets of different and sometimes overlapping communities, one of which should ideally constitute the national (political) culture.

Hermes' work on cultural citizenship, like Gordon's, brings media, news production and the internet to the foreground as important spaces for learning about democracy and citizenship. Young people are often portrayed as being generally apathetic when it comes to political news, but, we suggest, behind this accusation lies a complex relationship of mistrust, which may sometimes lead to increased civic engagement. In the next section, the relationship between young people, news media and levels of trust will be unpacked further.

Youth, News Media and (Lack of) Trust

News representation and reception are increasingly being seen as a crucial part of citizenship and of democracy. As Urry (1999, 318) pointedly asserts: "[c]itizenship has always necessitated symbolic resources distributed through various means of mass communication". However, this is not only relevant at a discursive/symbolic level of analysis, but as much at the level of everyday practices and performances and in the way in which media and news consumption fit (or fail to fit) into this everyday context. Bausinger (1984, 349) writes of the ways in which media and news consumption are intertwined with and influenced by "non-media related forms of behaviour". Further, news is also the object of much interpersonal communication in the everyday, between peers, between generations and between genders (Buckingham 2000; Noor 2008).

In relation to young people, media use and news consumption, we highlight three particular strands of research relevant to the argument developed here:

1. Those that focus on representation and framing.
2. Those that examine reception, and the theoretical nexus of news with consumption, values and beliefs.
3. Those that examine the interplay of reception and representation at the specific level of everyday life, charting shifts in news engagement, efficacy and political trust for particular spatially bounded communities of young people.

Media organisations, journalism and news production are contentious fields. They hold high degrees of symbolic, discursive and political power in society, which they do not always use to the benefit of society, leading to serious issues of (mis)trust (O'Neill 2002). From a critical tradition, the media, and journalism, has been seen at worst to fail and at best to contribute erratically in fulfilling normative ideals of objectivity, criticality and the protection of citizen interests. Media are "not neutral unselective recorders of events" (Oliver and Maney 2000, 464) and what is presented as neutral reporting is more often "an array of codes and practices which effectively rest upon a cultural imperative to hear the causes of disputes in one way rather than another" (Eldridge 1995, 212).

Although, as Cottle and Rai (2006) argue, the structured selection of communicative frames by journalists is not always implicated in processes of domination, this ideological bias can frequently be observed in the way mainstream media represents young people and protest. Studies attempting to ascertain how news media represent young people or protest conclude that young people are predominantly represented in negative ways as either unruly/immature, as victims or as criminals (Gitlin 1980; Banaji 2008; Wayne et al. 2008). It has to be noted, however, that as Wayne et al. (2008, 75) argue "the construction of young people as a 'problem'" dates back to the eighteenth century and increases or decreases in conjunction with other social and political changes and tensions. We could also refer here to the seminal work of Cohen (1972) in relation to youth subcultures, discussing how society, and media in particular, tends to construct folk devils, thereby inducing moral panics vis-à-vis youth culture. However, Wayne et al. (2008, 75) contend that "the sense of threat around media representations of young people has arguably become less ... restricted to subcultures of youth and increasingly prevalent across the category of youth itself". This sense of the increasing anxieties and tensions attendant on being young in Europe today is one of the central themes which will be seen to emerge from our data on young people, place, politics and news.

A number of studies have also examined the manner and implications of young people's political news encounters in an increasingly mediated and technologically innovative environment (Al-Ghabban 2008; Franssen and Daems 2010; Kahne et al. 2012). They confirm a shift away from traditional print media towards (satellite) television and online sources but take different views of the way in which this might play out in relation to citizenship and civic identity in local spaces and contexts. In general, these qualitative studies suggest that reliance on a diversity of sources can have a positive impact on political engagement, and exposure to snippets of contrasting information and ideology can lead to further information seeking.

It does appear, however, that for some researchers age remains an important determinant of being disconnected from news (cf. Blekesaune, Elvestad, and Aalberg 2012, 117). In this regard, what is considered to be news and how the impact of this "disconnection" is being assessed also matters. We draw attention to a problematic normative distinction which is constructed between fun/play, on the one hand, and civic engagement, on the other, whereby the former is dismissed as a distraction and the latter positioned as a serious worthwhile activity (Putnam 2001; Shah, McLeod, and So-Hyang 2001, 472). However, numerous studies have pointed out that for young people entertainment shows are a source of political news and instrumental in their political development (Barnhurst 1998; Calavita 2004). This also leads Buckingham (2000, 210) to conclude that we need to rethink "what is seen to count as news in the first place". Buckingham's study indicates the high degree of self-reflexiveness of young people, and their criticality, which shows itself in critiques of commodification, spin, sensationalism and lack of media content relevant to their interests and life-worlds.

Perhaps as a result of this reflexivity about news, the attitudes of young people towards the news media are sometimes fairly negative. Their low levels of trust in the news media may be seen as a response to the media's lack of objectivity and balance in reporting on young people and on democracy. Barnett (2008, 5), for instance, points out that this distrust is in line with rising distrust in other institutions, but maintains that journalism bears a specific responsibility in a democracy. Our own original data suggest that on average more than 60 per cent of young people from the age of 17–30 distrust the media. In the United Kingdom, this figure rises to a whopping 85 per cent (based on a re-analysis of the European Social Survey 2008 wave, Education, Audiovisual and Culture Executive Agency (EACEA) 2013). In what follows, after discussing our methodology and sample, we will assess the news consumption of young people, and their thoughts on political news and journalism in the context of the focus on representation, space, locality and trust emerging above.

Methodology, Data Gathering and Sampling

This article examines original data gathered on two distinct European projects. The first involves data from the FP6 European Commission-funded project "CivicWeb: Young People, the Internet and Civic Participation" (www.civicweb.eu), gathered by Banaji in the United Kingdom and colleagues in Turkey, the Netherlands, Slovenia, Hungary, Sweden and Spain between 2006 and 2009. CivicWeb involved in-depth focus groups with 70 cohorts of young people aged 15–25 drawn from a spectrum of activist and inactive; urban and rural; elite, average and socio-economically precarious groups, about their political and civic participation and efficacy on- and offline. The second, led by Cammaerts, Banaji, Bruter, Harrison and Anstead, discusses accounts of news viewing given by three groups of young citizens—heuristically named "excluded", "active" and "average"—in Austria, Finland, France, Hungary, Spain and the United Kingdom in early 2012 for the European Commission/EACEA study, "Young People and Democratic Life in Europe". While our knowledge that the heuristic categories of "active", "average" and "excluded" do not comfortably fit young people's political identities or social roots—something confirmed poignantly by discussions of acts of citizenship in school groups, critiques of politics and policy by "excluded" youth, and accounts of overcoming social disadvantage by "activist" youth—the categories also appeared to be ones understood and used by young people themselves in relation either to their family backgrounds or to their levels of political engagement. The key foci of these projects was the changing relationship between young people, democracy, media and technologies, and the groupings aimed to tease out reasons for similarities and divergences between and within high, middle and precarious socio-economic groups of youth in these regards.

The accounts generated are particularly salient here in relation to the geographic and class contexts of the young people, their own positioning in civic and mediated spaces *vis-à-vis* their positioning by adults and authorities, and the tensions revealed in these accounts. Both projects used a mixture of quantitative and qualitative methods and data, including original surveys involving questions about news and civic participation. The strand on which this paper primarily calls is the qualitative group interviews that allowed for a more nuanced discussion of issues of individual experience, trust and efficacy within particular social groups, while allowing for disagreement and challenge over the course of sometimes two- to four-hour long discussions. For the CivicWeb project, participants ranged from young political party cadres, students' union activists and high-income medical students through students in non-elite schools to youth in care or returning from encounters with the criminal justice system. To add contextual depth, excerpts used here are drawn from UK focus groups. For the more time-limited EACEA project, the "average groups" were drawn from local high schools or colleges with a non-selective social class intake. The "activist" groups consisted of civically active youth of various economic backgrounds and political persuasions from grassroots organisations, political parties, social movements or charities. Meanwhile, the diverse groups labelled "excluded" consisted of those in care, experiencing homelessness or prison sentences, young single mothers or carers in low-income situations, or those suffering mental illness, addiction and long-term unemployment outside stable family situations. Given that "excluded" groups are often under-researched because access to them is difficult, and because this particular group encounters very specific issues in their everyday lives, we treat this group separately in our analysis of empirical data. We remunerated young people for participation in the interviews, and maintained anonymity by changing names and salient details. Finally, given the sensitivity of discussions about local riots, for instance, or anti-fascist mobilisations with some of the groups, we endeavoured to be well informed about local political contexts prior to discussions.

This article pays particular attention to the connections between young people's experiences of news in relation to specific spatial, geographic, technological and political contexts, be these deprived inner cities, the countryside, homelessness, online or offline. Following manual coding, chunks of focus group data were extracted from the longer transcripts and categorised thematically in relation to: news consumption; access to news and the political sphere; orientations towards institutional politics and politicians; responses to mediated representations of young people; participation in and responses to depictions of non-traditional political activism; and news representations of spaces and places of civic life. In the following sections, these thematic excerpts are organised and presented in relation to the "activist", "average" or "excluded" groups from which they are drawn, and analysed with a view to understanding how particular geographical and spatial contexts intersect with social class and exclusion in inflecting youth responses to news about politics, youth and also local neighbourhoods.

Young People's Experiences of and Views on Political News in Europe

As outlined in the theoretical sections, the key concerns of this article are, first, how experiences of social disadvantage, exclusion or privilege inflect young people's physical and symbolic news consumption patterns and their interpretations of mediated politics and, second, how young people's spatial and interpretive encounters with news are connected to their levels of trust in or critique of media and political institutions. We begin this section with a summary of the main patterns observed across the data in relation to experiences of and attitudes to news in our sample. Selected points will be elaborated via attention to verbatim quotes, but our aim in this paper is primarily to cut across the sample to reveal and illuminate particular patterns. In the second half of this section, we home in on the views and experiences of "excluded" young people from different countries and walks of life in an attempt to clarify their particular concerns about news and its relationship to lived experiences of democracy.

Active Youth

Amongst civically and politically active and/or highly educated groups of young people in the age range 17–25, a proliferation of news sources and media sources is evident alongside new technological ubiquity, high levels of physical mobility through cities and generally personalised consumption of news in different spaces and places. Internet use for information seeking with regard to politics amongst these young people was steadily high in the focus groups taking place between 2008 and 2009, with some notable exceptions for activists working in deprived communities, and ubiquitously high in 2012:

> C: I use the internet all the time for news, mainly check *Telegraph* (paper version when I'm at home), *Washington Post*, then two blogs that I rely on. I also go to see what the enemy is up to—so I've read *Guardian online*, and even socialist papers.
>
> R: *Medicin Sans Frontier* website, *The Times* and *New York Times*, all online, but also watch the BBC and go to their homepage. I make factual comments and post opinion pieces too.
>
> A: Recently *Al-Jazeera* and *Al-Jazeera English*. I switch constantly, sometimes even within the same story, and I want to see what other sources say about it. We also put out our online newsletter for our [student organisation]. (High-income students, aged 20–21, UK, CivicWeb, 2009)
>
> For me, programmes that deal with topics more specifically are more exciting than this overview [available through traditional news on TV] because I can procure the overview on my own through the internet. (P, Active youth, Austria, EACEA, 2012)

Differentiating high-income young people, and activist youth regardless of their socio-economic background, from other socio-economic and politically non-active groups, these narratives and discussions reveal both a plethora of choices in relation to the spaces in which to consume news and increasing non-reliance on single mainstream news sources and outlets. In focus groups, this was evident in the amount of time devoted to discussions of technologies of access and news sources by average and active groups, while, as will be seen in the following section, excluded groups tended to move swiftly to discussions of representation on specific news outlets. For many interviewees in the activist and higher socio-economic category, this spatial cutting between channels and media is accompanied by critical and generally politicised online information seeking as well as political information promotion via newsletters, group emails, Facebook or Hyves groups, social media memes and symbols, personal or civic websites, and Twitter. Much political news is sought in this group, and most of it is experienced individually—often via online newspapers and the internet or documentaries and 24-hour news channels on satellite but is discussed with colleagues, friends, family or fellow activists on a regular basis. For the most part this brings with it a sense of being able to shape the news agenda; in about a third of cases it reinforces an awareness of the difficulty of shaping the mainstream news agenda, particularly with regard to young people and political causes, or austerity and other social issues facing young people in general and specific groups:

> I: With your Facebook profile, it's more about making people aware of the kind of situations that are happening in the world because with Facebook even if somebody's not watched the news they're going to realise when they see all these people changing their profile picture to the Palestinian flag that something's happening in the world.
>
> K: We diffuse! We are distributing tracts following the news. We are doing it all together during the weekend, it's nicer. (Young volunteers, CivicWeb, 2009)

[T]his morning we had street interviews, and we are going to make a video with it and post in our website ... We've got a website and accounts on Facebook and Twitter. In our personal [Facebook accounts] we also publish things. (M, Active youth, France, EACEA, 2012)

However, amongst this group we also witnessed frustration about having only a closed circle in social networks and hence ideological limitations of news gathered or disseminated via these:

Despite the good aspects I think the Facebook balloon has already popped. It's already obvious that after a while it becomes just as closed a system. You get the input from your acquaintances, your stuff reaches your acquaintances, after a while you ban those with whom you disagree or you're banned, and if you post something on Facebook and it reaches 10,000 people it will never reach the other 10,000. (D, Active youth, Hungary, EACEA, 2012)

Further analysis of transcripts reveals that activists at either end of the political spectrum are highly sensitive to the ideological opinions and biases prevalent in particular news sources and feel either confidence and ease, cynicism or profound discomfort when dealing with the most common news sources. Their comments suggest that they give more weight to social causes and to national or global news as opposed to hearsay, infotainment and sensational stories. Unsurprisingly, given the ideological heterogeneity of these youth, fractures open along ideological lines, with more elite and establishment-oriented activists suggesting they are often dedicated followers of particular mainstream sources and having high levels of trust in political parties, whereas others who are equally engaged display high levels of scepticism both about news agendas and about institutional politics in general.

Average Youth

Countering anxieties about a steady lessening of interest in political news amongst young people from non-elite backgrounds, our discussions with young people attending schools and colleges in non-elite neighbourhoods reveal high levels of interest in national and local events, informed scepticism about politicians' decisions, as well as generally accurate information about proposed changes to laws and economic systems that will have a direct impact on young people's lives. All of this knowledge is underpinned by news:

S: I'm more confident about documentaries and Q and A sessions with politicians where the general public's involved.

R: Best thing is to watch lots of different sources, not just one source. (Average youth, UK, EACEA, 2012)

Amongst these groups we noticed a tendency to favour snippets of news or even extended stories gleaned via social media sources and encountered online either alone or discussed with friends:

N: Facebook is huge for getting information. And Twitter too.

S: Podcasts are the best way to learn about things. Listening to different podcasts from different countries lets you see different views. That's better than just mainstream news.

R: This generation wants lots of different information from different sources. Different ways of learning are needed. (Average youth, UK, EACEA, 2012)

The findings of Holt et al. (2013, 31–32) about overall interest in political news remaining similar regardless of how the news is accessed are borne out by our data. The thoughtful comments in many of our "average" focus groups suggest that young people can be critical about interpreting old and new media sources:

T: Twitter means that you can say what you want and people can just believe. But the danger is that it can be completely false, so you've got to be good at reading it. Social networking helps us be more sceptical too. We learn not to trust it all and that's good.

G: Everyone knows that you have to be careful about how you interpret the news. You just know it's biased in someone's favour.

F: I actually believe my local newspaper more because you actually live there so you can judge how true they're being about what's going on. (Average youth, UK, EACEA, 2012)

These pedagogic and experiential emphases by young people in our "average" groups are indicative of one strand of young people's critical engagement with news, whatever the technology of access. Attention to local rather than national news sources can enhance civic and political efficacy and make the "daunting" sphere of national politics seem more approachable (Moy et al. 2004). F's comment that she has trust in her local newspaper because she can actually use her own experience to test their reporting of events and issues seems to bear out this assessment. It is highly salient because it suggests that it is not printed newspapers *per se* which do not appeal to young people but the distanced tone and ideologically biased or selective content of some national newspapers that may be alienating. What we also see developing, therefore, through analyses of the news consumption of both activist and average groups of youth, is a consistent attitude towards news content regardless of the spaces or tools of news consumption. Although de-territorialised spaces online or international channels on television may be increasingly where news is sought and encountered, the local or regional spaces known well by young people, rather than the national or global sphere, retain greater salience in terms of engagement. Thus attempts to displace onto technology or the medium *per se* blame for youth disengagement or dissatisfaction with politics and news media are disingenuous or at best naïve. This is confirmed by complaints across most groups of interviewees, except those from the socio-economic elites, about the demonisation of young people by national television news and mainstream national newspapers, and a growing anxiety about the side effects of such anti-youth discourse on their quality of life in particular geographical localities.

Excluded Youth, Spaces and News Media

The excluded groups in our sample were characterised by features which mapped neatly on to the empty spaces left by the elite, highly educated and/or activist young people in previous groups but overlap in places with the experiences of average groups.

Apart from young refugees and asylum seekers, and those who had entered the criminal justice system, many displayed low mobility in spatial and social terms, some having never left the section of the village, town or city in which they were born. As with Alexander's (2008) study, many demonstrated high levels of loyalty to their localities, neighbourhoods, municipalities, housing estates and/or boroughs rather than to cities, towns or the country as a whole. This group was additionally consistently more conscious than peers in other groups about social class and prejudice amongst the polity, the judiciary, the media and the "rest of society".

We include extended extracts to give a flavour of the ways in which conditions of political, economic and/or social exclusion intersect with the idea of "trust" in traditional civic authority and media:

> S: I think community is gone. They took away all the community centres, and all the youth clubs been taken away and all the services ... Community's been broken down. And now it's basically just people hanging around the streets. Trying to eat. Trying to survive.
>
> R: The more people, the more you get people saying "my mum can't afford me trainers".
>
> [Long silence]
>
> S: TV is controlled. The media is controlled. Everything's—anything political—got to be passed by the House [of Commons]...
>
> K: They approve information before they give it out ... the media's just a lie. They tell you what they want you to hear.
>
> T: They tell you about war and stuff but, lies ... I don't believe...
>
> S: The only news that I trust is internet news channels ... Worldwide ones. I'd rather watch some random news channel ... They're more likely to tell the truth ... if you get other channels, ones where government don't police it ... from abroad ... you get different information from the channels here. Here, there's so much they won't show you in the news... (Excluded youth, UK, EACEA, 2012)

Here, general scepticism about political control of the media has percolated through young people across all the different social categories and life circumstances. The lack of trust in mainstream media displayed by some of the socially active and politically leftwing young people earlier in this section is mirrored by the distrust and sense of political manipulation evident in this excerpt.

Indeed, the idea that national news channels are less likely to "tell the truth" about the nation than random foreign channels or internet sites or blogs was repeated in different formulations by several focus groups in all countries but was most starkly evident in the United Kingdom and Hungary. Furthermore, anxieties about the representation of youth on the news, shared with other groups, were compounded, for some, by anxieties about the effects of particular intersections of news stereotypes on their local areas and on the young people in those are as:

> P: ...I think there's too much killing of teenagers on the news and there's too much bad things happening to teenagers, they need like work.

B: On the news it brings up stuff about the economy and things I've read and things like when people gets hurt and stuff, they don't bring up the necessary things that [young] people are to be aware of.

C: People feel Moss Side is bad because they see guns, they see boys on bikes, they see all these boys and they don't ... but ... if you actually move in Moss Side and ... see what Moss Side is like, you would have a totally different opinion [People who have no idea of what a place is like] should keep their mouths shut. Just shut up. The television and newspapers for example. They think they can drive by in their cars and understand what's going on. No, oh, no ... [W]hen a black person gets shot or something on the news they say it's always got to do with drugs, or sometimes with guns... (Manchester, 15-year-olds, accessing the internet at a local library, CivicWeb, 2009)

In this extended excerpt we see clearly the relationship of news to place and space in the lives of young people from deprived neighbourhoods. Mainstream news media's fascination with youth crime and its emphasis on youth as victims or aggressors has been conclusively documented via content analysis (Wayne et al. 2008). It therefore becomes apparent that the expressions of frustration, anger and critique by the group of teenagers quoted above fall into the category of legitimate grievance and ideological critique. In other words, they identify recurrent biases against their age group, their locality, their race and their class in some news content, all compounded by their sense of the class position of the journalists. For instance, C's comment above stating that "[t]hey think they can drive by in their cars and just understand what's going on".

While young people in very deprived areas but in stable housing situations often have little internet access and low print media consumption, they generally tend to watch television on a regular basis, including television news. However, our data also show more extreme cases of media deprivation across Europe, a number of young people who almost never have unfettered access to the news unless the newspapers are left for free on trains and buses. Some have no access to television except in ambient areas, lobbies, train stations or shop windows. This was brought home to us by several discussions with young people in prisons or temporary accommodation or homeless shelters, such as this one in Hungary:

P: I don't know when the last time was that I'd watched the news. I don't listen to the radio. I don't know what's going on in the world. I sometimes stop at a shop window where they have a television set on display, but there's no sound ... I don't know about the catastrophes, about the good things that are happening.

N: Neither do I.

V: When I still had a job, back in Szombathely, I was interested in politics, I watched the news every night, I still had some interest in me ... but since there's no work ... I don't even remember watching TV. (Homeless, Hungary, EACEA, 2012)

The sense of exclusion and disenfranchisement harboured by many youth in excluded groups because of their economic situations appears to be ameliorated in circumstances where they can still access news about politicians and politics. Time and again it was made clear to us that it was lack of access rather than lack of interest which constrained news seeking in these extremely disadvantaged groups:

> O: I read a lot on internet, I don't like TV ... I read *Le Parisien*.
>
> N: Me too, I prefer reading little articles that are synthesis.
>
> J: I'm not looking at anything anymore. Because I can't really access internet. I try to go on Facebook but... (Excluded group, France, EACEA, 2012)

It is possible to take from these discussions several crucial points. First, with extremely low media access the salience of free newspapers rises exponentially. We were reminded of this poignantly in discussions in Austria, Finland and the United Kingdom with young people who either critically or favourably noted the tendency to social conservatism or even extreme rightwing sentiments in commuter newspapers. Some participants put this into the very local contexts of xenophobia that they now experience on a regular basis:

> A lot of agitation against foreigners stems from newspapers such as *Heute* or *Österreich* [free, highly circulated tabloids]. They write "The Turk (...), the Bosnian (...) killed (...)." If it is an Austrian, they only write "Andreas D. killed (...)". (F, Average group, Austria, EACEA, 2012)

Second, the previous discussion emphasises the fact that constant difficulties in daily life and lack of access to news can have a devastating impact on interest and efficacy with regard to national and local politics. Finally, regardless of a spatial locality's deprivation and stigmatisation in mainstream news, we noticed a high level of local loyalty, even pride, amongst some sections of excluded youth, alongside a wish for counter-representation.

This desire for better and more balanced representation was not matched by access to literacy, to political representation or to technology. In fact, we were told that, amongst other factors, such lack of access leads to high levels of frustration, anger and depression. It is apparent to us that low technological access, particularly to television and free broadband amongst already economically or spatially insecure young people leads to a spiral of *lack of interest* and *lack of engagement* with details of news and politics, a lower intention to vote and less sense of civic efficacy. In a 1997 paper on news and cultural citizenship, Buckingham (1997, 358) writes that:

> young people's uses and interpretations of news indicate that they do not simply adopt the position of the dutiful seeker of information or the deferential good citizen ... Their sense of exclusion and alienation from the adult sphere of political debate connects with a more general perception of their own powerlessness, to which a stance of boredom and deliberate ignorance may well represent a reasonable response.

Our data bear this argument out to a certain extent. We encountered numerous young people who did not sit down at home to read or watch the news, did not consider it with identical gravitas to parents and grandparents, and did not trust it as much as the makers of news would wish. Many also used personal and collective experiences to challenge and question news frames and agendas in relation to young people and local areas.

However, while engaged critique and cynicism were commonplace, complete disconnection was relatively uncommon. In fact, many of the young people we interviewed, wherever and however they engaged with national or local news agendas, did so in highly civic and/or political ways, contesting or supporting stereotypes of immigrants, ethnic minorities and youth, speaking in favour of their local communities and questioning the effects of national government economic and social policies. Only those whose stake in everyday life had been lowered through harsh social circumstances and whose opportunities to encounter news were highly circumscribed displayed a significant loss of interest in news and in politics conveyed via news.

Conclusions

Despite much nuanced and critical work in political science differentiating between normative and descriptive accounts of citizenship, there remains a crude and unjustified cluster of normative assumptions pervading some much-cited discussions of news and citizenship (cf. Putnam 2001; Galston 2004): that all citizens are equal, live how they wish to live and are equally powerful actors in the public sphere should they only choose to be, that the polity and the mainstream media are in the main unbiased and act in good faith, and that democracy works as it ought to in an ideal world. Our data tell a different story.

While it is undeniable that repeated quantitative studies suggest a decline in young people's engagement with formal political processes in Europe, many young people in our sample appear interested in politics. They engage with the world around them, specifically in relation to their local communities, leisure spaces (or lack thereof), schools, employment and housing prospects, and entry into adult life. This interest and indeed engagement is a feature common across nation, gender, ethnicity and class in our focus groups. However, in terms of physical and psychological access to political power, technology, the means of representation (both of themselves as a group, and of themselves as individual citizens) and even to the basic amenities of everyday life, there are huge and growing divergences. We have highlighted some of these in our paper.

In answering the first research question set out at the beginning of this paper, we found that factors such as economic status, geographical locality, proximity to political power and age are all axes for equality and inequality and strongly inflect the places and spaces of news reception as well as responses to news agendas on civic and political issues. The results of our analysis challenge several repeated fallacies about youth and news. The internet is not yet the sole or even the major source for young people's political information seeking, although it appears to be gaining ground amongst highly educated and/or highly civically active groups. However, while television remains the medium that young people refer to most often, it is also not a generally trusted source. Further, although factual news remains a key source of political information, humorous content, blogs, discussion forums on leisure sites and YouTube videos are repeatedly invoked as arenas for political debate and learning. Indeed, *a diversity of sources and formats as a desirable way of experiencing political news* is evident across all social groups of young people in our sample, and even named as a *prerequisite for informed citizenship by some*.

Meanwhile, it is also evident from our data that consuming lots of news and living in a high-income social group may be linked to less understanding of civic issues in other groups, and a more mechanistic conceptualisation of politics and the civic sphere. Thus life experience and the concomitant political values, rather than news consumption *per se*, play a major role in forming civic identities. In this regard and answering our second research question about the links between experiences of news representation and trust in news, our research sharply problematises evaluations which link higher "trust" in news media to good citizenship. Those youth who are most pathologised by news and who perceive themselves as being negatively represented both personally and via association with a particularly deprived or stigmatised locality or cultural space, are also most likely to have negative views about the news; i.e. the ones excluded from or demonised by the political system are also highly likely to show disaffection and critique in relation to news about politicians. These responses are *elements of, rather than counter to, engaged citizenship*.

Finally, we need to consider more closely what the impact of all this is on the sense of citizenship of young people and certainly those that come from disadvantaged backgrounds and/or those who are increasingly vocal about the way democracy and liberal mainstream media fails them. At the same time, our data also show that many *young people are critical rather than apathetic*. So while many young people from various backgrounds express disconnection from and are highly critical of political elites (including journalists), they are also politicised and have clear views and opinions about politics, policy and about the media. In fact, we argue that their at times *stringent critique towards the news media and journalism is a sign not of apathy, but of a heightened sense of critical citizenship*. From this perspective we should ask ourselves the question of how and in what ways can traditional news media and journalism build young people's trust?

ACKNOWLEDGEMENTS

We would like to thank our respective funders on the two projects, the European Commission and the European Audiovisual and Education Agency (EACEA) for enabling us to gather the data used here, and David Buckingham, the project director for CivicWeb. We thank also the EACEA project researchers, Eri Bertsou, Maria Pini, Emmanuelle Reungoat, Itir Akdogan, Judit Szakacs, Magdalena Schmidberger, Anna Clua and Melanie Pichler, for their meticulous focus groups and translations. We are hugely indebted to all the young people who volunteered their time and contributed to the focus groups on both projects.

REFERENCES

Alexander, Catherine Louise. 2008. "Safety, Fear and Belonging: The Everyday Realities of Civic Identity Formation in Fenham." *ACME: An International E-Journal for Critical Geographies* 7 (2): 173–198.

Al-Ghabban, Ammar. 2008. "Global Viewing in East London: Multi-ethnic Youth Responses to Television News." *European Journal of Cultural Studies* 10 (3): 311–326. doi:10.1177/1367549407079704.

Althusser, Louis. 1971. "Ideology and Ideological State Apparatuses: Notes toward an Investigation." In *Lenin and Philosophy and Other Essays*. Translated by Ben Brewster, edited by Louis Althusser, 127–188. New York, NY: Monthly Review Press.

Amadeo, Jo-Ann, Judith Torney-Purta, and Carolyn Henry Barber. 2004. "Attention to Media and Trust in Media Sources: Analysis of Data from the IEA Civic Education Study." College Park, MD: CIRCLE The Center for Information & Research on Civic Learning & Engagement FACT SHEET, January.

Banaji, Shakuntala. 2008. "The Trouble with Civic: A Snapshot of Young People's Civic and Political Engagements in Twenty-First-Century Democracies." *Journal of Youth Studies* 11 (5): 543–560. doi:10.1080/13676260802283008.

Barnett, Steven. 2008. "On the Road to Self-destruction." *British Journalism Review* 19 (2): 5–13. doi:10.1177/0956474808094193.

Barnhurst, Kevin G. 1998. "Politics in the Fine Meshes: Young Citizens, Power, and Media." *Media, Culture & Society* 20 (2): 201–218. doi:10.1177/016344398020002003.

Bauböck, Rainer. 1994. *Transnational Citizenship*. Aldershot: Edward Elgar.

Bausinger, Hermann. 1984. "Media, Technology and Everyday Life." *Media, Culture and Society* 6 (4): 343–351. doi:10.1177/016344378400600403.

Blekesaune, Arild, Eiri Elvestad, and Toril Aalberg. 2012. "Tuning out the World of News and Current Affairs—An Empirical Study of Europe's Disconnected Citizens." *European Sociological Review* 28 (1): 110–126. doi:10.1093/esr/jcq051.

Buckingham, David. 1997. "News Media, Political Socialization and Popular Citizenship: Towards a New Agenda." *Critical Studies in Mass Communication* 14 (4): 344–366. doi:10.1080/15295039709367023.

Buckingham, David. 2000. *The Making of Citizens: Young People, News and Politics*. London: Routledge.

Calavita, Marco. 2004. "Idealization, Inspiration, Irony: Popular Communication Tastes and Practices in the Individual Political Development of Generation X'ers." *Popular Communication* 2 (3): 129–151. doi:10.1207/s15405710pc0203_1.

Cammaerts, Bart. 2007. "Citizenship, the Public Sphere and Media." In *Reclaiming the Media: Communication Rights and Democratic Media Roles*, edited by Bart Cammaerts and Nico Carpentier, 1–8. Bristol: Intellect.

Carter, Cynthia. 2008. "Growing up Corporate: News, Citizenship, and Young People Today." *Television New Media* 10 (1): 34–36. doi:10.1177/1527476408325733.

Chaffee, Steven H., and Seung-Mock Yang. 1990. "Communication and Political Socialisation." In *Political Socialisation, Citizenship Education and Democracy*, edited by Orit Ichilov, 137–157. New York: Teachers College Press.

Cohen, Stanley. 1972. *Folk Devils and Moral Panics: The Creation of the Mods and Rockers*. St Albans: Paladin.

Cottle, Simon, and Mugdha Rai. 2006. "Between Display and Deliberation: Analyzing TV News as Communicative Architecture." *Media, Culture and Society* 28 (2): 163–189. doi:10.1177/0163443706061680.

Couldry, Nick, Sonia Livingstone, and Tim Markham. 2007. *Media Consumption and Public Engagement: Beyond the Presumption of* Attention. Basingstoke: Palgrave Macmillan.

de Certeau, Michel. 1988. *The Practice of Everyday Life*. Berkeley: University of California Press.

Eldridge, John. 1995. *Glasgow Media Group Reader, Volume One: News Content, Language and Visuals*. London: Routledge.

Esping-Andersen, Gøsta. 1990. *The Three Worlds of Welfare Capitalism*. Cambridge: Polity Press.

Etzioni, Amitai. 1993. *The Spirit of* Community. New York: Crown.

Franssen, Vicky, and Annet Daems. 2010. "Reflections on the New Peer News Paradigm as Exploited by Youngsters: The Influence of Sex, Educational Level and Type on News Participation, Seeding Behavior and Attitudes within Web 2.0 Environments." Proceedings of the Conference on Social Media for Social Inclusion of Youth at Risk, Leuven, Belgium, September13–14, pp. 102–120.

Galston, William A. 2004. "Civic Education and Political Participation." *PS: Political Science & Politics* 37 (02): 263–266. doi:10.1017/S1049096504004202.

Ginwright, Shawn, and Julio Cammarota. 2007. "Youth Activism in the Urban Community: Learning Critical Civic Praxis within Community Organizations." *International Journal of Qualitative Studies in Education* 20 (6): 693–710. doi:10.1080/09518390701630833.

Gitlin, Todd. 1980. *The Whole World is Watching: Mass Media in the Making & Unmaking of the New Left*. Berkeley: University of California Press.

Gordon, Hava Rachel. 2010. *We Fight to Win: Inequality and the Politics of Youth Activism*. New Brunswick, NJ: Rutgers University Press.

Graber, Doris A. 1988. Processing the *News, How People Tame* the *Information Tide*. 2nd ed. New York: Longman.

Gutmann, Amy. 1987. *Democratic Education*. Princeton, NJ: Princeton University Press.

Harber, Clive. 2004. *Schooling as Violence: How Schools Harm Pupils and Societies*. London: Routledge

Harber, Clive. 2008. "Perpetrating Disaffection: Schooling as an International Problem." *Educational Studies* 34 (5): 457–467. doi:10.1080/03055690802288445.

Hartley, John. 1999. *Uses of Television*. London: Routledge.

Hauben, Michael F. 1995. "The Netizens and Community Networks." http://www.columbia.edu/~hauben/text/bbc95spch.txt.

Hermes, Joke. 1998. "Cultural Citizenship and Popular Culture." In *The media in Question. Popular Cultures and Public Interests*, edited by Kees Brants, Joke Hermes, and Liesbeth Van Zoonen, 157–168. London: Sage.

Holt, Kristoffer, Adam Shehata, Jesper Strömbäck, and Elisabet Ljungberg. 2013. "Age and the Effects of News Media Attention and Social Media Use on Political Interest and Participation: Do Social Media Function as Leveller?" *European Journal of Communication* 28 (1): 19–34. doi:10.1177/0267323112465369.

Kahne, Joseph, Ellen Midaugh, Nam-Jin Lee, and Jessica T. Feezel. 2012. "Youth Online Activity and Exposure to Diverse Perspectives." *New Media and Society* 14 (3): 492–512. doi:10.1177/1461444811420271.

Moy, Patricia, Michael R. McCluskey, Kelley McCoy, and Margaret A. Spratt. 2004. "Political Correlates of Local News Media Use." *Journal of Communication* 54 (3): 532–546. doi:10.1111/j.1460-2466.2004.tb02643.x.

Noor, Habiba. 2008. "Assertions of Identities through News Production: News Making among Teenage Muslim Girls in London and New York." *European Journal of Cultural Studies* 10 (3): 375–389.

Oliver, Pamela E., and Gregory M. Maney. 2000. "Political Processes and Local Newsarticle Coverage of Protest Events: From Selection Bias to Triadic Interactions." *American Journal of Sociology* 106 (2): 463–505. doi:10.1086/316964.

Olsson, Tobias, and Peter Dahlgren, eds. 2010. *Young People, ICTs and Democracy*. Gotheborg: Nordicom.

O'Neill, Onora. 2002. "'A Licence to Deceive', Reith Lectures 'A Question of Trust.'" *BBC*. http://www.bbc.co.uk/radio4/reith2002/lecture5.shtml.

Pateman, Carole. 1972. *Participation and Democratic Theory*. Cambridge: Cambridge University Press.

Pateman, Carole. 1989. "Feminism and Democracy." In *The Disorder of Women*, edited by Carole Pateman, 210–223. London: Polity Press.

Putnam, Robert D. 2001. *Bowling Alone: The Collapse and Revival of American Community*. New York: Simon and Schuster.

Roker, Debi, Katie Player, and John Coleman. 1999. "Young People's Voluntary and Campaigning Activities as Sources of Political Education." *Oxford Review of Education* 25 (1–2): 185–198. doi:10.1080/030549899104206.

Shah, Dhavan V., Jack. M. McLeod, and So-Hyang Yoon. 2001. "Communication, Context, and Community: An Exploration of Print, Broadcast, and Internet Influences." *Communication Research* 28 (4): 464–506. doi:10.1177/009365001028004005.

Thomas, Pradip. 1994. "Participatory Development Communication: Philosophical Premises." In *Participatory Communication: Working for Change and Development*, edited by Shirley A. White, 49–59. Beverly Hills, CA: Sage.

Urry, John. 1999. "Globalization and Citizenship." *Journal of World-Systems Research* 5 (2): 311–324.

Valentine, Gill, and Tracey Skelton. 2007. "The Right to be Heard: Citizenship and Language." *Political Geography* 26 (2): 121–140. doi:10.1016/j.polgeo.2006.09.003.

van Steenbergen, Bart, ed. 1994. *The Condition of Citizenship*. London: Sage.

Wayne, Mike, Lesley Henderson, Craig Murray, and Julian Petley. 2008. "Television News and the Symbolic Criminalisation of Young People." *Journalism Studies* 9 (1): 75–90. doi:10.1080/14616700701768105.

Index

Note: **Boldface** page numbers refer to figures and tables, page numbers followed by "n" denote endnotes.

accusations of technological determinism 2
"action news" video format 47
Adler, Ben 18, 19
affective gestures 33–4
affective news streams 34–7
age of mediatization, cross-media perspective in 61–3
Alexander, Catherine 116
amalgamations *vs.* orientations **93**
ambient journalism 13, 15–18
Anderson, Benedict 13, 14
anticipatory gestures 34
Apple Daily 47
Apple Maps app 53
AR systems *see* augmented reality systems
Associated Press 51
asynchronous communication systems 17
audience logics 62
audience research 61
augmented reality (AR) systems 45
automatic tagging systems 52

Banaji, Shakuntala 5, 8, 9
Bausinger, Hermann 118
BBC 51
bin Laden, Osama 20
blogging platform 36
Boston Marathon bombings 17, 20, 22, 35, 60
Boston Marathon massacre 44
BrainPicker 15
breaking news 60
The Broughton Spurtle 49
Buckingham's study 119
business models of digital economy 98
BuzzFeed 15

Cammaerts, Bart 5, 8, 9
Carey, James 12
citizenship 116–18
CivicWeb 120

Climate Commons 53, **54**
Cobbett, William 107
commissioned research 49
Commons map 53
communication geography **81**, 81–3
communication systems 14
Community Reporter programme 100
community reporters (CRs) 97, 100, 107–8;
    motivations, relationships and skills 101–3;
    networked spaces of 106–10; sample 104
computer graphics imagery (CGI) animation 47
concept of flow (Williams) 19
Connected Cosmopolitans 93
Connected Locals 93
consumption of mass media 80
contemporary digital technologies 6
contemporary mobile media 43
contemporary news consumption 4; geo-social structuration of 80
contemporary transmedia textures 88
Copitch, Gary 103
cosmopolitan mode of news consumption 92
cosmopolitan news orientations 91;
    predictors of **90**
Couldry, Nick 5, 8
Courtois, Cédric 75
Creative Commons License 21
cross-media news consumption 61;
    typology of **71**
cross-media perspective in age of mediatization 61–3

Danes' news media consumption 64, 71
Danish informants 70
Danish landscape of news 61
Danish typology 71
data gathering 120–1
de Certeau, Michel 116
Deleuze, Gilles 43
Denmark: mobile news consumption in 7;
    news media use in different locations **73**; typology of cross-media news consumption **71**
de Souza e Silva, Adriana 14, 15, 20

INDEX

Dewey, John 99, 106
Dickens, Luke 5, 8
Digicel 21, 22
digital age 3, 97
digital imprints 37
digital journalism, "pivotal platform" for 16
digital media: ecology of 2; materiality of 18
digital oralities 36–7
digital screens 18
disaster 21–3
discursive spaces 33–4
distinct European projects 120
distinct mode of news production/consumption 103–6
"Do Not Track" (DNT) strategies 46
Dowd, Maureen 17
Dwyer, Tim 5, 7

Earth Journalism Network 53
echo-chamber effect 29
ecology of digital media 2
emerging patterns of cross-media 61
empirical audience research 61
empirical data 84–5
engineering advancements of industrial revolution 27
Euclidian approach 2
European Commission/EACEA study 120
Europe, political news in 121–4
"everyday life" 1; scholarly usage of 10n
"everywhere life" 1; mobility and flow of 6–7; news use in 4–6; place, space, and information in 9–10; politics and scale of 7–9
exchangeable image file (EXIF) metadata 52

Facebook 60, 64, 66, 87
"federated" websites 48
Fotopoulou, Aristea 5, 8
foundational stakeholder of journalism 2
Foursquare 23, 48
Frith, Jordan 14, 15
functional differentiation 61
functionalities of news 67

geo-social structuration 82, 88–92; of contemporary news consumption 80
geo-tags 52
geovisualisation tools 51
Giddensian approach 83
Gleick, James 17, 20
globally conceived and marketed geo-visualisation technologies, impact of 51
global positioning technology (GPS): chips 43; perspective of space 2
Goggin, Gerard 5, 7
"Golden Age" of mass communication 5
Google 46
Google Glass headsets 45

Google Maps API 51
Gordon, Rich 45, 118
GPS *see* global positioning technology
Greener Leith 49
Greenwald, Glen 20
The Guardian 16, 51

Haitian–Dominican border 21
Hermes, Joke 118
Hermida, Alfred 13, 16, 17
homophily 29, 37n
Hong Kong, multi-platform news in 46–8
Horst, Heather 21
human geography 4
Human Rights campaign 34
hyperlocal media 48, 49, 99
hyperlocal news 48–51
hypothesis 83

incorporation: of locative technologies 46; of social media 21
industrial practices of journalism 5
industrial revolution, engineering advancements of 27
Institute of Community Reporters: initiative 102; website space 108
interdisciplinary field of mobilities research 12–13
international mobility, different forms of **85**
international technology-company 48

Jansson, André 5, 7, 8
Japanese earthquake 22
journalism: foundational stakeholder of 2; industrial practices of 5
journalism scholarship, spatial awareness in 13
Journalism Studies 3

Kentishtowner 49, 51

Lai, Jimmy 47
landscapes of news media worthwhileness, mapping 64–70
Latour, Bruno 43
Le Corbusier 27
"legacy" media institutions 8
"Life is Crime," location-based mobile multiplayer phone game 48
liminality 30–3
liminal spaces 37
Lindell, Johan 5, 7, 8
literacies 36–7
live-blogging 16
Local Edge project 49
Localism Act (2011) 98
locan 4
locational data 42
location-based technology 43

INDEX

location search apps 52
locative journalism 45
"locative" media 42–4
locative news 44–6
locative technologies 44; incorporation of 46
longitudinal research, methodological challenges of 63–4
Lower Manhattan 22
Lull, James 75

manual drag and drop system 52
mapping citizen's news repertoires 70–2
mapping project 21
mapping systems, quirks of 53
mapping technologies 51–5
Martin, Fiona 5, 7
mass communication: "Golden Age" of 5; personal versus 4
mass media, consumption of 80
"materialist approaches," to media and mobility 12
materiality of digital media 18
media consumption: habits and patterns of 1; significance and meaningfulness of 4; temporal–locational ecology of 74–5
media group 47
media institutions, "symbolic power" of 5
media literacy 98–100
mediality 33–4
media, "materialist approaches" to 12
media repertoire 76n4
media sharing platform 52
media transformations 83
media use, temporal and spatial architectures of 2
Merton, Robert 88, 89; "locals" 89; Rovere study 90
methodological pluralism, spirit of 74
micro-blogging platform 16, 36
micro-level news 21
mobile application programming interfaces 43
mobile audiences 48–51
mobile communication devices 15
mobile interface 13; print news as 13–15
mobile media devices 43
mobile news 43–4; audiences 51–5; ecologies 46; "prosumption" practices 13
mobile news consumption: correlations between **85**; in Denmark 7
mobile privatization, concept of 29–30
mobile social media 14, 15
mobile technology, technological capacities of 7
mobile users 45
mobilities theory 12
mobility 14; "materialist approaches" to 12; older forms of 41; technologies of 30
mode of access 86

Monmonier, Mark 45
motion capture 47
Mubarak, Hosni 35
multidimensional scaling approach 75
multimedial QR advertising 48
multi-platform news in Hong Kong 46–8

NESTA 48–9; Destination Local programme 49; hyperlocal news report 52–3
NESTA-supported hyperlocal project 49
networked spaces of community reporters (CRs) 106–10
network society 3
new communication technologies 14
news 30–2; functionalities of 67; and spatial practice 85–8
news audiences, fluctuating 63–70
news consumption 81–3, 87; distinct mode of 103–6; locations of 72–4
news feeds 36
news flow 18–21
newsmakers 45
news media 12, 118–20, 124–8
news media–society nexus 61
news media use, surveys of 63
news media worthwhileness, landscapes of 64–70
news orientations, factor analysis of **89**
news repertoires, mapping citizen 70–2
news storytelling 36; new places of 28–30
Next Mobile 48
nexus of innovative technologies 60
nine-country Reuters study 41
nuclear meltdown 22

Øie, Kjetil Vaage 42
old distinctions 4
online "targeted display" advertisements 43
online technologies 68
open crowd-sourced maps 23
orientations, amalgamations *vs.* **93**
Oswald, Kathleen 13, 18, 19

Packer, Jeremy 13, 18, 19
Papacharissi, Zizi 5, 6
Park, Robert E. 88
participation in news communication (2011–2012) **69**
participatory journalism 99
participatory worthwhileness 68
People's Voice Media (PVM) 97–100, 102, 103, 105, 107, 108, 110
personal versus mass communication 4
Peters, Chris 13, 72
Pew News Media Consumption survey 41
Pew Research Center 42
phatic practices 31
"pivotal platform" for digital journalism 16

INDEX

political news in Europe 121–4
post-industrialized Swedish society 92
premediation 34
pre-social media era 14
print news 73; as mobile interface 13–15
"privatization" of public space 15
produsage 29, 30, 33
"prodused" feeds of storytelling 29
produsers 29
public sphere 3
"pushpin" system 52
PVM *see* People's Voice Media

Q-methodological task 70
quadrant model 81
quirks of mapping systems 53

radio news 74
Reddit 30, 35
Red Robot Lab 48
regression analysis **90**
repertoire, concept of 76n4
representative SOM survey 84
research context 100–1
Resistant Cosmopolitans 93
Resistant Locals 93
Reuters Institute Digital News Report (2013) study 74
robust comparative international statistics 42
Roskilde University's Center for Power, Media and Communication 61, 76n5

Samet, Hanan 53
sampling 120–1
scan QR codes 48
scholarship 3; spatial turn in 4
Schrøder, Kim Christian 5, 7
Secure Spaces: Media, Consumption and Social Surveillance 84
sensing technologies 52
Sheller, Mimi 5, 6
Snowden, Edward 20
social geo-mapping 52
"social licensing" franchise model 100
social media 64; incorporation of 21; platforms 32
social news climates 30–1
spaces 116–18, 124–8
spatial awareness in journalism scholarship 13
spatial turn in scholarship 4
Spinoza 33
spirit of methodological pluralism 74
structuration 81–3
subjectivity 30–2
Sunday Times 51
surveys of news media use 63
Sweden, dynamics of news navigation in 7
"symbolic power" of media institutions 5

tagging process 52
technological capacities of mobile technology 7
technological determinism, accusations of 2
technologies of mobility 30
temporal proximity 14
textural amalgamations 85–8
texture 81
3D modelling software 47
Tibbitt, Ally 49
Tiger Woods' 2009 car crash 47
Tigtag 49
"time-shifting" qualities 4
toponymic keywords 52
Toyota 22
traditional print media 13
traditional print news 13
transcend geographic scale 7
transformational condition 82
transmedia textures 82, 87; enactment of 80; expansion of 92; integrated and flexible nature of 86
transmediatization movement 86
trust, lack of 118–20, 125
tsunami 22
Turner, Victor 32
Twitter 17, 23, 30, 31, 35, 52, 60, 64

"unbounded" citizenship 118
US Climate Commons 53
US Federal Communications Commission 43
US Federal Trade Commission 45
Ushahidi's Crisis Map of Haiti 21, 22

Van Gennep, Arnold 32
vanguard digital media company 48
Värmland's news consumers 89

watching TV news on computer/mobile phone (2011–2012) **69**
Web 2.0 98
Web-based participatory news mapping projects 45
Web-based services 48
Web platforms 15
WhatsApp 23
Williams, Raymond 13, 18, 19, 107
WorstDrivers local initiative **50**
worthwhileness equation 63
worthwhileness of news sources, 2012 **65–7**

Young People and Democratic Life in Europe 120
youth 116–20; active 121–3; average 123–4; exclude 124–8
YouTube 47

Zite 16